FIFTY-SIX
WATERLOO CUPS.

GREYHOUNDS AND COURSING

THE AUTHOR

FIFTY-SIX
WATERLOO CUPS

By LOWIE HALL
(VINDEX)

GREYHOUNDS AND COURSING

PREFACE.

BORN, like good King Edward, in 1841, there being thus the burden of over four-score years to bear, it may be an unwise step to venture upon the task I am now taking in hand. Many kind friends, however, have urged me to it, and I have latterly been the recipient of so much generosity and evidence of goodwill from coursing patrons and devotees —which I here most gratefully acknowledge—that I should be an ingrate indeed if I were to shrink from attempting a requital of some sort. This may, perhaps, be open to a cynical rejoinder from younger coursers, but it would be mere affectation on my part, making pretence not to be aware of the general appreciation extended to my long past writings in connection with the sport.

Indeed—and I apologise for mentioning it—I had many proofs of this from leading coursers like Lord Lurgan, T. D. Hornby (for many years secretary of the Altcar Club and Waterloo meetings), B. Heywood Jones (father of the late Oliver Jones), Dr. Richardson (owner of King Death), Capt. Ellis (who has done more for the sport than any other man, and is happily still with us), as well as many others. Only a few years ago a letter appeared in the *Irish Field* from Mr. J. J. Ryan, that almost made me blush : it was in connection with something I had written in that journal.

He wrote : "It is a pity Vindex did not give a description of the famous final in the Waterloo Cup between M'Grath and Bab at the Bowster, probably the two greatest greyhounds of all time ; perhaps Mr. Hall will yet oblige. He stands alone as our greatest coursing authority, and his coursing articles will be long treasured by lovers of the greyhound." It is with no little diffidence that I append the above, and I hope my readers will excuse the seeming egotism : I am not unconscious of the truth of Pope's stinging lines—

> *Immodesty admits of no defence,*
> *A want of modesty is a want of sense.*

There was also a haunting feeling that I might be accused of having broken faith, an allusion to the story of the many Waterloo Cups I have seen bearing the inference that I intended to write it. Like rash vows, hasty promises are sometimes regretted ; but in this case altered circumstances afterwards interfered, and it would now certainly be very gratifying to myself if able fully to redeem what many of my readers regarded as a promise.

For the opportunity to do so I must acknowledge a debt of gratitude to Sir Edward Hulton, and the Editor of the *Sporting Chronicle,* for the old love naturally enough still burns brightly. To the real courser, which I claim to be, the sport never loses its charm, either to see it or to talk about it with a kindred spirit ; I might perhaps add, or to read or write about it. This at once recalls a passage in one of the several letters I had from Lord Lurgan, owner of the Irish prodigy, Master M'Grath, and one of the best judges of a course I have ever known. His lordship's health had given way, and he wrote : " My health will not now permit of my attending the meetings, but so long as there is breath in my body I must ever take a deep interest in coursing."

CONTENTS.

CONTENTS—*continued.*

LIST OF ILLUSTRATIONS.

CHAPTER I.

The Sport and its Intricacies.

COURSING is one of our sports that it is not given to everyone to thoroughly enjoy. Before it can be fully appreciated a discriminating knowledge is absolutely essential, and the mysteries of "turn, wrench, and kill" are somewhat profound. Of course, there are instances where exceptional brilliance has at once an inspiring influence upon the ordinary observer, especially if there be firstly an exciting tussle in the race to the hare ; but the majority of courses only appeal strongly to those "who know." And this perfect knowledge is not so easily acquired, except in certain directions where "it runs in the blood." Unfortunately, the want of it sometimes acts as a drawback to the sport in giving a false impression to the looker on.

This allusion to running in the blood reminds me of a pleasing fact that has not, so far as I know, even been referred to, and partly explains how it happened that the Duke of Leeds came to so quickly acquire a good knowledge, after only joining the coursing ranks towards middle life. His Grace is, so to speak, a born courser, being a direct descendent, on his mother's side, of the celebrated courser Lord Rivers, famed alike for the lead he took in advancing the sport, and for his splendid breed of greyhounds in the early decades of the previous century.

In the great percentage of courses run in good view of the crowd, even a casual looker on, let alone the great majority of regular followers of the sport, can form a correct estimate of which dog has won; but often enough with a circular run-up, and subsequent awkward angles, such a complex character is imparted that only a masterly penetration can give the necessary knowledge. It is this more often than not that leads to the judge's decision being sometimes impugned, though I do not suggest that coursing judges are infallible. There is such a thing as for the moment losing the particulars of a course, when the necessary concentration of thought has been at fault. I have no doubt whatever on this point, because

I have, in my time, seen such flagrantly wrong decisions that they could only be accounted for by the judge having forgotten the course and being compelled to guess as to how to decide. Better still, I can give an actual case that occurred :

Instead of being isolated on a horse, where no help is at hand, the judge was acting from a ladder, and upon descending when the course ended, he startled Mr. Harold Brocklebank, who was close by acting as flag steward, with the remark, " Which led up, Mr. Brocklebank ? I've forgotten the course." The desired information was quickly forthcoming, whereupon the judge, his remembrance then coming back, gave his decision. I was rather surprised that Mr. Brocklebank, in speaking at the N.C.C. meeting against the recent adoption of the new rule for "*all* dogs to wear collars," did not mention this incident in support of his argument.

To my mind the advantages of the new rule are outweighed by its dangers. The phases of the course have to be imprinted in the judge's brain all day long for him to decide correctly, and the strain is bound to be increased when he has to sustain his discrimination and recollection between four colours instead of two. It is not a new idea ; it was introduced some forty years ago, when flag stewards were perhaps less careful than now, and the more intelligent of our judges were against it.

It may, or it may not, be quite apropos, for in the old days even the honesty of coursing judges was sometimes called in question, but a remark I once heard made by a coursing judge in public was, in any case, piquante. It was at the coursing dinner of one of the Brougham and Whinfell meetings held in Lord Brougham's tennis court at Eamont Bridge. The judge, Mr. Anthony Dalzell, was one of the 200 or more diners, and his health had been proposed from the chair and enthusiastically received. In returning thanks the passage I so well remember was : "And believe me, gentlemen, that if I am unfortunate enough to give a wrong decision to-morrow it will be a mistake of the head, and not of the heart." Mr. Dalzell then left the room previous to the card being called over.

A remembrance of the little speech has sometimes made me wonder whether Sir Thos. Brocklebank in his tribute to

James Hedley that " he had raised the tone of the sport " had in his mind at the time honesty as well as competence. There is little doubt, however, but that the fact of the great northern judge having wiped out the abomination of so many undecideds was a pregnant factor.

Still, with all its drawbacks, difficulties, and disappointments, coursing in its best form, as seen at Altcar—and, may I add, Lowther ?—does and must ever possess genuine allurements.

As a field sport, giving six or seven hours in the open, its health-giving and exhilarating properties cannot be gainsaid, whilst even as a spectacle to the uninitiated it has its charms. It was Mr. Alexander Graham, who presided at the Waterloo Cup banquets for about thirty years, who wrote :—

> *Oh! what a noble chase!*
> *See how they twist and turn and fleetly race,*
> *Giving to scorn the critics who declare*
> *" Poor is the triumph o'er the timid hare."*

I must not, however, dwell upon generalities too long ; nor need I enter largely into the ancient history of coursing. That is amply and most interestingly treated in the third volume of the Greyhound Stud Book by the first " Keeper," Mr. David Brown, as well as the story of early English and Scottish coursing : Swaffham (Norfolk) in 1776, Ashdown (Berks) 1780, Malton (Yorkshire) 1781, Amesbury (Wilts) 1812, Altcar 1812, Ridgway Club between 1830 and 1840, were the chief of the earliest English meetings established.

The Ridgway Club.

The Ridgway Club meetings at Lytham, in the late sixties and the seventies, were amongst the best and most enjoyable of the season, and sometimes attracted extra large crowds of the visitors to Blackpool from 1870 onwards, when the early Octobers were sometimes as fine as in the present year.

Lytham coursing came to an end in rather a remarkable way. When the " Park " system came into existence, about 1877, there was great demand for live hares for the meetings run in March, and Lytham (always a prolific breeding ground) was a great source of supply. The hares taken away were, of course, nearly always " jacks," the does, after being released from the nets, being dropped on the other side ; and Isles, the Lytham keeper, told me that after the " jacks " (probably about two hundred) had been cleared off, hares always swarmed the following season. The eventual result, however, was perhaps instrumental in producing an evil that had not been foreseen. At any rate, a serious epidemic broke out, of such a virulent character that holding a meeting became impossible, and ultimately the surviving hares had to be killed off before the disease could be wiped out. The Ridgway Club meetings were afterwards, through Lord Sefton's kindness, held at Aintree for a few years, and eventually the Ridgway and Altcar Clubs were merged into one.

Returning to the earlier epoch, Scottish, like English, coursing flourished in the early decades of the eighteenth century ; but perhaps the zenith of its popularity was in the sixties and seventies, after the amalgamation of the Biggar and Caledonian clubs, the title then assumed being the Scottish National. Attending these meetings in the sixties was not all " sugar and spice." Headquarters were in the small village of Abington, on the Caledonian Railway, where accommodation was limited, many visitors having to tramp over the hills to an out-of-the-world village called Crawford John, their luggage being sent forward in farmers' carts. It was at one of these autumn meetings that the wonderful bitch Bab at the Bowster made her debut, and at once showed what a grand greyhound she was. Even over difficult ground she gave clear evidence of her sterling qualities, and after showing superiority in each of her five courses (there were fifty-two runners), divided the stake with Master Ivo. The latter's owner, Lord Lurgan, was amongst those present, and I remember well how he was impressed with Bab's excellence.

A few weeks later she divided the Croxteth Stakes (fifty-eight runners) with Brigade, both bitches running brilliantly throughout. At Waterloo she was beaten in the third round by the previous year's winner, Lobelia, after an undecided (which I thought Bab won), but that was her only defeat in her first season, whilst two great performances were yet to come. She ran clean through the Great Scarisbrick Cup of 128 dogs in the second week of March, and at the end of the month carried off the Scottish National Douglas Cup of 64 dogs, avenging the defeat she had sustained from Lobelia in the final course.

Their meeting naturally aroused much enthusiasm on the ground, and each had warm partisans. If I may be pardoned a personal touch, I had a triple wager on the course, half a crown on each event, the lead, the issue, and the kill, with Mr. Warwick, the then leading judge, who was present as a spectator only, Mr. Hay being the acting judge. I won two out of the three, and in paying his lost half-crown Mr. Warwick said it was the best-run course he had ever seen. He might, he said, have seen as good over the downs on the part of one greyhound, but never by both.

I remember the course well, and it is easily described, for there were no exchanges. Bab led fully two lengths, and at once setting to work in her best style, commanded her hare with splendid cleverness and force for a big sequence, before just failing in attempting the death (she was not a finished killer). Lobelia instantly spurted past for possession, and her style on the scut being even more brilliant than Bab's, the course soon became of thrilling interest. Indeed, it began to look like Lobelia winning, but her beautiful stroke that gave the *coup de grace* left victory with " the swift." Bab at the Bowster thus won twenty-five courses as a puppy and lost one.

She will come again under notice as runner-up to Master M'Grath in his second Waterloo victory, but I may at once mention that Bab ran over seventy courses in public and won sixty-seven of them. No wonder she failed to throw one nearly as good as herself, but through her son Contango super-excellence was reproduced. Not directly, perhaps, though the Waterloo winner and successful sire (after a fashion) Misterton was one of Contango's sons. But he also got Bedfellow when mated with Bed of Stone, a bitch almost the equal of Bab in point of endurance. Bedfellow then gave us the lion-hearted Greentick, who sired Fullerton (whose Waterloo exploits eclipsed even those of Master McGrath) and a host of good ones. And even apart from the Bed of Stone combination, Bab at the Bowster was instrumental, through Contango, in producing the great majority of our best greyhounds of recent years.

Coursing in Ireland.

So far I have been rather discursive, and have perhaps taken my story out of proper order of narrative, but having made allusion to early English and Scottish coursing, I must not leave Irish lovers of the leash out in the cold. When I first attended the great Lurgan meetings, over fifty years ago, I heard many wonderful stories of the grand coursing that used to be seen at The Curragh in bygone days, and enthusiasts never seemed tired of talking about Father Tom (the Rev. T. Maguire) and his bitch Lady Harkaway, described as the Bab at the Bowster of her day. Amongst the earliest Scottish supporters of the Lurgan meetings were Messrs. Ivie Campbell, Borron, Gavin Steele, and Lord Eglinton, the first-named winning the Brownlow Cup in 1864, with Calabaroono. After this English coursers began to venture upon the trip across, and the Yorkshire courser, Mr. Daniel Bateman, carried off the chief event in 1865 with his beautiful bitch Blue Belle.

In the following year Mr. G. A. Thompson's Trovatore won, and in 1867 yet another English greyhound was successful in Doctor Mould's Weasel. This bitch was trained by Archie Coke, who became a well-known formidable foe at the Lurgan meetings of this period ; and I may here interpolate an incident that gave me a rich experience regarding the value of emetics, which the Durham courser, Ned Dixon, owner of such greyhounds as Deacon (Waterloo Cup runner-up), Dalton, Dadda's Delight, Drawn Sword, Dead Shot, and others of renown, being his own trainer, made a practice of giving. It was a very rough trip across, and most of the Birkdale dogs were violently sick. I made a note of those that had suffered most, with, I need hardly add, a double object ; but the knowledge cost me dearly at the time, though it repaid with interest afterwards, when I had a few dogs of my own, and during the early years of my management of the Duke of Leeds's greyhounds, when I also trained them at Harraby before the Hornby kennels were built. These included the three consecutive Waterloo Cup runners-up—Lang Syne, Lapal, and Lavishly Clothed, as well as many other good ones.

Returning to Lurgan, Mr. Stocker's Sir William divided with Master M'Grath in 1868, in the autumn of M'Grath's first Waterloo year, and in 1869 Archie Coke won again with a moderate dog called Boy in Office.

The great Irish celebrity won outright in 1870 ; but I well remember that, failing to kill early, as usual, he was at one period of the course in great danger of defeat from Mr. W. Smith's Smuggler. The Scotch dog, however, was a nailing good greyhound, and caused his owner to be known as Smuggler Smith. I remember one very fine performance ; he ran through a Scottish National Douglas Cup in such brilliant style as to beat all his opponents nearly pointless. In 1871 Ireland again kept the honours at home with Double or Quits, but Scotland was next successful in 1872 with Contango, and in 1873 with Cockie Leekie.

Honeymoon then won in two consecutive years, and upon one of the occasions I well remember Lord Lurgan's remark : " That bitch might win the Waterloo Cup," which she did in 1875. Archie Coke then won again, with Mr. T. D. Hornby's Hematite, and the Irish dog, Wild Orphan, in 1877, won the last of the Brownlow Stakes, the Lurgan meetings ceasing upon the breakdown of Lord Lurgan's health. Lurgan must ever dwell in the memories of those who ever participated in its pleasures, for they were great meetings.

At its best it embodied three 64's—two puppy events and the Brownlow Stakes. They were all run once through on the opening day, involving over a hundred courses, including Mr. Warwick's usually big percentage of undecideds. The ordeal was a tremendous one for the slipper, for a wide face, when the Annoloist Moss was driven, often caused him to have to run a great distance. There is no doubt but that it destroyed Fred Hoystead's powers as a slipper of the highest class.

CHAPTER II.

Evolution of the Waterloo Cup.

I WAS only a little chap when I attended my first coursing meeting at Barrock Park, some five or six miles from Carlisle. I was on the way to school when the " dear old dad " and a friend picked me up, the school satchel going under the seat. I was interested in a red dog called Knight of St. George, through the dad, but he didn't win. Cumberland was a great hotbed of coursing in my very young days. In addition to the Border Union meeting—now held at Lowther, through Lord Lonsdale's kindness, and destined, I hope, still long to flourish—fixtures like Bridekirk, Brougham and Whinfell, and Brampton (not to mention many minor ones) could all claim class rank. The last-named was the first coursing meeting I ever reported, in 1864, and I well remember how the smart-looking white and fawn dog Tullochgorum ran through the Brampton Cup, a future Waterloo favourite in Bonus running up. Tullochgorum was own brother to the Waterloo winner, King Death, by Canaradzo—Annoyance, and the property of Mr. George Africanus Thompson, the foremost Cumberland courser of my day, and owner of many good greyhounds, his Tempest, Theatre Royal, Trovatore, and Tirzah, in particular, being all in the first flight. Two of this quartette figured prominently in the great match of Altcar Club versus the world, run in October, 1864, at that old queen of coursing arenas, Amesbury (Wilts), a few words concerning which may not be out of place.

Even in those days, when the club did not embrace, as at present, the great majority of leading coursers of the day, it was too strong for the world. In the Challenge Bracelet 16 bitch puppies owned by club members opposed a like number of the world's representatives, and the same arrangement was carried out with 32 dog puppies and 32 all-ages. In the bitch stake the club won eleven out of the sixteen courses in the first round, nine of the sixteen in the dog puppies, and eleven of the sixteen in the All-aged Cup, thus decisively winning the match on points. Ultimately two club representatives ran first and second in the bitch stake, Randell's Rising Star, by

Mr. FORD-HUTCHINSON.
Owner of Honeymoon, wearing the
Waterloo Collar.

LORD LURGAN,
Owner of Master M'Grath.

Early photo of Mr. N. DUNN,
Oldest Living Running Member of the
Altcar Club.

Mr. T. D. HORNBY.
Owner of Herschel, and Secretary of Altcar Club
and Waterloo for 26 years.

Beacon—Polly, winning, and Theatre Royal, by Cardinal York —Meg o' the Mill, running-up. The world balanced accounts in the dog stake, Mr. Strachan's St. George, by Seagull—Seaweed, and Mr. John Jardine's Jacob, by David—Goneril, dividing. The club, however, as in the number of courses, again took the lead in final results amongst the all-ages, being first and second with Lister's Cheer Boys, by Skyrocket—Clara, and Borron's Bit of Fashion, by Black Flag—Bit of Fancy, and Tirzah being third. In addition to the three Challenge Stakes, the programme embodied the Great Western Cup with 74 bitch puppies, and the Druid Cup of 46 dog puppies, no fewer than 216 greyhounds thus competing, and the meeting extending from Tuesday until Saturday; indeed, the final of the Druid Cup even then was left over until Monday morning. Randell's Revolving Light (brother to Rising Star) won it, beating Lord Craven's Cistercian Friar, the club thus beating the world in the closing scene of the meeting.

First Press Engagement.

If it will not savour too much of the personal, I may mention that it was the Mr. G. A. Thompson already mentioned who was directly instrumental in my being launched into a Press career. He and Mr. Walsh (Stonehenge), the then editor of *The Field*, travelled together as far as Carlisle back from a Scottish National meeting, which I had also attended. On the journey·Mr. Thompson, who was hon. sec. of the Brampton meetings, had asked Mr. Walsh why no reports of them appeared in *The Field*, and got the reply that he had no northern coursing correspondent. This led to Mr. Thompson introducing me to Mr. Walsh, and I somewhat doubtfully there and then accepted an engagement.

The Bridekirk Cup for 32 all-ages, at ten guineas (a high entrance fee in those days), invariably brought together greyhounds of high class. In the year that Annoyance won she beat the previous Waterloo Cup winner, Maid of the Mill, in the final, and a later Bridekirk winner in Beckford was a divider of the Waterloo Purse. The Waterloo winner, Roaring Meg, previously made a great impression by winning the puppy stakes at Bridekirk. There were also several links between Waterloo and the Brougham and Whinfell meetings. Maid of the Mill had previously distinguished herself on the northern ground, and I remember the two Waterloo Cup runners-up, Sunbeam and Deacon, both being beaten there. One of the earliest courses that made a lasting impression upon my mind was run there between the Waterloo Cup divider, Selby, and Attermire, a fine, handsome, deep-chested bitch, that was, together with Hardy, victimised at Waterloo, the pair going to slips three times.

Before commencing my story of Fifty-six Waterloo Cups in chronological order, a few words in connection with the varied changes that have marked the fleeting years will not be out of place. Present-day coursers have little knowledge of the old prestige and influence that attached to holding a Waterloo nomination, and the eagerness that then existed to possess one. Of course it is still the height of every courser's ambition to win a Waterloo Cup; but half a century ago the sterner battle was considered to be already half won if a nomination could only be secured. Only coursers of good reputation and position enjoyed the select privilege; to hold a Waterloo Cup nomination was, in fact, regarded as the hall mark of standard position in the coursing world. Proof of this may be cited in the fact that in stud greyhound and other advertisements, where the owner's name was given, the words " Waterloo Cup nominator " were not infrequently added.

'Midst many altered characteristics, perhaps the most striking one is with regard to the field management. Before the driving system was introduced, or rather fully developed —that is when the hares were mostly sprung from their forms— the whole Waterloo crowd, on certain portions of the ground, used to follow in the wake of the line of beaters, with the slipper slightly in advance. The pandemonium that often resulted can be more easily imagined than described, as drains had frequently to be jumped—the Altcar Club members mostly carried leaping poles—the spectacle of seeing hundreds of people in the air at the same time being a common one. Of course the amount of " grief " was enormous, and a golden opportunity was afforded the light-fingered gentry who visited Waterloo in swarms in those days. The favourite *modus operandi* was to spot a likely old gentleman who had jumped short and "help" him out. Two kind friends would each seize an outstretched hand and pull the unfortunate one just far enough towards the surface for a third confederate to do the rest. Mr. John Jardine, owner of the 1859 dividers, Selby and Clive, was in later years relieved of all he had about him in this way.

It need hardly be said that the Waterloo executive, including a long list of field stewards that afterward came to be appointed, had a very arduous task in those days, and upon one occasion—in one of Coomassie's years—the crowd got so completely out of hand as to swarm across the Church House ground, and form three solid sides of a square, the slips taking place from the open end, whence was the hare's only chance of escape should she be fortunate enough to break back.

In addition to the difficulties with the crowd, there was also a greatly increased risk, under the old system, of getting a second hare, this indeed being far from an uncommon occurrence. The Waterloo winner, Meg, might easily have been a victim in this respect. An undecided preceded her final defeat of King Tom, and whilst the latter had been readily picked up, Meg went careering away with a fresh hare. Luckily she pulled it down before serious harm resulted, and still carried "too many guns" for her far spent opponent. Smartness in picking up was consequently of the greatest importance, and this was recognised to the full by patriotic Irishmen in the days of Master M'Grath. I don't for a moment suggest that Lord Lurgan, who was a member of the Waterloo Committee, had any hand in it, the probability being that these volunteers were enthusiastic natives who had backed the crack ; but it was very wonderful, after Master M'Grath had run a course, to see half a dozen human forms suddenly appear on the surface, from various directions, like stage sprites ; they had evidently been secreted in, or along the ledges of, the drains.

A curious irony may be said to attach to this special safeguarding of the Irish idol, as the allusion naturally turns one's thoughts to the tragedy enacted in 1920, in the case of another Irish representative. The somewhat wild rush by two or three to pick up Honeyman after winning his course against Staff Job in the semi-finals, so scared the dog that he

B

bolted, and repeated the performance at the same spot in the final, before the course ended, with fatal results. It transpired that Honeyman has always been of a shy, nervous temperament, and this was further exemplified at the Altcar Club meeting in the following November.

Reverting to the fact that not a single nominator of my early Waterloo days is now in the list, I might have added that three treasured names were happily perpetuated. The Earl of Sefton (to whom the coursing world owes so much), Sir R. W. Buchanan Jardine, and Mr. Harold Brocklebank all followed in their fathers' footsteps, and the two first-named can be accredited with maintaining the traditional prowess of the Croxteth and Castle Milk kennels. Mr. Brocklebank, though infused with the old love, and still a " trier," anxious to get a good one, has been less fortunate, and must pine for another Bishop (Waterloo runner-up to Princess Dagmar), or, better still, another Bacchante or Brigade.

These were two brilliant bitches that required greyhounds of the calibre of Master M'Grath and Bab at the Bowster to beat them, nor was it any easy task even for these. The great Irish celebrity and Brigade met in the semi-finals at Waterloo, and it was as nearly as possible an undecided, great brilliance being displayed by both in a shortish course, run close to Hill House plantation. The tussle between " Bab " and Bacchante was, I well remember, a severe one, embodying fifty or sixty points or more, marvellous cleverness and determination being shown by each in turn. The issue several times hung in the balance, yet as " Bab," slightly the faster, had the beginning, I don't think Bacchante had ever quite turned the scales, although she looked like doing so more than once. It was undoubtedly one of the grandest contested courses ever witnessed : it was run at Southport, in one of the two 128-dog stakes that Mr. Blanshard's great bitch won in consecutive years.

In comparing the two eras of the Castle Milk kennel, some would say that the present Sir Robert has " gone one better " than his pater in winning two Waterloo Cups—one with such a brilliant greyhound as Long Span—against the previous single success of Muriel. But whilst also fully recognising the high class of other recent and present-day performers, Jibstay, Long Glass, and Jassiona amongst them, I incline to award the palm to the older lot. The kennel at one period, in Muriel, Progress, Joan, Carbineer and Lucetta sheltered a quintette that could have fairly challenged any other five in the world.

Blue Riband honours had never yet been won by the lord of the Altcar soil since the Cup became a 64-dog stake, although the beautiful bitch Sampler ran a good second to Maid of the Mill in the fourth year of its being promoted to its present importance. The present Earl of Sefton followed suit in 1908, Silhouette running up to Hallow Eve, after the pair had flukily beaten Long Span and Bachelor's Acre, and thereby prevented the most eagerly anticipated final of recent years. It was not a little singular that both cracks should fall, or rather " slip-up," upon reaching the hare near the same spot. The surface of the Withins that year was damp and not quite as smooth as could be wished, and it was decided to have it rolled on the Friday morning, with the unfortunate result that parts were somewhat glazed and rendered more slippery. It was hoped by many that a Croxteth victory was to be heralded in 1920, Staff Job having reached the semi-finals, and being manifestly the fastest greyhound of the quartette left to fight it out ; but it was not to be, though 1921 brought better luck.

In connection with the time-honoured name of Brocklebank, I am glad to have permission to also make allusion to the Rev. C. H. Brocklebank, who, under his pseudonym of " Mr. H. Charles," has been quite as ardent an enthusiast as his brother and late father. He patiently and pluckily " held on " under the fickle goddess's frowns for several years, and at last got a good one in Roving Stranger—perhaps the best puppy of his year. Then, as ill-luck would have it, the war stepped in, and the welcome Stranger, after his early successes, was cast aside until his own trainer (Tommy Amos) came back from France. Thereupon Roving Stranger reappeared upon the scene of mimic battle, but he was then in his fourth season, and his long inactive life had unfitted him to give more than a glimpse of his early powers.

" Mr. Charles," however, has latterly been a more prominent name than of yore, especially through his sons and daughters of Beaded Lil, and I remember having the pleasure of sending him a cheque for seventy-odd pounds—winnings at the Border Union (Lowther) meeting, last October.

What a model of order and good management, despite its crowd of ten thousand spectators, the Waterloo field is to-day I need hardly tell ; and it all seems so simple now that we have it. But only old stagers like myself can have a full grasp of the changes and improvements effected during the last fifty years, especially in connection with the legitimacy of the trials. During the first two decades of my earlier visits, and perhaps longer, a percentage of flukes was regarded as inevitable, the running at the Club meetings being always vastly superior to and much more legitimate than that in the great event. All this is now altered, and only a little reflection is required for it to be brought home, how much thought, work and expense must have been brought to bear during the last twenty years, since the present Lord of the Manor took personal and active control. Apart from the field management, the Earl of Sefton has always been most happy in associating with himself, as a committee of management, coursers who commanded the fullest public confidence, so that the internal administration of the Waterloo Cup should always be *sans peur et sans reproache*. The various secretaries, too, have been the right men in the right place. Mr. T. D. Hornby was assiduously careful in maintaining a high tone, as not a few coursers of his day found out ; and Mr. Harold Brocklebank, Mr. Hartley Bibby, and Mr. John Mugliston, have all proved worthy successors. It was Mr. Brocklebank who took the first steps towards freeing the Waterloo Cup from the thieves and welchers that used, in the old days, to infest it in gangs. He happily found Superintendent Jervis (Ormskirk Division) a willing agent, and the activities of this officer, with a large staff of police and detectives, soon had the desired effect.

My First Waterloo.

The first Waterloo Cup of the fifty-six I have seen was that won by the Yorkshire bitch Chloe, in 1863. She never came closely under my observation, but, judging from a photograph of her, in company with Cheer Boys and another kennel-companion, kindly sent by her owner, Mr. T. T. C. Lister, she

she was rather slenderly built. According to Captain Ellis's great book, " Winning Strains," she weighed 50℔, and was a pretty rather than a beautiful bitch. She was not much expected to win ; indeed, when her owner got back home his elder brother, Mr. S. C. Lister (afterwards Lord Masham), at first accepted the news of her victory as playful rather than true. Nor did her early courses, whilst very well run, suggest an absolute victory, and after she ran either two or three undecideds with the good Scotch bitch Spider (who, by the bye, had lost two-thirds of her tail) before beating her, she was the outsider of the four bitches left in—the other three being Reliance, Rebe, and Silkworm. She disposed of the Irish bitch easily enough, and then fortune favoured her, Rebe and Silkworm first running an undecided.

And thereby hangs a tale that may now be told without doing any harm. It was believed by Silkworm's owner (though by few others) that in the run-off Romping Girl had been substituted for Rebe, and when the latter's owner, Mr. Henry Haywood, was subsequently submitted to election for membership of the Ridgway Club, two excluding black balls were found in the ballot box. The stigma was deservedly resented by the general body of the club, and the *amende honorable* was made at a later election. Although she could not be ranked as a greyhound of the highest class, Chloe produced sons and daughters quite worthy of that distinction in Chameleon, Crœsus, Cymbal, Cock Robin, and Charming May. The last-named was one of the greatest artists on the scut I ever saw, and Cock Robin, as a puppy of rather massive mould, ran up to the great Master M'Grath in his first Waterloo Cup. There is a story in connection with this that will be told in the proper place. Chameleon, in addition to being a particularly handsome bitch, the very perfection of symmetry, was in the very front rank, and was perhaps an unlucky greyhound not to figure as a Waterloo Cup winner, as will be hereafter explained. In her puppyhood she hardly got fair play, as after running brilliantly through the Ladies' Plate over a big country like Amesbury, and winning her fifth course on November 5th, she was in slips again at Altcar on the 16th, and won three courses in the Croxteth Stakes before being beaten by Mr. B. H. Jones's Jew's Eye, a bitch not nearly up

to Chameleon's class.   The character of the Amesbury running
will readily be understood if I mention the fact that five horses
were sometimes provided for the judge; who not infrequently
had to change mounts every course.

Northumberland's First Waterloo Success.

King Death's year, 1864, was noticeable from the fact that
Rebe ran up, as she did the previous year, to Chloe, and she
was again to some extent unfortunate, the final being a
wretchedly poor trial, in which her slight deficiency in speed
told against her.   I do not wish, however, to detract from
the merit of King Death's victory ; he ran all his courses well,
and might have won in any case, but Rebe was a desperately
clever, determined runner.   With a third visit to Waterloo
she divided the Purse, though it was the general rule in those
days to run all the three stakes clean out—a practice now,
happily, revived through the Earl of Sefton's sporting inter-
vention, and handsomely giving a bonus, in the shape of a
cup, to the winners of both Purse and Plate, as well as the
Cup.   With yet a fourth visit to the classic ground Rebe again
showed a bold front by reaching the semi-finals ; and in the
succeeding year Mr. Haywood once more ran second to Lobelia
for the Cup with Royal Seal, thus being " so near and yet so
far " upon three occasions.

Whilst genuine running was well served in King Death's
cup, speed told its tale in the Purse, the winner being an extra
fast dog in Ivie Campbell's Calabaroono, afterwards sold to
Lord Uffington for £200, this being regarded as a big price at
that period.   The then aged Scottish courser about the same
time sold a brother and sister to his Waterloo winner Canaradzo,
afterwards known as Sea Pink and Sea Foam, and sold to the
Liverpool courser, Mr. J. Spinks, for a considerable sum.   He
was reproached by one of his friends for this transaction, as
the youngsters had already shown smart form as Coluxardo
and Corooreana, but a reply came which altered the complexion of affairs : " Aye, mon, I have a better at hame."
This, I believe, was actually the case, though the " better at
home " stories often prove unfounded ; but ill-luck came in
the way, the bitch in question, called Cioloja, breaking a leg
in a Waterloo trial : further allusion to this will be made in
Lobelia's year.

Meg's Year.

Au contraire to Cioloja's accident, it was a stroke of good fortune that enabled the Cumberland bitch Meg to figure in the scroll of Waterloo Cup winners. She was not at first included in the select sixty-four, but a postponement through frost gave opportunity for a change of entry, and she then appeared in the nomination of that fine sportsman and Crimean hero, Colonel Goodlake. Meg was a sterling good bitch (own sister to Bonus, who defeated the Waterloo winner King Death at Bridekirk before starting favourite for the Waterloo Cup), and went to Altcar cherry ripe, or she could hardly have won the Cup. For the final she and King Tom led off with an undecided, and before she could be picked up away she went with a fresh hare. I can see her stout owner-trainer, George Carruthers, now more florid even than usual, rushing away after her and crying, " She's dune noo, she's dune noo " ; but she came again wonderfully, and in the run-off led up and never left the issue of a nice trial in doubt. It was quite a North-country Waterloo year, for another Cumberland greyhound in Beckford divided the Purse, and the Northumbrian King Death, the previous year's Cup winner, won the Plate. According to Captain Ellis's invaluable book Meg only bred one litter, but she produced a smartish dog in Crossfell that figured to advantage at Southport more than once. Reverting to King Death, he made his mark as a sire, for in addition to Chameleon, Charming May, and Cock Robin, from Chloe, he produced many winners, including Ask Mamma, who won the Newmarket Champion Puppy Stake. He also bred for his owner, Dr. Richardson, several smart greyhounds, some of which were prettily named—Minute Gun, Miserere, and Requiem, to wit, the last-named being also a very handsome bitch.

I have advisedly touched only lightly upon the features of Waterloos at which I was merely one of the crowd, but I may now go more fully into detail where it seems desirable ; and if I may be pardoned mentioning it, it was from my pen in 1866 that the full description of Friday's Waterloo running first appeared in a Saturday's London journal. The preliminary reviews were sometimes adorned in rhyme in those days—more than half a century ago.

My First Waterloo "In Harness."

The Cup! Again to Waterloo the Northern spirit " drains,"
Fills up again the Southron guest to honest Altcar plains ;
Forgotten be the rod to-day, neglected be the chase,
Beshrew all those who breathe the " hare " in any other place !

No other course but ours to-day be welcome to our lips,
No Turf backslidings turn the mind from our discreeter " slips " ;
No boots and breeches lure the eye from sober " ties " and " cotes,"
No music and no " tally-ho " distract our ears and throats.

" Keep Warwick in my sight to-day," the noble Sefton cries ;
" Young blood and vigour must be served, and Scapegrace wins
        the prize ;
Already half the day is gained if either champion last ;
Our House will lead the common throng, for both its dogs are fast."

(Mr. Warwick was the judge).

Lord Sefton's " tip " did not materialise, Scapegrace being
beaten, after an undecided, by Lord Binning's Basil, but she
ran-up to the Irish bitch Golden Hair for the Purse. Saturn
was the Croxteth second string, and after going down before
the smart Castle Milk bitch, Annabelle, in the second round
of the Cup, he failed to do better than win a couple of courses
in the Plate, though one of those he vanquished was the
redoubtable Cumberland dog, Cauld Kail. The eventual
winner proved to be Brigadier, a black and white dog by
Boreas—Wee Nell, that had previously been sold by his
trainer, without the permission of his owner, Mr. James Bake,
for twenty-five shillings ! He stood at almost any odds on
the night of the draw, and as showing the difference between
then and now of the Waterloo Cup wagering, I may mention
that it was 20 to 1 on the field. These odds were accepted
about Bonus, Isaac, Gaudy Poll, and Cauld Kail, whilst several
were supported at 25 to 1, including the runner-up, Fieldfare,
and the previous year's winner, Meg.

The vogue of the bookmaker on the individual courses was
also then very different. There was no extra noise and confusion on the night of the draw by the double-barrelled offers
to take 100 to 50, and lay 60 to 40 the non-favourite. The
bookies of those days accepted the odds and took a sporting

chance, save when there was a natural change in the favouritism. Returning to my story proper, Brigadier being entered at all was quite a sort of fluke. Mr. Gorton's nomination, in which he ran, had been backed for " all the money " (and in those days a dog could easily be backed beforehand to win from ten to twenty thousand pounds), under the expectation that Bonus would fill it, a small syndicate having been formed to purchase the dog if needs be. The Bonus party, however, " got wind " of what was going on, and not only declined to arrange, but when purchase was attempted asked what was considered a prohibitive price, so negotiations fell through. It then became a case of looking round for a representative, Mr. Gorton having nothing of his own good enough, and Brigadier having in the meantime shown good form in a small stake, a satisfactory trial led to his being entrusted, as the best they could do. The luck, rather than the irony of the plot and sequel, is accentuated by the fact that Bonus failed to raise a flag in either the Cup or Purse.

The Waterloo Cup was full of romance about this period. It has already been explained how accidental was Meg's entry in 1865, and in '64 Doctor Richardson, his owner, sent King Death to Liverpool merely on the chance of getting him in, the nomination of Mr. Williams being only secured at the eleventh hour. Thus in three successive years was the Waterloo winner entered by a stroke of luck. Yet again was " the good fairy " playing a part in guiding to victory when Lobelia's Waterloo success immediately followed those of the other three, but before recounting particulars of 1867 I must add a few regarding '66.

Brigadier's year can hardly be described as a memorable one from an internal point of view, inasmuch as no great greyhound took part, though the winner certainly made a big mark afterwards in producing, amongst many other good ones, Honeymoon, the Waterloo heroine of 1875, and the grand bitches Brigade and Warwickshire Lass, the latter being " a nailer " over the downs. Brigadier ran all his courses well, showing great cleverness and determination, and only sterling qualities pulled him through in the final, the runner-up, Fieldfare, having the best of the early points.

The latter was a beautiful bitch by Dalgig (brother to the great sire Canaradzo) out of Woodpigeon, and a good performer ; she had won twenty-seven courses out of thirty-two when she went to Waterloo in her second season.   The good bitches Rebe and Theatre Royal (the first-named in her fourth season) each gave some sparkling displays, and were not disgraced when beaten in the semi-finals.   Before quitting 1866, a few words regarding both the double defeat of Bonus and the eagerness to secure him for Mr. Gorton's nomination may perhaps appropriately be given.   His first opponent was Isaac, and they ran a longish undecided, Bonus having the beginning and the finish.   Next time Bonus did not come again as well as the black, and was clearly beaten when he killed.   In his course in the Purse I thought he beat Sea Fly clearly, but Mr. Warwick decided against him.   Regarding his credentials, he had in the previous year started absolute favourite at 100 to 6, and on the first day inflicted defeat upon the flying Calabaroono and the 1865 winner, King Death, before suffering defeat from the smart Annabelle.   In the following autumn he had turned the tables upon the Castlemilk bitch at Bridekirk, and was fluked out after winning three courses.   He also won the Brougham Cup at the Brougham and Whinfell meeting, so that he had established a reputation, and had run like a good dog.

CHAPTER III.

Waterloo, 1867—A Great Ladies' Year.

IN addition to being signalised by the great luck that led to the winner Lobelia being substituted for the intended Saucebox, the Waterloo of 1867 was rendered memorable in other respects.

It was a red-letter year in connection with the "gentler sex," for not only were the last four in the Cup all bitches (Lobelia, Royal Seal, Trovatore, and Bettelheim), as in Chloe's year, 1863; it was also a case of *place aux dames* in the lesser events, Shy Girl and Woman in Blue (both Irish) being first and second in the Purse, whilst Princess Royal and Lady Cecil gained similar honours respectively in the Plate.

And " breathe it not in Gath," Christ Church bells rang out joyous peals when the news of Lobelia's and Mr. Stocker's success was brought to Southport.

It was not, however, I ought to add, a case of authoritatively linking coursing with the Church, for the " music " stopped when the vicar hurriedly arrived upon the scene, and learned to what it applied. Referring to such a remarkable chain of events as occurred in four consecutive Waterloo Cups, financial interests would hardly be conspicuous in connection with the victories of Meg and King Death; but, like Mr. Gorton (Brigadier's nominator), Mr. Stocker—identified with the big Southport meetings in the old days—backed his nomination heavily, expecting a different dog to fill it, and yet won all the money.

He had engaged to run the Newmarket Champion Puppy Stake winner, Saucebox, but she went wrong, and I am almost certain that there was a second disappointment when Cioloja broke her leg in a private trial at Southport.

All ended well, however, through Lobelia being secured, though confidence could hardly have been great at the outset. Lobelia, it is true, had given more than a glimpse of Waterloo

form in running clean through the Ridgway Club United
Produce Stake, but that ordeal involved six courses over the
Lytham country, and the meeting finished on February 1st,
leaving only an interval of eighteen days before Waterloo
commenced, and Lobelia was only a puppy.

Visitors to Waterloo this year were enabled to enjoy the
sport better than they had ever previously done. A number
of field stewards, elected from amongst leading coursers, were
for the first time appointed, and they were largely instrumental
in holding the crowd in position, instead of their being permitted
to follow the slipper and beaters, with the result that they
gradually became scattered all over the ground. The trials
were now less interfered with, and a better general view
obtained ; but, as was often the case in the 'sixties and
'seventies, there was " a fly in the ointment."

The judging was not free from blemish, the fiat in favour
of Rather Improved against Cauld Kail, and the undecided
(a long one) between Desperation and Basil being specially
condemned as wrong decisions. In the latter case Basil was
withdrawn, as his weakness throughout the late phases of the
course gave clear indication how hopeless was his chance of
landing all the money for which he had been backed.

Draw up once more the curtain, Fate, unveil thy hidden stores,
Teach how thy beaten followers may wipe off former scores.
Show in this game of Water-loo the secrets of thy hand,
Reveal the proper cards to " throw," the safest suits to stand ;
Yet more benignant than the last, unless thy favours be,
" Let slip the dogs of war," and leave their ordering to me.

Lobelia had suffered three defeats by Nimble, Batavia, and
Queen Emma, so that despite her later success she did not
figure amongst the favourites on the night of the draw. As
in the previous year, it was 20 to 1 on the field, Basil (who
ran in Mr. J. S. Bland's nomination, and included the leviathan
racing bookmaker of the day, John Jackson, amongst his
followers), Batavia, Marionette, Cauld Kail, and the previous
year's winner, Brigadier, being all backed at these odds.
Lobelia and one or two others were befriended at 25 to 1, the
runner-up, Royal Seal, and Trovatore, beaten by her in the

semi-finals, being on the 100 to 3 mark ; but the other semi-finalist, Bettelheim, was amongst the outsiders.

Lobelia's first course against Lord Soulis—a Netherby Cup divider—was very unsteadily run, and she was a long time in pulling her hare down. In the second round, despite her previous long twisting course, she performed much better against the fast South-country dog Catholic, and improving as she went on, ran each of her remaining four courses with exceeding smartness, her defeat of Royal Seal in the final being indeed a superb display. I believe Lobelia killed all the six hares : I saw her kill five, but the very finish of her course against Vyner's Vanity was just out of sight.

Of the other Cup runners, Trovatore ran clearly the best. In her defeats of Glideaway, Blue Rock, Fortuna, and Marionette, she each time gave a brilliantly inspiriting display, and her defeat by Royal Seal was quite a fluke. A partly cross slip led to Trovatore being momentarily unsighted, the black reaching the hare with a long lead ; and Trovatore, joining in at an unlucky moment, failed to displace her opponent.

Royal Seal thus had the credit of a good beginning, and though the red finished the course in her previous great style, and raised doubts, the fiat was for the black. Bettelheim, who was only entered through Isaac having injured himself, proved quite a worthy substitute, winning, and running her first four courses in most meritorious style. On the Friday, against the winner, she was unable to make much show, but Lobelia was now going " great guns."

Unlike the majority of Waterloo winners, Lobelia did not go into retirement for the season after her great triumph. There was an Altcar Club meeting in March that season, owing to the January fixture having been abandoned through frost, and in the Members' Cup she disposed of Jones's Jack-a-Dandy, Thompson's Trovatore, and Brocklebank's Isaac, then sharing in a division amongst four. She was also later entered in the Great Scarisbrick Cup, but after winning a course was then drawn. Lobelia was thus out seven times as a puppy, and ran twenty-six courses in public. This was hardly calculated to improve her future prospects, but she was of a small

(44℔), wiry stamp that would ripen early. She did not, as it were, flash upon the coursing firmament like those other grand bitches, Bab at the Bowster, Miss Glendyne and Bed of Stone, but I believe she was in amateurish hands at the outset, and her two early defeats were by good greyhounds in Nimble and Batavia. Her only other failure as a puppy was in the final at Lytham, when she had the worst of the handicap against Queen Emma.

Lobelia figured prominently in each of the next two Waterloo Cups, reaching the semi-finals before the great Master M'Grath both times barred the way. Like her sire, Sea Foam, and her uncle, Canaradzo (the king of the whites), she was the same colour, with a brindled patch or two, and cast in a pretty mould, with truthfully shaped limbs. She was the property of Mr. W. J. Legh (afterwards Lord Newton), of Newton-le-Willows. Lancashire thus followed up her previous success by Brigadier, these being the only ones gained so far by the County Palatine since the Waterloo became a 64-dog stake in 1857.

The first winner (King Lear) was Scotch, the second (Neville) Yorkshire, the third (Selby and Clive, both the property of Mr. John Jardine) Scotch, the fourth (Maid of the Mill) Cumberland, the fifth (Canaradzo) Scotch, the sixth (Roaring Meg) Durham, the seventh (Chloe) Yorkshire, the eighth (King Death) Northumberland, and the ninth (Meg) Cumberland, Brigadier being the tenth. Ireland had not yet had a turn, but she now followed with Master M'Grath's successes, to be supplemented later with those of Honeymoon in 1875 and Donald in 1876. Since then she has never headed the Waterloo scroll, though she has scored five seconds with Lord Fermoy's Zazel to Coomassie in 1878, Mr. Smyrl's Wolf Hill to Fabulous Fortune in 1896, Mr. Gaussen's Glenbridge to Long Span in 1907, Mr. Fullerton's Full Steam to Heavy Weapon in 1910, and Mr. Hearn's Honeyman to Fighting Force in 1920.

CHAPTER IV.

Waterloo, 1868.
Advent of the Mighty Master M'Grath.

IN winning his first Waterloo Cup, the now immortal Master M'Grath did not reveal all those transcendent qualities that made his name so famous, for though a little undersized (55℔) and squarely built, it took another year to fully develop his great powers.

But I may more appropriately deal with those when treating of his second success. Even in his early puppyhood he had shown in Ireland what a wonder he was, and led the then leading Irish judge, Ralph Westropp, into doing him an injustice.

An afterwards proved good bitch called S.S. had run through a puppy event in great style, and when shortly afterwards meeting M'Grath upon his first appearance, was led so far that Mr. Westropp's cap came off, the reply to an asked-for explanation being " The brindled was unsighted."

The lead, however, was the same in the run-off, and this time " Black " was sounded. I may here explain that it was a very slight white mark on his neck that led to his being described as black and white.

His form being little known on this side, his Irish friends got a good price about him at the calling-over of the Waterloo card, the favourites being Brigade and Bab at the Bowster each at 100 to 6, Improver, Patent Lever, Crossfell, and and Innkeeper at 25's, Cock Robin at 30 to 1, and Marionette at 100 to 3.

M'Grath was tackled in his first effort by a smart bitch called Belle of Scotland, the result being undecided, but he polished her off in great style next time, and gave a clipping display in the second round against Kalista. At night he jumped to the position of second favourite, the prices being 9 to 2 against Brigade, 8 to 1 each Master M'Grath and Stonewall Jackson, 100 to 8 each Patent Lever, Bab at the Bowster and Marionette, 100 to 7 Cock Robin, and 100 to 6 each Royal Seal, Charming May, Ghillie Callum, Peruvian, and Lobelia.

In the third round Lobelia beat Bab at the Bowster after an undecided (which I thought Bab won), but Master M'Grath in his defeat of Marionette, Brigade in beating Rustic Charms, Cock Robin in vanquishing Royal Seal, and Charming May in proving too good for Gipsy Jack, all won unmistakably and performed well.

The feature of the fourth round was the meeting of M'Grath and Brigade, and unfortunately it was a poor trial. They split wide in the run-up, Brigade hanging to the right when the hare was bearing in that direction, so that she was considerably thrown when puss at last bent to the left.

The black thus got up with a good lead, and wrenched strongly two or three times, being just ready to give his deadly stroke, whereupon Brigade came up with a wet sail, flashed past and killed. It was a wonderful shoot and stroke, but hardly balanced accounts; it was her own fault that M'Grath reached his hare so far in front.

The four left in to fight it out (three of them puppies) were the kennel companions Cock Robin and Charming May, who now came together; and Master M'Grath and the previous year's winner—Lobelia. In this course a roar of excitement was heard as Lobelia was seen to draw ahead, but before the hare was reached the Master had drawn clean past when the hare, after crossing the ditch, whipped to the left, down the roadway.

This favoured Lobelia under the red flag, but M'Grath, with wonderful quickness, again shot away in front, forced the hare back into the meadow, wrenched thrice and killed —quite a brilliant performance.

In connection with the other pair, a line of action was adopted that would be howled down in the present day. Cock Robin, running in Mr. C. Randell's nomination, had been the more heavily backed, Charming May being behind him in point of speed; and a very unsportsmanlike, and unwise, policy, as it turned out, was adopted in drawing the bitch.

She was put in to run the bye, which Cock Robin had necessarily to run, and by way of " piling up the agony," she beat her brother into smithereens, Robin having nothing more to do with a good trial, after leading up.

From Painting by Mr. J. Armstrong, Aglionby, Carlisle.

MASTER M'GRATH, Winner of Waterloo Cup, 1868-69-71.

From Painting by Mr. J. Armstrong, Aglionby, Carlisle.

BAB AT THE BOWSTER, Winner of 67 Courses; Runner-up to Master M'Grath in 1869.

I must not attempt to dim the morning star of the Irish crack's bright and brilliant career by saying that she would probably also have won the final, though it was a working course—the hare running in circles—in which she would have shown to the greatest advantage. · Long odds were offered on M'Grath beating Cock Robin, there being few takers of even 5 to 1, and the course was one-sided from start to finish.

Cumberland sent a few smartish greyhounds to Waterloo this year, and two of them appropriated the lesser events. Jane Anne, a daughter of Bonus, ran through the Purse, and Strange Idea, who afterwards sired the Waterloo winner Sea Cove, and many other good-class greyhounds, won the Plate. It was a year conspicuous for undecideds, there being no fewer than thirteen on the first day in the two rounds of the Cup.

The first brace, the Irish dog Hawk and the Croxteth bitch Symphony, went to slips four times. In point of production it may be considered a " vintage " year. Master M'Grath, Bab at the Bowster, Brigade, Cock Robin, and Charming May being entitled to special mention amongst a whole host of extra good, first-season greyhounds.

Waterloo, 1869.
How Master M'Grath Won Again.

NEVER before nor since has there been such a Waterloo as that of 1869. It was the best class 64, all round, that I have ever seen, and there were quite half a dozen fit to win a Waterloo Cup in an ordinary year ; yet the mighty " Master " quite overshadowed them all.

Happily the running was quite of a superior character, and with favourable weather throughout, in addition to a good surface, all " the swells " were enabled to give inspiriting displays. Luckily, I have records of my own writing to assist my memory, and any of my descriptive details may be accepted as correct.

Requiem led off with a stylish effort, but was severely run, it being a good performance, considering the handicap, to give such a licking in the next round to Crown Imperial,

C

runner-up to Bab at the Bowster in her first 128 stake victory the previous spring, and winner of a 64 Scarisbrick Cup the following autumn.   Lobelia in her first two courses showed all her previous brilliance, and the tussle between her and Requiem was regarded with much interest, the betting being very close. Mr. Warwick was unable to separate them the first time of asking, and Lobelia only won the run off by the narrowest of margins.

The Irish bitch, Woman in Black, made many friends on the first day, and went a step further before finding Lobelia too good, whilst Charming May gave two polished displays before falling foul of the champion.   Randolph showed fine speed in his first three efforts, but M'Grath then served him as he did the rest.   .

One of the best run courses on the first day was that between Lady Lyons (the only greyhound that ever beat M'Grath) and Bacchante, the latter afterwards running clean through the Purse. Lady Lyons won two more courses, and in the fourth round ran a couple of undecideds with Bab at the Bowster before suffering defeat.

Ghillie Callum fought his way into the semi-finals very meritoriously, but against his old opponent Bab at the Bowster shared the same fate that he had done twice previously, Bab giving one of the best displays of the week, despite her four courses the previous day.

M'Grath and Lobelia, were also old antagonists, and the great Master, leading the Lancashire bitch much further than in their previous encounter, beat her easily.

Now came the supreme struggle between, on the one hand, the most wonderful greyhound probably that ever was seen, and on the other, perhaps the best ; for the great Scottish bitch could run anywhere and everywhere : the adored of Erin's Isle was essentially an Altcar greyhound.

The course must have given a thrill to every looker-on, for electric quickness was shown by both greyhounds in their rapid exchanges, the hare being so hotly pressed that she could never race ahead for more than a few yards after once being reached. It was a closely-contested course throughout, the exchanges being evenly balanced, but the black always held his start to the good, and was a clear winner at last when he shot out and effected one of his deadly strokes.

It was unfortunate that in such a great final it was not made clear which would have led to the hare in a continued straight race. Beautifully delivered by Tom Raper, they came from slips smoothly together, and raced evenly for about eighty or ninety yards before puss broke sharply to the left to cross the drain by one of the hare bridges.

This, coupled with his own quickness in changing direction, gave M'Grath, under the red flag, a great advantage, as it enabled him to clear the drain inside the two posts at the mouth of the bridge, whilst Bab had to go beyond them to jump.

The black was then further favoured by the hare, after clearing the drain, again breaking to the left, and he eventually scored first turn fully three lengths ahead. A jerking hare avoided his first rush, but with great smartness he held possession for the second, Bab shooting in like a flash for the third : then followed those lightning-like exchanges already referred to. Old coursers were sent into raptures, and said they had never seen anything like it.

I may now go through the mighty one's thrilling performances in sweeping through the Cup. His first opponent was the smart Borealis (runner-up to Bacchante for the Purse), and they were slipped at North End on the flat adjoining what was known as the Salt Marsh, where, by the bye, M'Grath met with his only defeat, by Lady Lyons, the following year.

He at once fairly electrified lookers-on by the way he cleared the ground and reached his game fully twenty yards in front. The hare tried a break to the left, but M'Grath moved with her like a swivel, and, after another couple of drives, killed in great style.

In the first ties against Hard Lines he again led a great distance, and, though he failed to floor his hare as quickly, he allowed the white collar (they were both blacks) little or nothing to do with another short spin.

His third course against Charming May was a sensational one. Leaving slips like a bullet, and dashing ahead as before,

he went up ten lengths in front, and scored thrice before
blundering badly as a strong hare nicked short to the right.
Before the white could reach her game, however, he raced
clean past, and fell in just failing to kill—the fur flying.

This enabled Charming May to again show well in front,
but the black, as before, went streaming past, dusted his hare
merrily a few times, and again just failed to effect the death,
coming a regular purler this time in the attempt. Charming
May now obtained clear possession, and, setting to work in
her well known beautiful style, ran up point after point until
the spectators fairly held their breath.

The " Master " was a long way behind when the game
little Yorkshire bitch killed, whereupon a loud roar of cheers
went up from the bookmakers suggesting her success, but
Mr. Warwick was not to be coerced, and he galloped back
hard to let the flag steward, Mr. Nathan Slater, hear his cries
of " Black, black."

Against the wind, Mr. Slater would not have the flag
hoisted until he was sure between " black " and " white,"
and I may here appropriately mention that he was one of the
few flag stewards who never sent up the wrong colour.

After M'Grath's long course, and seeming distress, he was
strongly opposed in the fourth round when he met Randolph
(from the Rebe, Royal Seal, and Romping Girl kennel). This
dog had so far shown a great burst of speed, but against
M'Grath he was not revealed as such a flyer. The crack
rattled ahead about five lengths, and very quickly gave one
of his masterly strokes.

Coming out like a lion refreshed on the Friday morning, an
outside in the run-up did not prevent his leading Lobelia some
four or five lengths, and, though she contested the course well,
he was the pronounced winner of a good trial, when he killed.

The " Master's " flying pace was thus clearly shown against
five good class opponents, and though in the final course
(already described) Bab at the Bowster fairly held him, this
was not a true index of the best speed that each possessed.

It is true that Bab's three slips with Lady Lyons on the
second day were a stronger dose than M'Grath's exhausting

course with Charming May; but she possessed marvellous powers of endurance, and could " come again " after a gruelling that would have settled any other greyhound of my time, except Bed of Stone. Through Lobelia it is made clear that, both fresh, M'Grath would have led Bab quite three lengths.

M'Grath's Killing Powers.

In this connection I may be permitted to reproduce something I wrote in the *Irish Field* some few years ago.

" Anything and everything appertaining to such a phenomenon must have a fascination for all coursing devotees. I think I saw the immortal black run all his courses in public after his initial effort in his native land, and certainly no other greyhound ever made my blood tingle in the same way; it was often quite thrilling to see the truth and force with which he lined his hare.

" It used to be said that he seemed to hypnotise his hares : I think I can give an explanation of this seemingly mysterious effect. During one of his courses at a Lurgan meeting, against a white dog called Precentor, belonging to Doctor Eltringham, of Southport (owner of Master Sam, expected to win the Waterloo Cup in Coomassie's first year), I was out in the running field (with Lord Lurgan's permission) behind a tree, and it happened that they came very closely past, a spectacle then meeting my gaze that made a lifelong impression.

M'Grath was driving closely on the scut, with marvellous movement, the entire length of his back being in visible play, just as though it were a mass of hingework, whilst his eyes looked more like two balls of fire than ordinary optics. A stout hare kept gallantly feinting first to one side and then the other, but M'Grath's suppleness and electric quickness were such that he seemed to almost anticipate her moves, showing her that any attempt to break at much of an angle would simply present a wider target, and meant certain death. Vainly she pressed forward, until the foeman's superior speed placed him within certain reach of striking distance, when the deadly stroke was instantly made."

Master M'Grath Beaten in 1870.

MASTER M'GRATH, backed at 3 to 1 and beaten. Over half a century is a long vista to look back upon, but many incidents attached to the anniversary of 1870 still live strongly in recollection.

Of course the crack's defeat was the great feature, and Mr. Borron's famous objection also led to much excitement at the time. The committee had, owing to unpropitious weather, perhaps unwisely deferred the completion of entry and draw for 24 hours, and Lord Lurgan and Mr. B. H. Jones having, amongst others, failed to name their dogs, Mr. Borron lodged an official objection against their afterwards being allowed to do so.

The then N.C.C. rules were certainly infringed, and the Waterloo circular programme of the period gave no powers of exceptional action. The committee, however, declined to entertain the objection, and the frost, meanwhile giving way, the entry was completed on Wednesday evening, the draw afterwards taking place.

The matter was later brought before the National Coursing Club, and the action of the committee was upheld. In the following year, and ever since, the words " or on any day to which the draw may be adjourned " follow those of " Dogs to be named and stakes paid, etc.," in the Waterloo circular.

A fiasco also occurred in connection with the running, the last brace in the fourth round of the Cup (Sea Cove and Commodore) running an undecided and being unable to run it off owing to the failing light. I remember that it was already dusk when Bab at the Bowster and Lady Lyons went to slips for the third time the previous year.

Hitherto it had been the practice to begin with the Purse the second day, as it was a 32 against the Cup's 16 ; but to avert further danger to the chief event the order of the second day's running was next year altered to the Cup first, and, rightly, still remains so.

Both the objection and a course having to stand over were, however, side shows compared with the great M'Grath's signal defeat. His opponent was Lady Lyons, and they were slipped on what was known both as the Cylinder Marsh and the Salt Marsh, lying between the river Alt and the Liverpool and Southport railway, on the north end portion of the Altcar ground that has now for some number of years been abandoned.

A tremendous roar went up from the crowd as Lady Lyons was seen to at once draw ahead, and in a longish run up she led between two and three lengths. Sweeping grandly on the scut as puss broke to the left, she also took the second turn, at which she stumbled.

The black instantly shot in, and for a moment looked like retrieving the situation, but after a few points he blundered just as the bitch had done—the ground no doubt being slippery after the frost, and in a short time he became quite helpless. He got several openings, but could not take advantage, the red going past to regain possession several times.

It was a long course, Lady Lyons still blowing hard when she came back past the crowd, and M'Grath narrowly escaped being drowned. The Alt was half frozen over, and he got under the ice, only being rescued with difficulty.

The crack's display cannot be regarded as his true form, for his collapse was too early and too complete for him to have been anything like fit. The greasy condition of the ground after the frost, especially on the wheat—on portions of which the course was run—was all against his rapid action, and no doubt prevented his usual great burst from slips.

All the same, he was beaten by a high-class greyhound, and it is probable enough that Lady Lyons would have won that year's Waterloo Cup had My Goodness been drawn after their undecided in the second round. Through starting stiffly, she was led the first time, though she was winning in a canter when she killed, and at the second attempt she went up well in front, and showed great superiority.

Unluckily, a stout hare gave her another gruelling, and in the third round she went under to Bendimere, the runner-up, though not until after two undecideds. She was quite a victim of Mr. Warwick's cap at Waterloo, for she ran two undecideds the year before with Bab at the Bowster.

CHAPTER V.

More About 1870—Sea Cove's Year.
Defeat of Bed of Stone and Bab at the Bowster.

THE year 1870 was further marked by the defeats of M'Grath's great compeer also another queen of the leash in Bed of Stone. "Bab," however, was carrying Contango and four others at the time, and Mr. Warwick's decision in favour of the speedier Commodore against Mr. Briggs's unique heroine of the triple crown—Purse, Plate, and Cup—in successive years, was at least open to doubt.

As "all's well that ends well," the extra course that Sea Cove had to run on the last day was not of serious consequence. In it she polished off Commodore in grand style, and was still equal to disposing of her other two opponents Chivalry and Bendimere, and winning the Cup.

This pair, like the winner, were first-season greyhounds, and so were Bed of Stone (winner of the Purse) and Waywarden and (Dunlop's) Pretender, winner and runner-up of the Plate, so that, like 1868, it was quite a puppies' year.

Sea Cove, as Covet, had previously made her mark at one of the big Bothal meetings promoted by Captain Ellis (yet happily still in the flesh) by dividing the Bothal St. Leger of 142 runners, and was afterwards sold to Mr. Spinks for £150. In all her Waterloo courses she showed the qualities of a high-class greyhound, leading every time, though I well remember what a near thing it was between her and Bacchante in the third round.

The course was exceedingly well run by both, and Sea Cove both led up and went a little the faster in the stretches, but the black ran with great cleverness and desperate determination all through.

Without wishing to detract from the merit of Sea Cove's victory, the honours of the week could perhaps fairly be claimed by Bendimere.

He had been very hard run when he went to slips for the final, and the ground was all against a big dog puppy. The going had been a little treacherous from the start, and with a partial return of the frost on Friday night the ground on Saturday, on which day the meeting that year finished, was hard in places, and not the best of going anywhere, though a cheerful sun was doing its best to improve it.

The going, more than likely, explains the fact that there were this year fewer brilliant performances than usual, as well as more surprising results ; there were also an extra number of greyhounds so severely run that their prospects of going further were virtually destroyed. Brigade was a special victim, for after beating Enchanter and giving a magnificent display, she got amongst a drove of hares, and was run to a standstill.

Amongst the best performances of the week were those of Bed of Stone and Waywarden in respectively winning the Purse and Plate.

In the first round of the Cup Requiem gave such a stylish performance in beating the smart Irish bitch S.S. pointless that she was then freely backed to win outright at 100 to 15 ; but she ran disappointingly afterwards, and probably enough struck an unlucky patch of the going. S.S., on the contrary, did well in the Purse, her defeat of Black Huntsman being as inspiriting a display as anything seen during the week.

Waterloo, 1871—Master M'Grath Redivivus.

AFTER his defeat the previous year, it was not intended that the dethroned idol should ever run again. Lord Lurgan himself spoke to that effect, and when in a conversation shortly after the course I mentioned, in extenuation, the condition of the ground, and the fact that we had never seen a third season greyhound win a Waterloo Cup, I well remember his lordship's rejoinder, made with emphasis, "And probably enough, never will."

Little did either of us then think that even fourth season greyhounds of super-excellence would be equal to the task which both the mighty M'Grath and the great Fullerton accomplished.

In pursuance of his noble owner's intention not to run M'Grath again, he was advertised at the stud, and I glean from Captain Ellis's book of "Winning Strains," so rich in coursing lore, that at least four bitches visited him in the spring of 1870. When the autumn of that year came round he was taken out on one of the trial days to help in giving the Brownlow Kennel youngsters a lesson, and showed such superiority in each of his spins that Lord Lurgan decided to run him at the forthcoming Lurgan meeting.

He was, accordingly, on October 25, entered in the Brownlow Stakes, and ran clean through it in brilliant style, though without showing all the superior speed of his earlier days; and the stout-hearted Scotch dog Smuggler gave him a good challenge in the fourth round.

Several English dogs were entered, including the previous Waterloo Cup winner and runner-up, Sea Cove and Bendimere. The latter was drawn through severe running after winning three courses, and Sea Cove was beaten in the third round by Fritz, the runner-up.

This led to Waterloo being thought of again for the Irish wonder, and continuing to give every satisfaction in his trials, M'Grath again crossed St. George's Channel in February to add to his now imperishable fame.

The most romantic canards went the round of both the English and Irish Press after his triple-crown victory; Lord Lurgan was credited with having won £150,000 and taken out an insurance policy for £6,000 to cover the sea risk back home, before the dog sailed from Liverpool for Belfast. It was also gravely announced that Master M'Grath was to be "presented at Court."

This implication, however, was correct enough, as Lord Lurgan had a letter from Sir Thomas Biddulph, the then Lord Chamberlain, that "Queen Victoria would much like to see Master M'Grath at Windsor Castle," but there was no truth about the insurance, and Lord Lurgan's winnings did not exceed £2,000. Many of his friends, however, "threw in" for good stakes, as no secret was made of how well he had done in his trials.

On the night of the draw M'Grath was backed freely at 10 to 1, 100 to 12 being the best offer at the close. Bendimere was also supported at 100 to 10, Fritz being third favourite at 100 to 6.

Countryman, a Newmarket puppy that had won a Brigg Cup, and divided at Marham, together with the stout-hearted Scotch dog Smuggler, and the eventual runner-up, Pretender, were each backed at 20 to 1, and Waywarden and Chameleon each at 100 to 4. Bed of Stone, known to have an injured hind leg, stood at 100 to 3 offered, whilst Sea Cove and Chivalry, each known to have recently been suffering from sexual causes, were out in the cold. The speedy Cataclysm, a daughter of the flying Lady Stormont, was well befriended at 1,000's to 30, but only longer odds tempted backers of the remainder.

My mention of Brigg reminds me of one of several incidents that occurred during my many years of constant travel. Before reaching Retford from London, *en route* for the then famous Lincolnshire meeting, our Great Northern express was pulled up, the line being blocked with a wrecked luggage train, and the delay looked like being a long one from the way in which the breakdown gang were operating.

A consultation took place amongst the coursing *voyageurs*, and a way out of the difficulty was soon found, the foreman of the gang offering no objection. A long, strong rope was soon forthcoming, and Mr. C. F. Allison, who was something of a yachtsman, as well as a courser, together with his friend, Colonel Goodlake, took charge. The rope was always properly adjusted, and with plenty of willing helpers it only needed the " Now altogether—pull," for each wagon to be toppled over out of the way, there being, luckily, plenty of room on the near side.

How Master M'Grath Won.

It could not add to his glory and fame to make a long story of M'Grath's victory and last appearance in public, and though luck was on his side in a year that was marked by wretchedly poor trials, through hares running so badly from the effects of a very severe winter, he gave a strong glimpse of his early greatness on the last day.

In a shortish slip he went up some considerable distance ahead of the tired Black Knight (who had three slips with Chameleon in the fourth round), and kept so closely on the back of a good hare that he and she were twice over in the air together.

To explain more fully, the hare crossed the grass roadway at the now slipper's end of the Withins, with a wideish drain running along each side, and in both jumps M'Grath had each time taken off before the hare landed.

She next manœuvred at a gate, but the black could not be baulked, and holding on to the scut in the most marvellous manner, gave one of his master strokes at the finish.

In the final, with 2 to 1 on him, the champion could only just draw clear of Pretender, but, commanding his hare with all his old force, almost instantly gave the *coup de grace.* Quite an indescribable scene followed, and Lord Lurgan was over $yhelmed with congratulations, whilst cheers again rose, time after time, for the gallant M'Grath, as he was led back past the crowd.

The runner-up, Pretender—a Newmarket Champion Puppy Stake divider—acquitted himself exceedingly well, and so did another youngster, Latest News, in winning the Purse. The latter's sister, Letter T, also gave three sparkling displays in the Cup, being then put out by M'Grath in a course that ought not to have been decided.

Bed of Stone gave striking evidence of her gameness in winning the Plate, virtually on three legs, in addition to being very hard run ; and her companion in misfortune, Bendimere (they ran three undecideds in the Cup), was fearfully handicapped when beaten by Favorita in the fourth round of the Purse.

Before taking leave of the great Irish idol, I may appropriately mention that a Dublin reader of my reminiscenses as they were appearing weekly in the *Sporting Chronicle* drew my attention to the fact that " it was not only at Altcar where M'Grath's wonderful powers inflamed men's minds. The excitement in Dublin, great at the outset, grew in intensity year after year : there is nothing of the kind now."

CHAPTER VI.

Waterloo, 1872—Bed of Stone's Victory.

IN adding the Cup to her previous Purse and Plate laurels, Bed of Stone stands alone in being able to claim premier honours in all the three Waterloo events ; and perhaps the full story of the career of such a wonderful greyhound will be more acceptable to my readers than a lengthened review of the Waterloo Cup she won.

It was an outsider's year, for the winner stood at 40 to 1 on the night of the draw, and though the runner-up, Peasant Boy, was supported at 100 to 6 the two beaten in the semi-finals, Iron Shell and S.W., were in the outside division. Iron Shell was befriended at 1,000 to 10, but offers of 50 to 1 against S.W. elicited no response. Chameleon was favourite at 1,000 to 100 taken—Double or Quits and Pevensey being next in demand—and she went down in the first round and the first course run.

This, I have reason to believe, had something to do with her defeat by the good Scotch dog, Dr. Dougal's Glen Avon. It was in the days before much telegraphing was done, and Boynton, her trainer, who always made a practice of giving his dogs a fairly good breakfast, was unaware that she was in so early. Chameleon was in great form at the time, and not only ran through the Purse in great style, but won all her courses unchallenged, a good dog in Dr. Lawton's Liberty running-up.

Chameleon and Liberty were both by King Death. Mr. B. Heywood Jones's Jewess, by Ewesdale out of the good bitch Tamar, won the Plate in capital style.

I will now only add that the year was made conspicuous by the general stoutness with which the hares ran. They mostly gave only poor trials the year before, and extra care was taken this time, Lord Sefton (the present Earl's father) personally ordering carrots and oats to be freely put down, though Flatman, the head-keeper, used to say that the rooks got most of the oats.

This, coupled with favourable weather, had the desired effect, and many of the hares reached quite abnormal size and weight, especially for Altcar. The hare that Bed of Stone killed in her course with Lurline was weighed, and found to scale 10½lb., and the one she floored in the final with Peasant Boy weighed 9lb. Many of my readers may be somewhat incredulous at least about the 10½-pounder, but my information at the time was quite reliable.

Bed of Stone first saw the light in the spring of 1868, and was bought, together with her sister, Bill of Portland, by Mr. Briggs from his friend Mr. Frank Johnston as whelps at eight weeks old out of a litter by Purser's Portland (by Effort, by Larriston, by Littlesdale, by Bowhill) out of the good and beautiful bitch Imperatrice, by David out of Java, by Judge.

The combination of the David and Judge blood was then regarded with great favour, just as the intermingling of Greentick's and Herschel's descendants was at a more recent period. Although a South-country dog and a great-grandson of King Cob, David sprang from the North. Mr. John Jardine sent Matilda Gillespie to King Cob (the great Judge James Hedley taking her when a lad) and bred The Tollwife, who produced Motley, the sire of David.

In point of " class " regarding running abilities, Bed of Stone would be assigned lower rank than those grand bitches Bab at the Bowster and Miss Glendyne, but though they would both have certainly led her and probably beaten her, she was in some respects superior to either.

As I wrote in the *Irish Field* a few years back, the particular feature of her super-excellence was the " electric quickness with which she could win a course, after it was apparently lost. After being led a couple of lengths, or even more, and losing also the second point, and perhaps the third, she could turn the tables with dazzling rapidity.

" This was the result of the brilliant way in which she could, after once obtaining possession, shoot round any class of opponent, no matter how great the angle, to retain it : in running a course her frame seemed to consist more of whale-bone than bone and sinew. This bodily suppleness it was that enabled her to maintain such close possession that puss was rarely able to elude her; nor did her opponent, during her puppy career, often get a second chance.

"She did not kill her hares in the thrilling style, *a la* M'Grath; she did not possess the same speed and power of forceful movement on the scut, but she could spin with her quarry at whatever angle it broke, and the result—at least in her early days—was almost equally deadly.

"Before entering in detail upon Bed of Stone's career I ought to say something of her conformation, and this I am easily able to do, for her beautiful shapes are often under my eye from a perfect painting, presented by her owner, hanging in my dining-room. Without being such a perfect model of symmetry as, say, Mr. Lister's lovely Chameleon, she was, as is recorded in Captain Ellis's winning strains from 1880 to 1911, 'beautifully moulded'; but her best points are not given sufficient prominence.

"The perfect balance struck the eye at once, so did the clean-cut shoulders and her beautifully-shaped limbs and perfect feet. More conspicuous still was the forefront, and rarely has the old description been more fully verified:

A head like a snake,
A neck like a drake.

"And this was, doubtless, one of the secrets of her fine killing powers. And in addition to her charming shapes, 'Bed,' at least during her puppy season, was invariably in silken sheen, presenting thus a very pleasing picture to gaze upon. Her weight is given as 47lb., but that must have been when she was finely drawn, as she did not strike the eye as being at all undersized. She carried no lumber, being clean-cut and bloodlike, from her snake-like head to her rat-like tail.

"Her first appearance was in October, 1869. at Southport, in the South Lancashire Oaks (27 runners); this she divided with Morning Star after an undecided. She also beat Jerry for the Silver Vase, run for by the winners of the Derby and Oaks. A fortnight later she ran clean through the Ridgway (South Lancashire) Stakes (40 runners), and, upon making a second visit to Lytham in December, divided the Clifton Cup with her kennel companion, Duty Repealed, Mr. Briggs being in great form in those days.

" At Waterloo she met with her only puppy reverse, a speedy greyhound called Commodore leading her some distance. ' Bed ' was not long in getting to work, but this time her kill came too quickly. She carried off the Purse, however, beating the Irish bitch, S.S., in the final, after an undecided that was particularly well run by both.

" A fortnight subsequent to Waterloo Bed of Stone paid a third visit to Lytham, and won outright the combined North and South Lancashire Stakes, beating in the final Dr. Mould's My Goodness, who ran an undecided with Lady Lyons, after she had beaten Master M'Grath at Waterloo a fortnight previously.

" Yet another call was made upon ' Bed ' in her puppy-hood, and, disdaining defeat of juveniles like herself, she vanquished all opposition in the Douglas Cup (Scottish National), beating in the final a smart-running bitch called Sarah Ann. She, in the semi-finals, had (after an undecided) disposed of Cataclysm, who a fortnight earlier had, in the fourth round of the Waterloo Cup, beaten Bab at the Bowster.

" As a puppy Bed of Stone ran 38 courses (including undecideds) over all sorts of ground—the Southport fallows, the Scottish National undulations, the Lytham and Altcar flats, and only lost one.

" Whether from excessive early strain or kennel vicissitude, Bed of Stone did not evince all her pristine vitality in her second season, a natural sexual visitation interfered in the autumn, and an attack of rheumatism supervened, causing an anxious time as Waterloo drew near.

" However, before the day she acquitted herself sufficiently well in private to be again selected as the champion of the now famous Blackburn kennel. In the draw she came against Bendimere, the previous year's runner-up to Sea Cove, and the pair, under Mr. Warwick, ran no fewer than three un-decideds, Bendimere being at last drawn.

" Being thus handicapped with extra running, and being also lame from injury in a trial the previous Thursday, ' Bed ' was next outpaced by Fancy and beaten in a poor trial. On the second day she ran a smart course in her easy defeat of Primrose in the Plate ; but on Friday morning, when opposed

From Painting by Mr. J. Armstrong, Aglionby, Carlisle.

BED OF STONE, Winner of Waterloo Cup, 1872; Purse, 1870; and Plate, 1871.

COOMASSIE, Winner of Waterloo Cup, 1877-78

to Sandridge, was so lame that she would have been drawn on any reasonable terms.

" The proposal, however, was not entertained; as a matter of fact the Sandridge party were wishful for the course to be run, as there had been some heavy betting on it overnight. Consequently they went to slips, with the result that ' the fat was in the fire,' ' Bed,' a little favoured in the run up, being first to the hare, and winning in a canter.

" The die being now cast, the lame 'un was sent to slips against two other Scottish opponents, Avonside and Duke of York, and she led and easily beat them both, thus virtually winning the Plate on three legs.

" It was left for her third season to give the crowning triumph to Bed of Stone's career, though its early stages gave little promise of such an appropriate denouement. At the outset she made, like ' Bab,' an ill-starred visit to Lurgan, and though she escaped the humiliation of defeat, a single-handed ' pounding ' in the second round, through both being unsighted, necessitated her withdrawal.

" My days of severe criticism being long past, I will only make gentle allusion to the incompetence of the slipper of that period (it was not Hoystead, whom one great day at Lurgan virtually destroyed); but my reflections on past experiences often lead me to think how much present-day coursers owe to the ability and rectitude of a slipper like Edward Wilkinson. And yet, when the Massereene executive, recognising his priceless worth, gave Irish coursers the benefit of his services, they had to endure reproach from some stupid quarter for engaging an Englishman !

" Three weeks later Bed of Stone figured in the Netherby Cup, but after winning her first two courses easily, and cutting each fairly short, she got two terrible gruellers the next day, and, being injured as well, had to strike her flag to Kingcraft, the divider. Ill-luck again attended her next effort (at Lytham) in December, for in defeating Adelaide, after a no-course, she was run to a standstill and drawn; and at the Altcar January Meeting, after beating Cripple, Lignum Vitæ, and Jew, she went down before Lady Grafton, in the final.

D

A Waterloo Triumph.

" Many now thought that Bed of Stone's sun had set, but Waterloo told a different tale. She led off by smartly disposing of Eyes of Fire (who ran an undecided with Master M'Grath the year before), and polished off Princess in the same finished style. This gave her a considerable jump forward in public favour, for, after starting at 40 to 1, 10 to 1 was now eagerly taken, Peasant Boy being favourite at 7 to 2.

" On Thursday she showed her superiority to Grig in a short spin, and also gave Lurline a terrible trouncing, but this course seemed to about extinguish her chance of winning the Cup. A rare hare persistently ran in circles, and stood up so gallantly that the trial extended to distressing length. In the evening 7 to 4 was laid against her going further, but her powers of recuperation came to the rescue, and she vanquished Iron Shell in her best style.

" For the final Peasant Boy was a strong favourite, and in a grandly-contested trial he made a good fight ; but ' Bed,' after reaching the hare first, under slight favour, always had the best of it, her beautiful finish and stylish kill leaving no doubt which had won.

" A tremendous cheer went up as the white flag was hoisted, ' Bed ' being a great Lancashire idol and her owner exceedingly popular. The bitch's fame had also much to do with his brother, Mr. W. E. Briggs, barrister-at-law, being returned member for Blackburn."

Bed of Stone ran over 80 courses in public, and the great treasure house of her valuable blood was very nearly lost, for she only reared one puppy—by Contango. That puppy was Bedfellow, who produced the lion-hearted Greentick, sire of the great Fullerton and a host of good ones.

Bed of Stone died in pupping to Blackburn in 1875, and, by a singular coincidence, Bab at the Bowster died in pupping to the same dog, in the same year. Blackburn himself was the victim of misfortune, as he broke a leg in his second season at an Altcar Club January meeting.

He ran three undecideds with Muriel, the latter being then drawn, and in the final course of the Members' Plate, led Crœsus three lengths in the run-up, but broke his leg in landing over a drain, and lost the course. Five weeks later Muriel won the Waterloo Cup.

CHAPTER VII.

More about Bab at the Bowster.

LINKED together as they are in the lineage of so many of our most distinguished greyhound families, it seems quite fitting that Bed of Stone and (in some respects her prototype) Bab at the Bowster, should also be in juxtaposition where their active careers are concerned. There was much in common between the two, for though their styles were dissimilar, Bab's, like Bed's, transcendent qualities were her wonderful endurance, and great powers of recuperation.

As a pair, they certainly stand alone in this respect amongst all the greyhounds of note that I have ever seen. *En passant,* I ought perhaps to add that the famous bitch Riot was slightly before my travels. Her owner, Mr. C. Randall, often mentioned her; her excellence was early evinced, and winning two sapling stakes did not prevent her lasting on, and winning five stakes in her fourth season. She ran over eighty courses in public, and won seventy-four of them.

If Riot, however, vies with Bab and Bed in regard to their active careers, she did not make the same indelible imprint upon the future. Bed of Stone's son, Bedfellow, gave us Greentick, and Bab's son, Contango, through his grandson, M'Pherson, gave us Herschel—the two greatest sires of modern days, the co-mingling of whose blood was the best mixture of my time.

Numbers of good greyhounds were thereby produced, including the two grand bitches, Fearless Footsteps and Lavishly Clothed, winner and runner-up of the Waterloo Cup, 1900. Both were by Herschel's son, Fabulous Fortune, and respectively out of Greentick's daughters, Fille de Feu and Irish Queen.

The Waterloo winner in 1895, Thoughtless Beauty (another brilliant bitch), was by Herschel, direct, out of Greentick's daughter, Thetis, and another Waterloo winner, Wild Night (in 1898), was produced the reverse way, her sire, Freshman, being a son of Greentick, and her dam Fine Night, a daughter of Herschel.

A still stronger instance of the combination's value is given by Farndon Ferry, entitled perhaps to rank next to Master M'Grath, Fullerton, and Herschel in point of excellence amongst his sex. His dam, Fair Florence, was by Herschel, and his sire, Fiery Furnace, was by Sir Sankey, by Greentick.

There is not much honour in self-praise, but with due modesty I can claim a hand in producing Farndon's sire. Tom Wright had an attack of distemper at Saughall, whilst Flying Fancy was carrying Fiery Furnace, so he brought the bitch to Carlisle, out of the danger zone.

I pupped the bitch, and put the litter out to walk. Fiery Furnace was reared by a country bread baker, and always had the run of the bakehouse, often sleeping there on cold nights, hence his name.

Like Bed of Stone, Bab's first attempt in public was signalised by more than a glimpse of those great powers that were to make her name famous. Much of the running, too, was over uneven ground, abounding with great grips, where present-day greyhounds would be more likely to break their legs—or their necks—than to kill the hare, but Bab, inexperienced as she was, showed even then that she could run over any sort of ground.

In all her career, I only remember her being once at fault. It was at Altcar, and she was pressing her hare very closely whilst running parallel to a drain. Puss feinted as though intending to cross it, and Bab, in her eagerness to follow closely, could not avert a side-slip into it. She reappeared, however, in a twinkling, and was very quickly again in front.

A few weeks after her initial success Bab appeared at Altcar and divided the Croxteth Stakes with Brigade, both puppies showing such smart form that they were then kept in reserve for the Waterloo Cup. How they were both beaten has already been told.

Bab's transcendent merits and amazing vitality, even as a puppy, were strikingly exemplified before her first season closed. Early in March she ran clean through the Scarisbrick

Cup of 128 all-aged dogs, good greyhounds like Joan of Arc and Crossfell being amongst the seven she vanquished; but she was still called upon for another effort, and proved equal to the occasion.

In the Scottish National Douglas Cup (64 all-ages) she swept away all opposition, taking a sweet revenge upon Lobelia in the final course. Bab thus won 25 courses, and lost one during her puppyhood.

Bab's Second Waterloo.

Despite her heavy juvenile efforts, Bab came out the following autumn with her energies unimpaired. She led off by winning the Altcar Club Cup (20 runners), beating Mr. Spinks's Sea Rocket in the final, and the following month divided the Elsham Cup at Brigg (32 runners), being then accorded a rest before attempting a Waterloo triumph.

In the great event she did not represent her owner, Mr. George Blanshard, and it is regretful to add that this was not through any mistaken judgment as in several other cases. Of these special mention may be made of Lord Haddington running Haidee in preference to Honeywood, and Mr. Postle relying upon Palm Bloom rather than Princess Dagmar, the second string in each instance winning.

More recently it will be remembered that Mr. Fawcett in 1900 made the mistake of entering in his own name Father of Fire instead of Fearless Footsteps, who beat the Duke of Leeds's Lavishly Clothed in a memorable final; and in 1903 it proved an error of judgment to entrust the previous year's victor, Farndon Ferry, in preference to the stout-hearted Father Flint.

Reverting more closely to my text, the money kept pouring in for Mr. R. Paterson's Waterloo nomination (there was considerable ante-post betting in those days), and, as the day of running drew near, it became known that Bab at the Bowster would fill it. Mr. Blanshard himself ran Bab's brother, Bethell, who lost his first course, and only raised two flags in the Purse. This was the year of Bab's thrilling final with Master M'Grath.

As in her puppy days a visit to Southport followe Waterloo, and here a second great triumph in the Scarisbric

Cup (128 runners) awaited her. I may mention that much of the running was over rough fallow, and the hares were all "walked up," but Bab was quite at home on any sort of ground.

A further repetition of her puppy achievement by adding a Douglas Cup success was frustrated by accident. She was in slips with a black bitch called Miss Lizzie, and during a short change of beat a hare sprang up unexpectedly, with the result that they freed themselves close to her.

The black had the luck to gain first possession, and put in three or four smart points before Bab shot up and killed. It was, to all intents and purposes, a "no course," but the judge, Mr. Hay, decided it for Miss Lizzie.

Re-entered in the Biggar Stakes (32 runners) Babs gave some clipping displays, and divided with Captain Watson's Witchery, her second season's record being thus—winning 24 courses and losing two.

For the third time in succession Bab opened her autumn season successfully, an early start at the end of September gaining her further Douglas Cup laurels, though two subsequent reverses were in store. A trip to Ireland resulted in defeat in the second round of the Brownlow Cup by the Irish greyhound, Sir James, but I was not present that year, and cannot say how it occurred. The English dog, Boy in Office, trained by Archie Coke, proved the winner. Mr. Caulfield's Come-take-Care, who beat Sir James in the third round, running up.

A visit to one of her old haunts next resulted in summary dismissal by a dog called Sailor, but it was a palpable fluke. The course was run on wheat, and the ground was in such sticky condition that Bab, losing her position unluckily after leading three lengths, was unable to displace her opponent until he had a winning balance, Bab then destroying her chance with her teeth. The Elsham Cup was a 64-dog stake in those days, and Bab was backed freely at 5 to 1, second favourite, at 100 to 15, being the Irish bitch, S.S., who landed a good stake for her party, the two leading Nottingham book-makers (one of them the present Sir J. Robinson) jointly making a large book.

Bab next essayed Waterloo honours for the third time, but a Blue Riband triumph was still denied her. She led off by beating a good bitch in Jaunty Jane, but after also disposing of Inkstand and Albatross, she was beaten by Cataclysm, though the latter had the luck to be slightly favoured for her lead. Bab made yet another appearance, and it is noteworthy, and probably unique, that she began and ended each of three running seasons successfully.

Bab's Farewell Appearance.

Her closing effort was at Lytham, where the Ridgway Club held court so pleasantly and successfully over a considerable stretch of years, and she shared the honours of the Clifton Cup with her Waterloo victress, Cataclysm, a fast bitch by the good dog, Patent, out of the flying Lady Stormont.

This bitch was the dam of Cashier, whose mating with Bab at the Bowster resulted in the production of Contango, whose blood few greyhounds of note are without.

It will have been gleaned that Bab had a very strenuous career, and in addition to the great number of courses she ran, not a few of them were extra severe. I used sometimes to hear reproaches cast against her owner for his apparently inconsiderate treatment of such a gallant greyhound, but there were difficulties in the way of which the public were unaware. Bab refused resolutely to be left at home, and " would," I was assured, " have torn the place down, or injured herself seriously in the attempt " had a team been taken away to a meeting without her being included.

Bab and Bed of Stone were related, their respective sires, Boanerges and Portland both being great-grandsons of the Scotch dog Liddlesdale. Boanerges was by Canaradzo (Waterloo winner, and one of the illustrious Beacon and Scotland Yet family) out of Baffle, by the perfectly moulded dog Hughie Graham (see picture, Cerito, Mocking Bird, and Hughie Graham), a son of Liddesdale and Queen of the May, respectively son of Bowhill and daughter of King Cob, " Bab " and " Bed " thus inheriting the same blood in two directions.

CHAPTER VIII.

Short Allusion to Pupping.

FROM the fate of these two famous bitches—I might say world renowned greyhounds, wherever coursing is known—a short allusion to pupping might perhaps not be out of place here. Not that I suggest the least likelihood of there having been any neglect ; they were getting on in point of age, " Bab " being nine and " Bed " seven years old, and both went through running ordeals that perhaps no other greyhound would have survived sufficiently to breed at all.

But from my own actual experience—I bred all the Duke of Leeds's greyhounds—I know how preliminary trouble can sometimes be relieved without much risk. Of course, all breeders will know the necessity of the bowels being kept open and free as pupping time approaches, and the usual precautions will be taken.

If all is going well, it is no doubt best to secure quietude, and leave the bitch to her own devices ; but if in trouble she will come to her best friend, and in her own way ask for help, which must then not be withheld.

I experienced this more than once, and successfully applied hot flannels and gave a dose of oil. I particularly remember Lemon Squash at one of her puppings—perhaps when carrying those grand bitches, Limetta, Limonum, Lavender, and Laurifolia, the first three of which could all lead and beat Lonely Star—being in sore straits. She kept up a continual whine, going into and out of her pupping bed, and at last I ventured an extra big dose of chilled castor oil—fully two large tablespoonfuls, with a little syrup of buckthorn added.

This proved quite a complete remedy, for within a short time the first puppy was born, and the entire process of whelping five bitches and one dog occupied less than the half usual period.

Valuable aid can also be given by saving the mother from having to dry a whelp a second time. This also conserves the strength of the whelp, thereby helping it to find a teat. Once dried, the puppies ought to be gently moved with a warm hand from the whetting zone at each subsequent birth.

Value of Personal Assistance.

I am here reminded that there is sometimes great danger from the bitch being worn out in the case of big litters. It is no uncommon thing to hear of a litter including a dead one ; but this, more often than not, is through the mother having crushed it, or still more probably from her having been so exhausted that she failed to break the case in which each puppy is enveloped, so that it quickly dies of suffocation.

A more serious drawback in connection with parturition is where the brood bitch is constitutionally deficient ; and I can here tell a rather interesting story. A bitch called Irish Queen, possessed of above average running qualities, was being sent to the Barbican for sale during the Duke of Leeds's early days.

Being by Greentick out of Miss Glendyne, and thus possessing also the blood of the other two wonderful bitches Bab at the Bowster and Bed of Stone, I journeyed to London for the purpose of buying her unless the price proved prohibitive.

To my surprise, I got her for a moderate price—I believe, less than forty guineas—but there was a secret, and I was not in it. Irish Queen was the property of Sir George Irwin, who was selling off, his coursing manager being Mr. George Lister, of Kirkstall, near Leeds, whom many of my readers will remember.

George was a kind-hearted chap, and finding that Tom Wright (Messrs. Fawcett's trainer) was after her, he warned him and also one or two others of his friends against buying the bitch, and this was how I came to get her for so little money. The " murder was out " soon afterwards, and Irish Queen was not expected to prove of much value. She had a litter to Ascestes the previous spring, and, as I heard the story, just escaped with her life : the record of the litter in Captain Ellis's book is one puppy.

Irish Queen was looking well when she visited Fabulous Fortune, and she successfully gave birth to six puppies—afterwards to be known as Lavishly Clothed, Lightly Clad, Letters of Gold, Laurels Galore, Letters of Marque, and Lady Eden's Mythology.

But it was only by the greatest good fortune that any of the family were reared : the warning note had been a " true bill "—the mother would not allow the puppies to suckle. As luck would have it, however, a collie bitch, quite freshly pupped, was quickly secured, and the puppies never looked behind. Not so the mother.

Poor Nellie had a terrible time from inflammation, and I can here illustrate the value of long-sustained fomentation. The veterinary in attendance had done her up for the night, swathed in cotton wool under her clothing ; but she was evidently in such great pain that I said to my then housekeeper (one of the best), " Jane, I don't think Nellie will be alive in the morning." She replied, " Well, is there anything we can do ? " It so happened that I knew the great virtues of hot water.

I mentioned this to Jane, and the pair of us, instead of going to bed, put the bitch through the same process, from about 10 p.m. until nearly breakfast time, when we were at last rewarded by seeing Nellie shrink from the heat : the inflammation was at last subdued.

There was rather a pathetic sequel to this incident which I may as well relate. For a change I had sent the bitch to one of the walks where a couple of our saplings were being reared. One day she surprised us by putting in an appearance, but we thought it was simply a case of home-sick and took little notice. Next day, however, she began to whine a little and follow me about, and I sent for her old vet. He did not diagnose that there was much wrong, though he took what he considered prudent precautionary steps, but next morning I got the shock of finding her dead in bed.

Upon revolving everything in my mind it became quite clear that Nellie had found herself again in trouble, and came back home for another happy relief, which was this time so cruelly, though unwittingly, withheld.

CHAPTER IX.

Waterloo, 1873.
Muriel's Year.   A Missing Link.

THE marks of "times effacing fingers" were conspicuously and regretfully in evidence this year, and the passing of two such prominent and popular Waterloo figures as Mr. Alexander Graham (chairman for so many years) and Mr. B. Heywood-Jones (President of the Ridgway Club) claims special mention.

With the exceptions of Master M'Grath and Fullerton, Peasant Boy (the previous year's runner-up) could claim to be the greatest favourite that had ever been so freely supported on the night of the draw. There was almost a scramble to catch the eye of the bookmakers, who offered £100 to £15, and he only just failed to land his backers home.

Bed of Stone, in "the sere, the yellow leaf" of her fourth season, was backed at 1,000 to 60, and Chameleon was on the same mark; but both to some extent proved to be "lights of other days," though in justice to the latter it must be added that she was the victim of a gruelling on the first day, before suffering defeat from the winner, Muriel, in the third round. She had a double go with Diacticus to start with, and in the second round ran three undecideds with Gone before winning a punishing course.

Muriel did not make any special impression on the opening day, whilst the favourite, Peasant Boy, as well as Crœsus, Satire, and Magenta, did. The betting at night was 3 to 1 against Peasant Boy, taken freely, 5 to 1 Crœsus, 9 to 1 Satire, 10 to 1 Magenta, and 100 to 7 Muriel.

On the second day Peasant Boy polished off his first opponent, Amethyst, in capital style, but he was fairly tackled by Cymbal in the fourth round, and had the judge given the undecided to Mr. Lister's bitch there could have been no complaints. In the run-off Cymbal was unluckily unsighted for some distance, and the crack made such good use of his advantage that Cymbal only got in to kill and lose.

Muriel had an easy task against poor Chameleon, and again

going " great guns " against Crœsus, led him some distance, and won in a canter. Magenta also went fast and well in her defeats of Magnano (the next year's winner), and Satire—one of the Larkhill lot that Lord Sefton bought upon Mr. B. Heywood-Jones's death.

On Thursday night a shade of odds were laid on Peasant Boy winning, though 105 to 100 was taken several times. Muriel now became second favourite at 4 to 1, Magenta and Madeline standing respectively at 5 and 8 to 1.

What would otherwise have been a grand Waterloo—for the weather was favourable, the ground in splendid order, and the trials excellent—was seriously marred by the behaviour of an angry and excited portion of the crowd.

The Plate and the Purse were run once through without incident, and in the semi-finals of the Cup Peasant Boy polished off Madeline so decisively that her being unsighted for a short distance from slips clearly made no difference to the result. Muriel and Magenta then ran an undecided, the removal of Mr. Warwick's cap giving rise to indications of disapproval. Next time Muriel led a considerable distance, and won quite decisively.

Hare and Dogs Mobbed.

In the final Muriel outpaced Peasant Boy, and had a meritorious beginning, and as soon as Peasant Boy obtained possession a portion of the crowd rushed forward from the Withins bank, and mobbed both the dogs and the hare, interfering with the black's chance of rubbing off the early points. Before Mr. Warwick could give his decision they also surrounded him, and only the fiat in favour of Muriel saved him from violence.

" It was a most 'deplorable spectacle to see both hare and dogs mobbed in the deciding course for a Waterloo Cup, and it is melancholy indeed to reflect on the possibility of its recurrence. But it was even worse to see the judge threatened, and the evil consequences of heavy betting were never more forcibly illustrated. Greatly incited by a particular section of the professionals—whose unguarded and unbridled mode of speech cannot have other than a most degrading influence upon the sport—a large proportion of the public (not the coursing public be it remembered, but the Lancashire roughs) got it into their heads that Mr. Warwick intended nothing else but to pull Peasant Boy through, and determined to frustrate his designs if possible.

" In running through the Cup Muriel proved herself a really good greyhound—possessing fine speed, great quickness, and a ready mouth—and although very nearly beaten by a ' fluke ' in the first round she polished off all her subsequent opponents in brilliant style.   Prince reached the hare in front of her, but not on merit, as after getting the worst of the slip Muriel quickly drew past, and only lost the lead by slightly faltering upon landing over the drain through overjumping herself.

" It was quite clear to me that Muriel had the pace, although she lost first turn, and she ran in such magnificent style after the hare came round that Prince was never afterwards in it.   Her defeat of Chameleon did not possess much merit, as the ' old 'un ' was completely ' settled ' the night before ; but the style in which she ran clean away from Crœsus ought to have opened everybody's eyes to her great chance for the Cup.   It gave a direct line that she had the speed of Peasant Boy, as the latter had already shown himself to be only two lengths faster than Amethyst, who, at New-market, proved herself of about the same pace as Crœsus.

In her undecided with Magenta she made an unpardonably unsteady dash, and the Cumberland bitch made such good use of the advantage that she would have won had she succeeded in killing, but Muriel shot in at the first fair opening, and made such a brilliant finish that Mr. Warwick might fairly have decided for her.   At the same time, it was nothing like the decisive win a great many made it out to be ; and, as I have already intimated, I have no doubt in my own mind but that Mr. Warwick considered the points equally balanced.

" At the second time of asking, however, Muriel made a most decisive job of it, and the superiority she displayed, of course, confirmed those who thought she won the undecided in their opinion.   The course being a longish one caused odds of 5 to 2 and 3 to 1 to be laid against her for the ' decider,' but, like Bed of Stone last year, she was destined to dash the Cup from Peasant Boy's lips.   Upon that occasion the Boy's friends argued that he lost through the hare favouring Mr. Briggs's bitch, but they have to go on another tack this time.

" The hare favoured Peasant Boy very considerably in the run up, and the style in which Muriel shot past to obtain possession was meritorious in the extreme. Peasant Boy got every opportunity of taking the early points, and was fairly unequal to the occasion. His defeat led to a most exciting scene, and no victory could have been more popular than that of Muriel. Immediately she was seen to forge ahead in the run up a roar of satisfaction rent the air, and the final hoisting of the white flag was the signal for such an outburst of enthusiasm as was never before witnessed at Waterloo.

" Mr. Jardine's triumph did not end with his carrying off the Cup, for his smart Joan divided the Purse with Contango, and it was a ' red letter day ' for Scotland to snuff out so decisively the mother country in both events.

Mr. Jardine's First Cup.

" I need hardly tell my readers that it was Mr. Jardine's first Waterloo Cup victory (Selby and Clive, the dividers in 1859, were the property of Mr. John Jardine), but he has shown a bold front upon most of the occasions on which he has essayed to win it. The first year he held a nomination was in 1866, when he ran into the last eight with Annabella, then he ran second to Strange Idea for the Plate with Improver, and afterwards second to Latest News for the Purse with Favorita, whilst last year he ran into the last four for the Cup with Mr. G. Bell-Irving's Iron Shell. He can boast of having won the Blue Ribands of both the Turf and the Leash.

" Before leaving Muriel's year I may mention that it was the last of the series judged by Mr. Warwick, and when the voting of the nominators in 1879 was against him, he found consolation in the remark, ' I have judged thirteen Waterloos : it will never be done again.'

" This was a striking acknowledgment of the difficulties of the position ; but Mr. Warwick was not a true prophet ; his successor, Mr. James Hedley, ' held the field ' for no fewer than 24 years, and Mr. Robert Brice wore the Waterloo scarlet from 1898 to 1911 inclusive."

CHAPTER X.

An Outsider's Waterloo, 1874.

MAGNANO'S year was not marked like many Waterloos with a favourite in slips and an exciting finish, the finalists having respectively stood at 1,000 to 7 and 1,000 to 10 on the night of the draw, and never once having come prominently into favour. Even on the last evening they stood at longer odds than the other two of the final quartette.

The prices were 7 to 4 against Fugitive, taken in hundreds, 75 to 20 Diacticus, taken freely, and 9 to 2 against each Magnano and the runner-up Surprise. Like the winner and runner-up Diacticus was originally an extreme outsider, his price being 1,000 to 15. Magnano outpaced Fugitive and beat him well in a capital trial, but Mr. Hedley, who made his debut as Waterloo judge, was unable to separate Surprise and Diacticus.

In running it off, however, the Irish dog went up well ahead, and showed marked superiority in a nice trial, which he ran exceedingly well. These courses, as well as the two rounds of the Purse and Plate, had been run on Rye Heys (the flat below Hill House Covert), but for the finals a move was made to the Withins, which was not very sound going this year, and favoured the bigger and stronger-built dog, Magnano. It was a ding-dong struggle in the run-up, the son of the stout Cauld Kail only towards the finish drawing out a good length, and sweeping with his hare in fine style he made a good start by holding strong possession.

At the first opening Surprise shot smartly to the front, and the remainder of a capital trial—well run by both—was stoutly contested, the balance in Magnano's favour being only slight when Surprise killed.

Gallant Foe and Her Descendants.

There was also a beautifully-run final in the Plate between Gallant Foe and White Slave, but the first-named having the better speed always had the course won. Gallant Foe was a great performer, and also bred a wonderful litter to Contango's son Ptarmigan, embracing Princess Dagmar (Waterloo Cup winner), Paris (sire of Miss Glendyne), Peter, Prenez Garde, Palmbloom, Pathfinder, and Assegai, all very handsome greyhounds.

I am hardly disposed to say it was the best litter of my time ; indeed, I am inclined to the opinion that both the first Herschel—Fair Future litter, embodying Fabulous Fortune, Fortune's Favourite, Fortunæ Favente, Fair Floralie, and First Fortune ; and also the Duke of Leeds's four bitches, Limonum, Limetta, Lavender, and Luarifolia, by Tuddenham—Lemon Squash, stood on quite as high a plane in order of merit in the field ; though as show greyhounds the Ptarmigan—Gallant Foes would have won easily enough, for they were a handsome crew.

The Waterloo Purse, as in the previous year, led to a division, but this time it was not after two undecideds but between the two kennel companions, Muriel and Progress, and, judging by the way they improved as the week wore on, the result of the Cup might have been very different but for the contretemps that preceded it.

Frost had prevented preliminary trials at home, and the hazardous, not to say dangerous, risk of running trials on the Ince ground, contiguous to Altcar, on the Saturday before the meeting, was resorted to with most disastrous results. I may add that the Ince hares were well-known to take some killing, but the class of the Castle Milk greyhounds at this period was such that it was thought the risk might safely be taken. Alas ! for the weakness of human foresight ; but I will let what I wrote at the time tell its own tale :—

" ' Muriel and Progress were both run to death on Saturday ' was the first piece of news with which we were greeted on Monday ; and, whatever their fates may be, it is quite certain that their respective chances of winning have been considerably prejudiced, even if not effectually destroyed. I will not here enter upon the question as to the policy of trying so near the time—and surely such judges as Mr. Robert and Mr. John Jardine ought to know whether circumstances rendered such a proceeding politic—but the slipping together

CERITO, MOCKING BIRD, and HUGHIE GRAHAM.

LANG SYNE, LAPAL, LAVISHLY CLOTHED.

Consecutive Waterloo Runners-up in 1898-99 and 1900.

of Muriel and Progress was nevertheless attended with the most disastrous results.

" Muriel had already led and polished off White Slave, whilst Progress had a short go with Lucetta, in which there was not room for any distinctive merit to be displayed, Lucetta gaining the run-up by favour, and had matters rested here, ' all would have been well.' But it was decided to put Muriel and Progress together, and ' a demon ' of a hare to which Progress led over two lengths and had matters nearly all her own way for some time, ran both almost to a standstill.

" Then, to pile up the agony, Progress got away with a fresh one, Nanny O and Lucetta being let go, in their sheets, to help her, and the old hare even defied the lot for some time, Lucetta being the one to dispatch her at last. The consternation such a contretemps created in the minds of Mr. Jardine and his friends present can be better imagined than described, and their mortification must have been quite sufficient punishment for any indiscretion—even admitting that it was an indiscretion—without such uncomplimentary remarks as have been so inconsiderately launched.

" As is not unusual in such cases, wildly exaggerated stories got into circulation during the latter portion of the day, and to show what *canards* were afloat I may mention that a prominent bookmaker offered to lay 40 ponies against Mr. Jardine's nomination, and a level pony that Muriel didn't run."

Of course all the nursing possible was given to Muriel and Progress, and instead of being knocked out, their respective prices after the draw were 100 to 8 and 100 to 6 taken. Peasant Boy (runner up to both Muriel and Bed of Stone) was a strong favourite at 7 to 1, Fugitive being next in demand at 100 to 12.

The latter justified his favouritism in so smartly defeating his first four opponents, but being only a puppy, was clearly going off when beaten by the winner. The favourite gave indications of " the sere, the yellow leaf," and after receiving a severe licking from the runner-up, Surprise, in the second round, was withdrawn from the Plate.

E

CHAPTER XI.

Waterloo, 1875—Honeymoon Supplements Master M'Grath's Victory.

PARTLY owing to there being no public idol, Honeymoon's year was comparatively tame at the outset, but it culminated in a most exciting finish, Corby Castle, against whom 1,000 to 10 was on offer on the night of the draw, only just failing to repeat the success of the previous year's extreme outsider, Magnano.

The Scotch puppy Sirius started favourite, 100 to 12 being taken freely, and the Border crack, Fugitive, was strongly supported at 100 to 10. Honeymoon had also a strong following at 100 to 8, but 1,000 to 60 was on offer against the 1873 winner, Muriel, now in her third season.

Sirius was bowled over in the first round, and after winning two courses in the Plate was beaten by the winner, Goodlake's Gilderoy. Fugitive won a couple of courses, but then made a sorry exhibition against Lucetta after they had been severely mauled in slips.

The winner's form was good throughout, as will be fully gleaned from the sketch of her career that appeared in the *Irish Field* from my pen a few years ago, and now repeated here.

" Honeymoon cannot claim to stand upon the same elevated pedestal as her great compatriot, nor as a few of the best English bitches ; but as an Irish greyhound of considerable distinction—a winner of two (Lurgan) Brownlow Cups as well as the Blue Riband of the leash—she may not inappropriately be included amongst the ' great ladies ' of the past. She was a fine raking bitch of 55lb. or 56lb., cast in a handsome mould, and was the only piebald greyhound that has ever won the Waterloo Cup.

" She is described in the records as a bk. w. b., but she was distinctly more white than black, though the balance of colour was not much. Whelped in 1872, I do not know that she made much of a mark in her puppy season (1873-74) ;

but in the autumn of the latter year she asserted herself by carrying off the Brownlow Cup for 64 all-ages ; winner £300 and cup, presented by Lord Lurgan ; entrance fee, £11.

" Oddly enough, Honeymoon was not then deemed to be the best in the kennel, her owner (Mr. Ford-Hutchinson) preferring to rely upon the faster Hopeful Joe, who, however, went down in the third round before Rover, and he in the next ties was beaten by Donald.

" In the semi-finals, the two subsequent Waterloo Cup winners, Honeymoon and Donald, came together, the bitch winning a shortish trial easily, and, though she was favoured a little in the run up, she clearly went the faster in the course. The final tussle was between Honeymoon and Mr. H. Haywood's good bitch, Ruby, who started second favourite to Surprise for the stake at the outset, and advanced to the premier position at 5 to 1 after the first round.

" Honeymoon went too fast for the Blakemere bitch, and the hare was not good enough to give the latter an opportunity of bringing her wonderful working powers into play.

Her Waterloo Triumph.

" Still further developing her powers (as a bitch of her build would), Honeymoon came out brilliantly at Waterloo, and even at the outset, in her first course, truthfully foreshadowed her ultimate success. Quoting from my own report : ' Honeymoon drew out fully half a dozen lengths from Master M'Turk, and, coming round cleverly at the turn, went off with a good lead for the second, then handling her hare with the greatest cleverness, never left the scut until she killed.' In the second round she rattled out six or eight lengths from Pearl, and instantly floored her hare.

" Commenting on the day's running, I wrote : ' The best performance of the day was Honeymoon's first course, and she supplemented it with a second smart display.' Her third opponent, Indian Star, was enabled to make a lucky undecided, but at the second attempt Honeymoon led three lengths and beat him pointless. In the fourth round Darcarolle (a very fast, though only moderate, dog) had the foot of her ; but in the semi-finals she shone as brilliantly against Lucetta as against Master M'Turk, leading many lengths, giving a polished display, and winding up a grand performance with a smart kill.

" Here I may interpolate an explanation of why Honeymoon's third and fourth courses (on the middle day) compared so unfavourably with her others. She was in very capable hands, Joe Chestnut being her trainer, but on Thursday morning he could not succeed in getting relief to her bowels. Joe thought the matter over, and decided that to give the bitch her ordinary feed in the evening might make matters worse for the finish.

" ' Do you know where I could get some buttermilk ? ' was Joe's inquiry at his training quarters, and, though it took some finding, the desired supper was secured, no solids being added. The result was a complete success, the bitch being full of spirits, and ' fit to run for her life ' when she went to slips with, and polished off, the Castle Milk bitch, Lucetta, on Friday morning.

" It now looked all over but shouting, her last opponent, Corby Castle, having shown no pretensions to deprive her of a great triumph. And yet the final only missed being a tragedy by a hair's breadth. They were slipped down the famous Withins, Honeymoon quickly drawing in advance, and scoring the initial point four lengths ahead. Puss, however, nicked short back, which enabled the outsider to gain possession, and, handling his hare with desperate cleverness, he quickly ran up a clear balance in his favour, backers of Honeymoon meanwhile holding their breath at the seemingly tragic turn of events. Fortunately, Corby Castle just failed in his attempt at the death, and the bitch, instantly dashing past, wrenched and killed, Judge Hedley at once signalling an undecided.

" The run-off gave another thrill of even more pronounced character than before. Honeymoon again stretched away well in front, but puss beginning to circle to the right the red crossed behind for a short cut, and actually reached the hare first. The white and black was not long in displacing him, but, to escape her too eager attentions, puss broke at a sharp angle, which gave Corby Castle another opportunity, which he very smartly took. And now came the thrill, ' Corby ' sticking closely and resolutely to the scut for such a strong sequence that his success seemed almost certain. At last the hare broke sufficiently clear for Honeymoon to shoot to the front, and this time, commanding her game with beautiful cleverness before giving the *coup de grace*, the flag went up in her favour.

"A memorable finish was thus not spoiled by the inferior greyhound being at last successful; and, if Honeymoon cannot take rank amongst the greatest Waterloo winners, this much can at least be said—that in all my long experience I have never seen a greyhound (Master M'Grath alone excepted in his second triumph) gain Blue Riband laurels in more meritorious or brilliant fashion. Her success led to much enthusiasm amongst the Irish Brigade, of which a strong contingent were present, and she was heavily backed at the draw at 100 to 8, taken freely.

"There were two better favourites—Sirius at 100 to 12 and Fugitive at 10 to 1. Several good stakes were landed, one of the largest winners being the late Lord Lurgan, who fancied Honeymoon very much after her performance at the Lurgan meeting the previous October. It is, perhaps, worth mentioning that her owner was not amongst the fortunates, apart from the stake-money. The bitch had not entirely pleased him in her last trial, and Mr. Ford-Hutchinson, who at any time bet very little, also thought the price a short one.

Donald's Revenge.

"Her Lurgan and Waterloo successes were Honeymoon's only efforts in her next season and she came out the following October with her energies unimpaired, adding another Brownlow Cup to her laurel crown; her honours, too, being gained in great style. Trusting to what I wrote at the time rather than to memory, I read: 'Honeymoon eclipsed even her previous day's brilliant performance in her defeat of Regalia, and it was a sight to see her make such an example of so good a greyhound.'

"Her final victory over Heath (owned by the father of that staunch sportsman, Mr. Michael L. Hearn) was equally brilliant, and made such an impression that £700 to £100 was taken upon the field that she repeated her previous season's double by again winning the Waterloo Cup. In attempting this, however, she failed, her own countryman, Donald, in the fourth round taking his revenge for her defeat of him at

Lurgan the previous season, and eventually adding his name
to the scroll of Blue Riband winners. Honeymoon had
previously disposed of Warren Hastings, Mr. Hornby's good
bitch Handicraft, and her old opponent Lucetta.

" It would hardly be profitable to follow her career further
—indeed, I am not certain whether she ever ran again. She
was purchased by Mr. W. H. Clark, of Howden, Yorkshire,
who bred largely at the time for sale, the price being £500
and two pups from each litter. At the stud, however, she was
not a success, and, though mated with Bedfellow (sire of the
lion-hearted Greentick), and respectively son and grandson of
those wonderful bitches Bed of Stone and Bab at the Bowster,
no great result followed."

Waterloo, 1876—Ireland follows on.

DONALD'S year was, comparatively speaking, quite a
tame one, the 64 embracing few greyhounds of renown
to help the excitement beyond the previous year's winner,
Honeymoon. She was a strong favourite, £1,100 to £200
being one of the last bets taken, a smart Scotch bitch called
Greenburn being second favourite at 100 to 7.

Mr. Hornby's Hematite was third favourite at £1,000 to
£60, and Mr. N. Dunn's King David was backed at 20 to 1,
after which the prices rapidly expanded. Col. Goodlake, V.C.,
as in the few preceding years, presided, and a conspicuous
figure during the evening was Mr. Ford-Hutchinson, wearing
the Waterloo collar (then already in double or treble folds),
which had been in his possession since Honeymoon's victory
the year before.

The collar is formed of small gold medallions with owners'
and winners' names engraved, and it is, or at any rate was,
passed on year by year. The last time I saw it it had attained
unwieldly length.

The opening day's sport this year was marked by a series
of excellent trials, and not a few well-run courses. The
Squatter made such a good impression that at night he
advanced to the position of second favourite at 9 to 1 taken
freely, his price at the start being 1,000 to 15.

Honeymoon, however, remained a strong favourite, there

being far more would-be takers of 5 to 2 than could be accommodated. She still further increased in favouritism after repeating her previous year's defeat of the Castle Milk bitch, Lucetta, in the third round, being then backed at evens to again win the Cup. Her downfall, however, was at hand, Donald reversing their previous Lurgan form by showing the better speed, and beating her cleverly. On Thursday night the four left in were Donald against Huron and Lord Glendyne against The Squatter. The favourite was beaten in the latter course, but Donald easily landed the odds, and the final was a virtual walk-over for him. Lord Glendyne's gruelling in the semi-finals was contributed to by an extraordinary incident.

The South-country slipper, Luff, had little or no previous experience of the Altcar country, and in attempting to clear a drain with Lord Glendyne and The Squatter in slips all three were immersed for several seconds, Luff at last dragging his charges out. The Squatter was fawn when he went in, but he was now nearly as black as his companion.

It was a source of wonder to me that the trainers did not run up to at least scrape the mud off, especially as it was some time before another hare came forward, but they were finally dispatched in a shivering condition and with most of the slimy mud still attached. No wonder a clipping good hare was more than a match for them.

Donald was bred by his owner, Mr. R. M. Douglas, who sold several good greyhounds to Mr. Leonard Pilkington. After his Waterloo victory he was bought by the very successful Scottish courser, Dr. Dougal, for £300, but he failed to make any great name at the stud. The runner-up, Lord Glendyne, was previously bought by Mr. Paterson after seeing him lead and beat his good bitch Polly Perkins. He was a grandly bred dog by the game Smuggler—the only greyhound, in addition to Bab at the Bowster, that ever fairly tackled Master M'Grath—out of Fanny Warfield, by the stout Cauld Kail out of Leah, by David's best son, Patent.

Lord Glendyne had only a short career at the stud, but distinguished himself as the sire of Lady Glendyne, dam of the peerless Miss Glendyne. I say peerless because I think she would have beaten any other bitch I ever saw—both fresh— for a single course.

CHAPTER XII.

Waterloo, 1877.
Coomassie's First Year: A Brilliant Victory.

THE outstanding feature of Coomassie's first year was her marked superiority over all her opponents, together with the brilliant way in which she each time spun with her hare and gave a sure stroke at last, when the correct moment arrived. She killed every one of her six hares, and never was a Waterloo Cup more meritoriously won, not even in the best years of those splendid greyhounds, Master M'Grath, Fullerton, and Miss Glendyne. Under such circumstances a review of her career may very fittingly take precedence of the general features of the years she made memorable.

Coomassie was the property of a Mr. Caffley, a Norfolk man—when she opened her career by dividing the Oaks at Beckhampton (over the Wiltshire Downs), and though evincing marked excellence by the style in which she won and ran her courses, he sold her to Mr. R. Gittus, who, I believe, also hailed from Norfolk. For this gentleman she divided the Newmarket Champion Puppy Stakes (64 runners) in November, 1876, under conditions which at once stamped her as one of the gamest of the game, and in the following January won the Newmarket Stakes (at the local meeting there) outright; yet he also parted with her (for a greatly augmented sum) to Mr. "Tommy" Lay, a London bookmaker of considerable substance at that time, who used to make a biggish book on the Waterloo Cup.

The merit that attached to Coomassie's Champion Stakes victory was hardly estimated at its full value at the time, for in her very first course, which she ran beautifully and won in one-sided fashion, she cut herself severely under one of her stoppers through killing a bouncing hare on the turnpike road. She limped away lame enough, but came out in wonderful spirits next morning, and, easily beating The Boy, luckily cut her course fairly short with a smart kill.

On the third morning she was stiff and sore and unwilling to leave her bench, yet proved equal to defeating both Delusion and Pin Wire. On the Friday she declined all invitation to get up, and it was necessary to lift her off her bed. Her opponent in the semi-finals was Deceit—a fast, good bitch that had already won at Worcester and divided at Amesbury, so that Coomassie's chance of success seemed somewhat remote; and so it did in the early part of the course.

They were slipped on wheat, all in favour of Deceit, as she was a much bigger bitch than Coomassie, but as soon as the hare came half-round the lame 'un shot to the front, and Deceit never got another look in until the little fawn's victory was quite secure. Coomassie was now in quite a crippled condition, but the other left in, Paul Jones, had been very hard run, and a division was easily arranged.

A second visit to the Turf Metropolis, in January, resulted in absolute success, and, though styled " Newmarket Local Meeting," it was quite an important three-days' affair. Coomassie was entered in the chief event, for all-ages, with 22 entries at 10gs., and amongst those she defeated were two fast greyhounds in the Duke of Hamilton's Hot Shot and Mr. Wilkins's Warren Hastings. The fact of Coomassie's outpacing Warren Hastings in the final had something to do with Mr. Lay buying her, and it was in Mr. Wilkins's nomination that she made her first Waterloo mark.

It is no exaggeration to say that a Waterloo Cup was never more brilliantly won ; moreover, Coomassie is the only greyhound that ever achieved the distinction, after running the first course on the dreaded Ince side of the North End ground. She was one of the first brace in slips, her opponent being a red dog called Cæsar that had shown good form, 6 to 4 being taken on the course.

A stag of a hare quickly sprang from its form, and Cæsar was soon left in the rear. He contested a few points in the early part of the course, Coomassie running with more fire than steadiness, but she was not long in settling down, and then gave quite an artistic display.

Puss was so hard pressed that she dare not jump the drain, and began running in circles to get a better lead ; but

Coomassie all the while stuck to the scut like glue, and finally effected a fine kill. She next met one of the favourites for the stake, Master Sam, and to the general surprise went to the hare in front. Nor did she make the least mistake when there, and, soon bringing her teeth into play, I do not think the crack scored a single point.

Her two performances brought about a considerable change in the betting, for, after starting at 40 to 1, she now advanced to 11 to 2, Braw Lass being favourite at 9 to 2, and, as they ran first and second, " the talent " were thus early well on the mark. In her third course Coomassie made quite an example of Aunt Fleda, and finished another clipping display with a stylish kill. Against Conster, too, she showed almost equal superiority, and he was a dog of no little reputation.

In the semi-finals she met the Irish bitch Serapis (a Lurgan winner), and showing great fire after taking a strong lead to the hare, never allowed the brindled a look in, making the course fairly short with another smart kill. In the final Coomassie and Braw Lass, after being delivered beautifully together by Hoystead, raced neck and neck for some distance, but the fawn drew well clear at the finish, and with a smart sweep at the turn held stylish possession for a nice beginning before puss threw her out.

Braw Lass, like a flash, shot on to the scut, but had not squared accounts before Coomassie returned the compliment, and this time she held possession until she quickly gave the *coup de grace.* It was a brilliantly run course by both, and though beaten, the Lancashire bitch was far from disgraced. She was by Mr. Briggs's own unfortunate dog Blackburn. Coomassie's entire performance, however, stands out clearly as a great one, and her superior displays were against at least four proved good greyhounds in Master Sam, Conster, Serapis, and Braw Lass, all of whom had been at the end of big stakes.

There was an incident in connection with the course between Coomassie and Master Sam that recurs forcibly to mind. They were slipped on the Church House section of the broad meadows, which at this period were all in grass, and Doctor Eltringham, of Southport, in charge of Master Sam, was out in front ready to pick him up. He was so taken aback, however, at seeing the despised Coomassie come away in front—on a very slight inside—and shoot away from the turn with a still stronger lead, that he became transfixed to the spot, and, statue-like, never moved for several seconds, being evidently in wonderland when Coomassie clinched her one-sided victory with a fine kill.

I ought to mention, by way of explanation, that Master Sam in his first spin had increased the confidence of his party by leading and decisively beating Barabbas (a leading favourite) in one of the heaviest betting courses I ever remember, and now to be polished off in such style, too, by the diminutive and despised little fawn would be a terrible blow.

Waterloo, 1878.
The Wonderful Little Fawn Scores Again.

COOMASSIE'S second Waterloo victory is quite a different story, though from one aspect even a more remarkable achievement than her first. She was in no condition to run : her coat flew off with the least touch, and she was not very long over her pupping time. For the truth of this I can personally vouch, as I squeezed the milk from her teats with my own fingers in the smoke-room of the Adelphi Hotel within a few hours of her success !

The wonder is, therefore, not that her second win compared unfavourably with her first, but that she was able to win at all under such physical disabilities, and it says no little for the cleverness of her trainer, Jack Shaw, of Northallerton, to get her so clean in her wind under such circumstances.

On the first day she outpaced both the Irish bitch, Joy Bells, and Penrith, and had the early points, but each time looked not unlike being beaten. Joy Bells was fast squaring accounts when she killed too soon, and Penrith looked like rubbing it off when she drove puss into the drain.

On the second morning Dear Shamrock led her, and had the best of it for some time, Coomassie's extra cleverness and better staying winning this course ; but Dear Shamrock was a soft bitch. The only time she gave a glimpse of her real form was in the fourth round against Mr. Hornby's good bitch, Handicraft.

They first had an undecided, in which the little fawn showed speed, Handicraft having the finish. In the run off Coomassie increased her lead up to three lengths, and, in a very smartly-run course by both, always had the best of it, finishing with a good kill. Coomassie showed remarkable dexterity in this course by jumping over Handicraft's quarters to avoid a cannon.

In the semi-final she had an easy task, Whistling Dick showing a striking falling off from his previous form, and all sorts of stories got afloat. The other pair, Zazel and Rival Belle, started with an undecided, and in running it off got a gruelling, Lord Fermoy's bitch being heavily handicapped for the final. Consequently, 5 to 1 was vainly offered on Coomassie, who went up in front on an outside and scored the early points.

Zazel warming up then made a game challenge, but killed with a good balance still against her. It is perhaps not very chivalrous to belittle the merit of such a wonderful victory, though it certainly looked as if Zazel on fair terms would have followed in the footsteps of Master M'Grath, Honeymoon, and Donald. On the other hand, what would Coomassie have done with Zazel, and the rest of them, in her true colours, as guaged by her previous year's form ?

If all the stories that got into circulation were true, the gallant little fawn (she scaled 43lb.) was already third season, but she was put into training for the following year's Cup, and broke her leg in a trial on Everleigh downs, at almost the same spot as the Duke of Leeds's good bitch, Livid Light, happened on a similar accident at an Everleigh meeting, some years later. Coomassie was preserved for breeding, but was not a success at the stud, though her son Middleton ran exceedingly well in Mineral Water's Waterloo Cup, and very smartly disposed of Plymouth Gin, Irene, False Standard, and London before suffering defeat from the winner.

Her origin is uncertain, and when she won her first Waterloo, as a puppy by Celebrated out of Queen, Mr. S. J. Binning, of Carlisle, thought he recognised her as a bitch by

Master Birnie that he sent up as a puppy in a draft for sale the previous year, on account of being undersized. She ran 28 courses in public without ever suffering defeat, and after her first Waterloo victory Mr. M'Culloch, a leading Australian courser, offered £1,000 for her.

Waterloo, 1879—Four Puppies Fight it Out.

MISTERTON'S year does not awaken many agreeable recollections; indeed the Waterloo records would be all the richer in pleasant memories if the anniversary of 1879 could be blotted out. Bad coursing weather through January and early February gave way in time to admit of the meeting commencing according to date, but owing to dogs not being properly trained, and several of the hares running indifferently, the first day's results were all " topsy turvey," such a slaughter of the favourites never before being seen.

Matters went from bad to worse. A return of the frost, together with a fall of snow, caused a suspension of hostilities over Thursday, but on Friday, though the ground wore a white mantle, the stewards decided upon running. The coursing was a complete fiasco, the trials mostly being a run-up and kill, and if the leader failed effectually to use his teeth he never got another chance, every hare being quickly dispatched. It was simply a burlesque upon coursing, and despite Mr. Hedley's masterly discrimination, his nerve must have been often sorely tried; with a less skilled and determined judge we should have had one undecided after another. On Saturday morning there was less snow on the ground, and though the air was frosty, the going was fairly safe when the stewards present, Mr. T. D. Hornby, Mr. J. Briggs, and Colonel Goodlake decided upon a start in Church House meadows.

The four now left in for the cup were all extreme outsiders on the night of the draw; and the point of correctly foreshadowing the final result was never reached, though in the semi-finals the winner (Misterton) and the runner-up (Commerce) were each favourite against their respective opponents, Regal Court and Plunger.

They both justified the odds by leading and winning well ;
but though Misterton got off more lightly than the bitch he
was non-favourite in the final.   It was a fluky course, for
Commerce was clearly showing speed until the hare broke
short round to Misterton's side, and puss again favoured him
at the turn.   Shortly afterwards he made a wide sweep, and
Commerce setting cleverly to work, looked all over a winner
until the white collar cross-cannoned into her.   This settled
the issue, for Misterton, getting away well in front floored
the hare without the Scotch bitch getting another chance.

Mr. R. B. Carruthers, amongst the best judges of a course,
and one of nature's own gentlemen, was thus unluckily
deprived of the highest Waterloo laurels with one of his own,
but he had the honour, and the profit, of nominating three
distinguished winners later in Lord Haddington's Honeywood,
Mr. C. Hibbert's Miss Glendyne, and Mr. Leonard Pilkington's
Thoughtless Beauty.   Misterton and Commerce were both by
Mr. Carruthers's famous sire Contango, and so was Dear Erin,
winner of the Purse.   The Plate was won by Mr. Marfleet's
well-named Musical Box, by Handel out of Spice Box.

Misterton was a handsome, bloodlike greyhound, and
making some good hits in his early efforts at the stud, especially
with a litter from Annie M'Pherson, was largely patronised.
His owner, Mr. H. G. Miller, told me that Misterton had
earned him nearly £5,000.   He never, however, produced a
greyhound of great fame, and many of his get inherited his
own softness.

CHAPTER XIII.

Waterloo, 1880—A Memorable Year.

HONEYWOOD'S Waterloo is quite entitled to take high rank in the records. Leaving out the giants, Master M'Grath, Fullerton, and Herschel, I am not sure that I have ever seen a better dog (as distinguished from bitch) than Honeywood was at this point of his career. In the early autumn he made a most vivid impression by the brilliant style in which he ran through the Culhorn Cup at Stranraer.

The ground was very hard that autumn, but Honeywood never flinched, and won the final course under the greatest difficulties. In the run-up the hare made almost a cart-wheel circle, yet Honeywood got up on the outside and won in a canter. Being a rather heavy-bodied dog he must have been a bit shaken, but with only a shortish rest he came out in the Netherby Cup, and divided with his kennel companion Honeybuzzard, again running like a great greyhound.

This was in the autumn in which the Earl of Haddington accomplished the great feat of sweeping the Border Union decks. The programme at that time consisted of two 64's; Honeywood and Honeybuzzard divided the senior, and Hornpipe and Halcyon the junior event! As Waterloo approached I never tired of singing Honeywood's praise, and though the result of a home trial between Honeywood and Haidee induced their noble owner to run the latter in his own nomination, Honeywood running in that of Mr. R. B. Carruthers, public form was thoroughly vindicated.

The two were the leading favourites on the night of the draw, 100 to 8 being freely taken about each, the next in demand being the previous year's winner, Misterton, Dalcardo, Lady Lizzie, Truthful, Star of Woodcote, Coquette, and Debonnaire. Most of these, together with Haidee, figured in the Purse or Plate, and though Honeywood kept rejoicing his backers with his grand displays, the other three left in on the last day, Mr. Hinks's Plunger, Mr. Swinburne's Surpriser, and

Mr. N. Dunn's Nellie Miller, were all originally in the extreme
outside division, each oddly enough being on the same mark
of 1,000 to 10.

Plunger and Nellie Miller first tried conclusions in the
semi-finals, and the Northumberland bitch was snuffed out,
without getting much of a chance. Plunger, partly by favour,
was up two lengths in front, and the hare breaking to his side
at the turn he held possession, and quickly finished a poor
trial with his teeth. The other pair, on the contrary, were
well tried. They first had a no-course, but a fine trial followed
in which Honeywood's great superiority was conclusively shown.

An Exciting Finish.

The semi-finals had been run in what was then described
as the meadow adjacent to Hill House plantation, and it was
more spacious then than now, as the further end of the Rye
Heyes had not been broken up.

The final was run on the famous Withins, where so many
Waterloo Cups have been won and lost. Despite Honeywood
having the worst of the handicap 7 to 4 was laid on him, so
strongly were the public impressed with the great form he had
displayed. Delivered beautifully together by Tom Wilkinson
(uncle of our present *facile princeps*) they raced neck-and-neck
for some fifty yards when Honeywood forged ahead and reached
his hare fully two lengths in front. Puss breaking short to the
left, he swept smartly with her, half-round his opponent, but
as she circled further round to Plunger's side the latter shot
up and killed, whereupon the cap came off.

This, of course, was a wretched trial to decide a Waterloo
Cup, but I had a perfect view, and, though a close shave, it
was an undoubted win for Honeywood. Next time, over the
same stretch of ground, Honeywood increased his lead to fully
three lengths. The hare again broke to the left, but the white
collar forging grandly on the scut held close possession, and
when Plunger, under greater favour, attempted to wrest it he
went sweeping past, the issue looking all over but shouting.

A rare hare was not done with, and some eager pickers-up
helping to throw Honeywood out Plunger at last got well
placed. Right gallantly, too, did he stick to his work as the
hare broke back down the Withins towards the end from which

Sports and General

BORDER UNION (LOWTHER) COURSING MEETING, 1921.

A Group of well-known Owners, including LORD LONSDALE, Hon. H. E. LOWTHER, EARL of SEFTON, Mr. P. NOBLE,
LORD TWEEDMOUTH, Major HUGH PEEL, Mr. J. BELL-IRVING, and SIR ROBERT JARDINE.

they were slipped. The excitement soon reached fever heat, for Honeywood was in a rearward position, and Plunger was not merely chasing his hare but clouting her about.

The very finish of the course was out of my sight, the crowd rushing in from the bank, and the hare at last being killed in the drain. It was an anxious moment or two before the white flag signalled Honeywood's victory, but it would have been nothing short of a tragedy had he suffered reverse. He was not only manifestly much the superior greyhound ; it was one of the few weak moments of Mr. Hedley's career when he gave the first spin undecided, simply because it was an unworthy trial.

The Purse was won by the fast Cumberland bitch Shepherdess, the Northumberland dog Delcardo (by Diacticus) running up. Another speedy bitch in Douglas's (afterwards Pilkington's) Debonnaire ran through the Plate, going too fast in the final for that good runner Trevors' Truthful. Truthful was one of a particularly good litter out of Warwickshire Lass, one of the best of her day over the Downs. Debonnaire was by Master Sam out of Death, dam of the speedy Marshal M'Mahon, and the good bitch Dear Erin. Honeywood was in-bred to the Border celebrity Cauld Kail, being by his good son Cavalier out of Humming Bird, a daughter of Cauld Kail's son Bendimere.

One of the few instances of a leg being broken at Waterloo occurred this year, and it happened in a heavy betting course between the good bitch Lady Lizzie and a fast flash dog called Decorator. The latter only just secured the run-up, but the brindled shot in at the turn, and was making an example of him when she broke a foreleg near the very spot where Blackburn broke his leg in a course with Muriel at an Altcar Club January meeting the month before she gained her Waterloo honours.

Lady Lizzie gave an extraordinary display of gameness in running on, and even trying to spurt to the front as the hare came round in her favour. Such a gallant performance, coupled with her brilliant running previous to the accident, led to much sympathy with her plucky owner, for he had backed his bitch to win a big stake.

F

CHAPTER XIV.

Waterloo, 1881—Princess Dagmar's Success.

COINCIDENCE and romance are both much entwined with a long story of Waterloo, and Mr. Postle, just as the Earl of Haddington did in the previous year, made the mistake of relying upon home trials, and running Palm Bloom in his own nomination, in preference to the "Princess," it being left for the lucky Mr. Miller, owner of Misterton, to nominate the winner.

Palm Bloom was no doubt a good bitch, but Princess Dagmar (a grand-looking greyhound) had shown such great form in public, especially at Plumpton the previous month, that "Vindex," as in the other case, stood staunchly by public form. In this case the choice of owner and advisers was perhaps influenced by the knowledge of coming danger, and sure enough the Princess was attacked on the eve of the meeting, the " weeping " process having strongly developed by the opening day. Some bitches—probably the great majority —would have " fallen to pieces," and been utterly incapable of giving their true form ; not so the Princess.

She was a " waggon-horse " of a greyhound, though nevertheless of exquisite mould, and never lost either her spirits or her strength : she was a 60lb. bitch. The chair at the dinner was, this year, taken by Mr. T. (afterwards Sir Thomas) Brocklebank, and on his right and left sat the Marquis of Anglesey and Lord Wodehouse (the present Earl of Kimberley).

Honeywood, the previous year's winner, although now in his fourth season, was a strong favourite at 8 to 1, Mr. Pilkington's Debonnaire and Mr. N. Dunn's Dulas being next in demand. All three were beaten early, Honeywood being led and well beaten in the first round by the runner-up, Bishop. Dulas also went down before Mr. Mather's Meols Water—a good dog and winner of an important Scarisbrick Cup—but his victory was partly due to being more expert at the drains than the bitch. This often told its tale in these bygone days.

Debonnaire survived the first day, but on Thursday morning, after a great race to the hare, she was polished off in style by the smart Northumberland dog Free Flag. After this course there was quite a furore to back Free Flag for the Cup, as little as 7 to 4 being taken ; but with 3 to 1 on him for his next course, against Vindictive, he joined the ranks of the many other departed favourites, Mr. R. C. Vyner's bitch, who had been running well all along, being too smart for him at close quarters.

Princess Dagmar, Bishop, and Cui Bono all won their courses in capital style, respectively against Shipmate, Clyto, and Assault, and now only four outsiders were left in. It was thus a comparatively tame finish, and the three results were all as expected.

The last day's meet this year was at Church House, this portion of the ground being the soundest, after such a wet season ; indeed, I may mention that within a few days of the fixture a postponement was feared, owing to the flooded conditions. Bishop sustaining his good form, led and vanquished Cui Bono in such decisive fashion that great hopes of a final victory were entertained ; but Princess Dagmar followed with an equally good display, and after leading Vindictive several lengths never gave her an opportunity of bringing the smartness she had hitherto shown into play.

For the final 6 to 4 was laid on the " Princess," but there were plenty eager takers of the odds. The hare coming forward rather wide on Wilkinson's left, Princess Dagmar, under the white flag, was quickest into her stride, and she soon drew well in front. Also gaining an advantage as they cleared the drain, she was fully three lengths ahead as she swept round with her hare. Keeping well to the scut, she never gave the slightest opening, and quickly ended a poor trial for a Waterloo final with a smart kill.

Bishop was a complete surprise packet, as being a late July puppy he never ran in his first season, and in this, his second, his previous form had not revealed him as up to Waterloo class. He gained his five victories here, however, like a good greyhound, though his superiority, in the fourth round, to the sterling good dog Clyto (whose counterfeit resemblance adorns the stud book cover) was not made clear, Mr. Clift's dog getting a terrible purler upon landing over a drain when leading in the run-up.

The Purse was won by " Smuggler " Smith's good, game little dog Sapper, by Master Avon (by Master Birnie out of Wee Avon) out of Wideawake, by Smuggler. Sapper was a great performer as a puppy, and after his early efforts had told against him in his second season (as it did to a lesser extent in Bed of Stone's case) he came out " like a giant refreshed " in his third, and ran through a 64 at Gosforth (when the hares were so strong that shorter slips could be given) within a very short time after winning at Carmichael.

Like the Cup, the Plate was won by a second string in Mr. N. Dunn's Dodger, by Fugitive out of Ellen Johnson, Herschel's sire, M'Pherson (by Master Sam) running up. Dodger was nominated by Mr. Dunn's friend, Captain Ellis, a surviving twain of the Old Guard, of which so few are left. Their association here recalls that they are linked together in another respect. Mr. Dunn gave valuable assistance to Captain Ellis in the production of his imperishable as well as invaluable book " Winning Strains," without which there would be a great blank in the history of the sport.

Unhappily, it only runs up to 1911, and Captain Ellis being nearer ninety than eighty, can hardly be expected, with all his loving ardour, to push his weighty labours further. Mr. Dunn, too, must be "getting on"; he raised a flag in the Roxburgh Stakes at Kelso, in 1863, and fifty years later, in 1913, won the stakes with Dualine and Droughty. In his early days Mr. Dunn was a favourite personality, tor he was the fortunate possessor of a charming tenor voice, and I have a vivid recollection of many delightful evenings at the pleasant Wigtownshire Club (Stranraer) meetings, when Mr. Dunn and the late Mr. S. J. Binning, of Carlisle, were present together. Song and toast then never failed to go merrily round until, sometimes, late into the night.

CHAPTER XV.

Waterloo, 1882—Success of Snowflight.

SNOWFLIGHT'S year was amongst the most memorable ones that Waterloo records supply. Even the dinner imparted an exceptional touch, for it was the only occasion upon which the then Earl of Sefton ever presided ; and the wholesale slaughter of the favourites on the opening day, together with a sensational finish, conduced to making the anniversary one of green memory.

The previous year's winner, Princess Dagmar, now the property of Mr. W. Reilly, started favourite at 100 to 11, but she was amongst those early bowled over. Her victress, Mr. Jos. Hutchison's Clyde Pearl, followed up her unlooked-for success by also disposing of the previous year's runner-up, Bishop, before being outpaced and beaten by Assegai (late Patchet and brother to Princess Dagmar), for which the Marquis of Anglesey paid 300gs. at the sale of Mr. Postle's greyhounds.

Like Coomassie's, Snowflight's career only extended over a couple of seasons, but it was eventful enough while it lasted ; indeed, it may not inappropriately be described as romantic, sensational, and tragic. She may in a manner be almost considered at the outset a chance greyhound, romance being attached to her birth and the way in which her excellence was discovered ; then, her Waterloo Cup victory was sensational as well as wonderful, whilst her defeat in the final the following year partook quite of the tragic, especially to her then owner, Mr. "Will" Reilly, who had backed her to win many thousands of pounds, and would not hedge a penny.

She lost the course through leading too far ! Captain Ellis, in whose nomination she gained her Waterloo laurels, tells her early story in that valuable book, " Winning Strains from 1880 to 1911."

He describes her as "A model of a greyhound, weight 47½lb., fast, clever, and resolute," and then goes on :—

" Her story illustrates the luck of breeding in every way

and encourages us all. Her dam, Curiosity, was bred by a working man. She was a strong, thick-set, hardy bitch, very stout, and of a good constitution, and one of the few descendants of the fast, smart dog, Kingwater (who was fluked out of Roaring Meg's Waterloo Cup in the semi-finals by Bowfell.—L.H.). Another ancestor was the Bounding Elk, brother in blood to Ladylike (thought by James Hedley to be one of the best he ever saw.—L.H.).

" She had run respectably in seven stakes, but had never seen the end of one. Her owner went to New Zealand for a while, and Curiosity was handed over to a farmer to kill hares ; he was of a sporting turn, and wanted to buy the bitch to breed from, but the wife would not sell. It happened that there was a well-bred dog running about in the neighbourhood called Bothal Park, belonging to a pitman.

" This dog had nothing but his breeding to recommend him, but he was by a son of Bab at the Bowster, and his dam was choicely bred. So the farmer put Curiosity to this dog, and the result was Snowflight, Waterford, and Clyde Sphinx. The farmer kept some of the puppies, sold others, and gave Snowflight to a Miss Hall, aunt of a neighbouring farmer, as a pet dog ; but she and her nephew cared nothing about coursing. Then Cutter, the owner of Curiosity, came back from New Zealand and looked up this daughter of hers, was pleased with her looks, and persuaded Miss Hall to let her run at a local meeting. She ran so well that she was next entered at Gosforth, where she won unchallenged."

There was a wide difference, however, between what she had already accomplished and a Waterloo task, few of the general public supporting her ; and, neither owner nor nominator being of a speculative turn of thought, Snowflight started at 1,000 to 15. Hornpipe, the runner-up, I may mention, also figured in the outside division at 1,000 to 20.

The previous year's winner, Princess Dagmar, was favourite at 100 to 11, Mary Morrison, Alec Halliday, and Witchery being next in demand, each at about 100 to 7. Rosewater was heavily backed at 100 to 6, and Debonnaire was well supported at a point longer odds. Marshal M'Mahon was also in the inner circle, 1,000 to 45 being taken.

It was a memorable year for slaughter of the favourites, not one of those enumerated getting far into the Cup except Witchery, whilst Princess Dagmar, Mary Morrison, and Alec Halliday all failed at the first attempt. Snowflight, on the contrary, won her course against General Wyndham in one-sided fashion, and in a trial of fair length was never at fault.

In Rhodora she met a fast, good-class greyhound, but Snowflight proved a full length the faster, and though the white and brindled offered a stout resistance in the early part of the course, Snowflight was an easy winner when she finished with a brilliant sequence and fine kill.

In the evening's betting Snowflight's two meritorious displays were reflected in the shortened price of 9 to 1 being taken, the two favourites being Witchery, at 11 to 2, and Rosewater, at 7 to 1, these two having to try conclusions in the third round.

This was an exciting course, for Rosewater had been backed for a pot of money, and she went to the hare in front, but being a bit hasty in attempting the death lost position, and Witchery finishing in great style was a clever winner when she killed.

Snowflight had the best of the luck in rather a tricky run-up with Whipsnake, and gave an exceedingly smart exhibition before the black and white shot up inside for a couple of wrenches and a good kill, leaving Snowflight with plenty in hand. Against her fourth opponent, Sugarcane, she stretched ahead nearly four lengths for first turn, at which she was thrown out a bit awkwardly, but, quickly dashing to the front with great fire, then ran up a series of brilliant points before effecting a fine kill.

The final quartette were now Witchery v. Snowflight and Hornpipe v. Leader, the first-named brace being equal favourites at 2 to 1, 7 to 2 being laid against Hornpipe, and 6 to 1 against Leader.

Maintaining the improvement she had shown throughout, Snowflight made a magnificent display against Witchery and created general surprise by the superiority shown over such a doughty opponent. She drew out nearly three lengths for first turn, and after a few brilliant points looked like losing possession. But almost instantly regaining it under difficulties, she again drove resolutely on the scut and quickly effected the kill.

This performance caused 7 to 4 to be freely laid on her for the final against Hornpipe, although the latter had polished off Leader quite as decisively and almost as brilliantly. A sensational denouement followed, and when they went to slips a second and a third time 2 to 1 was freely offered on Hornpipe.

At the first attempt it was a grand race for some distance, but Snowflight had drawn clear when a second hare sprang up close to them, and they separated, with the result that Hornpipe quickly killed, whilst Snowflight went streaming across the meadows and got something approaching a grueller. We were running on the Engine House section of the Church House ground—not on the famed Withins, where so many Waterloos have been decided.

After half an hour's delay they were again handed to Tom Wilkinson, uncle of the present slipper, and this time Hornpipe, of course, showed speed, leading up a clear length, although the hare kept bearing from her. The red collar, however (they were both black), shot in at the turn, and with a wrench and kill brought the cap off. Snowflight's chance still looked forlorn, certain bookmakers who were bad against Hornpipe being most anxious to " hedge," but the short undecided had warmed up the Northumberland bitch.

At the third attempt, from a pretty slip, Snowflight gradually drew nearly clear, and the hare, then bearing in her favour, she was out two lengths when she came round beautifully on the scut, wrenched strongly, and quickly cut matters short with a fine kill. It was a most surprising, as well as great, performance, and elicited such sustained cheers as have not often been heard at Waterloo, except, perhaps, in the days of Master M'Grath, when such strong Irish contingents used to cross the Channel.

Being under two years old (she was whelped in April), it might, after such an ordeal, have been wise policy to retire her for the season ; but Gosforth Park held out alluring attractions with £500 and a gold cup for the winner, so Snowflight was entered, and started an equal favourite with the fast Irish-bred bitch, Debonnaire, at 8 to 1, Alec Halliday,

Match Girl, Marshal M'Mahon, Rhodora, and Princess Dagmar being the next best favourites. Snowflight led and disposed of the good dogs Glenlivet and Aydon, but in the third round was outpaced and beaten by Mr. Alfred Brisco's fast bitch, Ben-y-Lair. Alec Halliday proved the winner, beating Rhodora in the semi-finals, and Snowflight's brother, Waterford, in the decider. Alec Halliday was English-bred (by Fugitive out of Free Trade), but was the property of the Irish courser, Mr. G. J. Alexander.

Waterloo, 1883—Wild Mint's Victory.

BEFORE another Waterloo came round Snowflight was sold for £500, and, as previously mentioned, was backed by her owner to win a big stake. She started a pronounced favourite at 8 to 1, Spick and Span being second in request at 100 to 9 ; Hornpipe, Rhodora and Witchery were the next best favourites. The odds against Wild Mint, the ultimate winner, were 1,000 to 8.

In her first effort Snowflight was fully held for speed until nearing the hare, but she shot well ahead of Glenburn at last and began the course very smartly. The white collar, however, then joined issue, though the crack was a decisive winner when she floored her hare. She improved upon this display against Petrarch (who ran into the last four the following year), leading up over three lengths, giving a polished display and allowing the white and red little but the kill.

When the card was called over at night Snowflight's price was 3 to 1, taken in hundreds, Spick and Span still being second favourite at 9 to 2, the two being due to meet in the fourth round. Rhodora was backed at 10 to 1, but beyond these three longish odds ruled, Wild Mint's price being 66 to 1. Snowflight was favoured with an inside against her opponent, Glenlivet, and, going up well in front, held absolute possession, and killed without allowing him to score.

Her defeat of Spick and Span was equally decisive, though the trial was a poor one. It was a tight race for some distance, but Snowflight, again having the best of the luck, was well clear as she gained possession, and, covering the scut closely, killed without the fawn ever getting a look in.

It now looked " all over but shouting," and in the evening 55 to 40 was laid on Snowflight winning, whilst 9 to 2 was laid on her beating Waterford.   The other brace were Wild Mint and Hotspur, the latter being favourite at 2 to 1.   In this case the odds were floored, Wild Mint easily beating her faster opponent with extra cleverness.   Snowflight drew well ahead of her brother, and after scoring smartly several times flecked her hare and came down, Waterford soon finishing the course.

For the final 3 to 1 was freely laid on Snowflight, and when she stretched ahead fully half a dozen lengths down the Withins it looked all the odds.   An unsteady dash to kill, however, caused puss to jerk short back, and Wild Mint, getting well placed, at once began to be busy.   Snowflight got an opening through the fawn attempting the death, but she failed to take full advantage, and Wild Mint, again sweeping on the scut for a couple of wrenches and smart kill, upset one of the apparently greatest certainties even seen in connection with a Waterloo final.

Three weeks later Snowflight again tried her fortunes in the Gosforth Gold Cup, and made a good show by surviving the fourth round, but in the fifth she was outpaced and beaten by Mr. Vines's Markham (the winner), running in my own nomination.   This finished Snowflight's public career, Mr. Reilly afterwards selling her to Messrs. Fawcett for the same price that he had given for her—£500.

She never bred a good one, though her daughter, Fleet Flight, threw Flying Fancy, dam of Fiery Furnace, who was so splendidly successful at the stud, and sired two Waterloo Cup winners in Farndon Ferry and Father Flint, as well as a host of good ones, including Fleet Footed, Lottery, and Lonely Star.

Excepting its sensational finish, Wild Mint's year can be classed as only prosaic.   Few greyhounds took part that live in the memory.   Markham and Maid Marion were first and second in the Purse, and Rota and Manager divided the Plate. The Cup winner, Wild Mint, ranks amongst the least worthy that have gained the great distinction.

CHAPTER XVI.

Waterloo, 1884—Mineral Water's Year.

AS in the three previous years that had followed Honeywood's success, the winner again proved difficult to find, actually starting at 1,000 to 12, and the runner-up, Greentick, 1,000 to 20. The leading favourities were Mr. L. Pilkington's Phœbus (late Black Peter, a good performer and subsequent Kempton £1,000 winner) and Dr. W. Irving's Irene (running in Mr. T. Stone's nomination), who had performed very smartly the previous week at Haydock. Mr. Miller's Manager, Mr. E. Dent's London, Mr. Fletcher's False Standard, Mr. R. Jardine's Gladys, and the Scotch dog, Ballangeish, winner of a Kempton Park £1,000, being next in demand.

It was emphatically a year of genuine coursing, the ground being in good order and the hares running well. For once in a way, too, backers had a royal time, the opening day in particular being greatly in favour of the layer of odds. A great proportion of the trials, too, were well run, and, the weather being favourable, I never remember a finer first day's sport over the famous battleground.

The second day hardly equalled the first in grandeur, but, nevertheless, was again of almost super-excellence, and the Cup was still very open, with only four left in. That the final issue was still regarded as doubtful was proved by the betting at night, 2 to 1 being offered on the field.

Middleton was, however, freely supported at these odds, and I may mention that he started as Mr. Miller's third string, Manager and Madeline both being better favourites on the night of the draw. 105 to 40 was accepted about Greentick, 75 to 20 Petrarch, taken ten times, with Mineral Water (the winner) the outsider of the party at 4 to 1—800 to 200 being taken and still offered.

So far as recollection goes, there has never been closer betting than this on the last night ; but it was equally remarkable after the first day's running, for, with only sixteen dogs left standing, it was 10 to 1 on the field.   500 to 50 was accepted about Petrarch, and the same odds were taken about Markham, London and Phœbus being each close up at 100 to 9.

The last day's meet was fixed for Hill House, and the assemblage was accordingly there, but shortly afterwards the order was given for Church House.   It transpired that a strong feeling had been expressed in favour of the change, Wednesday's and Thursday's running there having been so eminently satisfactory, and there being now only a small card to get through.

There was also the recollection of the fiasco, on the Withins, in the final course the previous year.   The committee and stewards, I believe, favoured the idea, and the Earl of Sefton having personally consulted the owners of the four dogs left in the Cup, Mr. Harold Brocklebank, who had succeeded Mr. T. D. Hornby as hon. secretary, shortly before, gave the necessary order.

The result was a triumphant success, the meeting ending, as it began and progressed, with a series of glorious trials.

Before referring to them in detail, I may mention that the inexorable scythe bearer has left few of those chiefly concerned that day.   The then lord of the soil, together with the committee, consisting of the Earl of Stair, Major-General Goodlake, V.C., Messrs. T. Brocklebank, T. D. Hornby, R. Jardine, M.P., J. Briggs, and G. J. Alexander, and the Stewards, Marquis of Anglesey and Sir W. C. Anstruther have all been gathered to the fold.

Of the owners, too, whose names figure in the year's records, only their memories remain, so far as the Cup and the Purse are concerned ; but happily the Plate brings a gleam of brightness, Mr. J. R. Marshall, owner of the winner, Cocklaw Dene (and present treasurer of the N.C.C.), and Mr. J. T. Crossley, owner of Cyril, the runner-up, being still able to enjoy and pursue the sport they both love so well.   The results were :—

Mineral Water beat Middleton ; betting, 5 to 4 on the latter.   They were delivered beautifully together, and a most exciting race commenced.   They ran quite sixty yards before it was at all certain which would lead, and then Mineral Water, slightly favoured, could barely draw clear for first turn. Puss breaking short back, Middleton was the quicker round, but in the good stretch that followed Mineral Water fairly collared him, and a little outside fairly forged his neck in front for the second point.

Puss then shifting further to the right placed Middleton, but he was not running with his previous cleverness, and Mineral Water twice over stretching to the front in the give-and-take work that ensued was a good winner as he knocked his hare into the drain. Puss regaining the bank in safety, the course still went on, and the black was a bit the cleverer afterwards, but Mineral Water never flinching again dashed up in front, and although Middleton finished with a wrench and kill, the white was left a gallant winner.

Greentick beat Petrarch ; betting, 7 to 4 on Greentick. It looked for a few strides as though Petrarch was going to lead, being a neck in front as they landed over the first drain. Greentick then began to go the faster, and quickly dashing to the front was three lengths ahead on the outside as he drove puss short round by the right. Petrarch was thereby placed, but Greentick fairly struggled past him for the second point ; puss again shifting in Petrarch's favour he scored the third, and looked like holding his position for a dangerous score.

As puss broke down the meadow towards the crowd Greentick made a strong point by stretching clear past, and for some time he had decidedly the best of it. A terrific course ensued, for although they in turn flecked a rare hare, Greentick all but settling her, she was not to be so easily disposed of. Petrarch, staying the longer, had all the best of the finish, but good and game dog as he ran, his last three wrenches and fine kill left a balance of a few points still against him.

Deciding Course.

Mineral Water beat Greentick ; betting, 9 to 4 on Mineral Water, who quickly showed his heels to his handicapped opponent, and gradually widening the gap was up fully four lengths first. Moving resolutely with his hare he went round in good possession, and it was some time before the black could fairly contest the course. He made a plucky effort after warming up, but in a capital trial could never look dangerous,

Mineral Water having a strong balance in hand when he nailed puss as she tried to break round.

This was Greentick's first season, and though well beaten in the final, the show he made after such a gruelling with Petrarch so shortly before stamped him as a puppy possessing extraordinary grit ; of course, it was the combination of the Bab at the Bowster and Bed of Stone blood that gave it.

The Purse was divided by Mr. R. Jardine's good bitch Gladys, and Mr. Evans's puppy Escape, both having performed exceedingly well, and been very hard run in their respective defeats of Countess of Sapey and Pious Fraud. The first and second for the Plate, Cocklaw Dene and Cyril, also gained their positions with meritorious running, especially the first-named, his defeat of Hand in Hand being a clipping performance that clearly stamped him as a puppy of the good class he afterwards proved to be.

Greentick's Career.

I have come across a rather interesting reference to his exploits which I wrote in connection with a Haydock Park meeting, I am sure it will be acceptable as a tribute to such a great greyhound :—

Excepting the two immortal celebrities, Master M'Grath and Bab at the Bowster, no greyhound of modern times has made such a vivid impression upon coursing men's minds as the lion-hearted Greentick, grandson of Bed of Stone and great grandson of " Bab." He has in his time received many well-deserved tributes from my pen, but it would be difficult to mete out the full reward earned by his latest achievement. Times and oft has he been one of the heroes of the hour, and many bitter throbs of disappointment has he caused.

As a set-off against these may be cited his memorable victory after that never-to-be-forgotten struggle to the hare with Nolan, and his glorious triumph of the present week. But it is not simply his bare successes that have so stirred the enthusiasm which every real courser's heart is capable of feeling. It is the marvellous amount of pluck and endurance he has shown that have worked such magical effect.

Let us take a glance through the salient features of his career. It was at a very early age that he gave his first promise, for I think he commenced by winning a sapling stake. He was unlucky enough to get several severe dressings as a puppy, both in public and private, and few who saw it will ever forget the terrific course run by him and Lady Abbess at the Altcar Club Meeting.

Mr. Lea's bitch was a puppy of high promise up to that time, but she was never a good greyhound again. It was generally thought that Greentick's prospects were also settled, at any rate for that season ; but he came out at Waterloo with his powers unimpaired, and made a gallant fight with Mineral Water in the final course, even handicapped as he was by his heart-breaking trial with Petrarch in the previous round.

Passing over such comparatively minor achievements as his division of the Altcar Club Cup, as well as his defeat by Pinkerton in the fifth round of the October Stakes at Haydock Park, the next sensation he created was at Waterloo the following year. It was the most exciting feature of the draw when he and Gay City fell together, and the sequel intensified the situation greatly. They ran two undecideds, after which Greentick's owner would have gladly come to terms.

But Gay City's owner was also interested in both Bit of Fashion and Miss Glendyne (the two ultimate dividers), and naturally enough wished such a redoubtable foe as Greentick handicapped, if not knocked out altogether.

They accordingly went to slips again, and long before the terrific course was finished it was seen that both their chances were effectually destroyed. Gay City's owner was sufficiently indiscreet to send him to slips in the next round against Petrarch, but Greentick did not come out for the Purse. With a few weeks' rest, however, he once more showed what extraordinary powers of recuperation he possessed, and it was not until the sixth round of the Gosforth Gold Cup that he fell an unlucky victim, partly to his own momentary hesitation, and partly to the brilliant Canaradzo shoot made by Mineral Water with a quickness that can only be described as resembling an electric flash.

Greentick's first appearance the following season at Haydock was nearly a tragedy.

Through rushing at his hare as she made the escape in his course with Hand in Hand he struck one of the hurdles with great force, the violence of the blow being such as to cause him to lie prostrate for some minutes, and to give rise to the impression that he was dead.

Two certain individuals, evidently more intent upon their own pockets than about a good greyhound, and with an utter absence of all good taste, began offering 100 to 2 against Greentick, but even they seemed to catch quickly the infection of gloom and sorrow that had spread with such intensity. It would, indeed, have been a tragic ending to a disappointing career had the worst fears been realised, and great was the cheering as the gallant dog was seen to shortly afterwards walk towards the exit gate at the top of the ground.

He had just run one of his very best courses, and this no doubt stirred sympathy still more strongly in his favour. It was doubtful for some time whether he would be able to again go to slips, but his owner was not one of the dividing sort, and, moreover, there was the handsome solid silver punchbowl for the winner if the stake were run out. Indeed, it was not a question with Mr. Gladstone of dividing at all.

Had Greentick not sufficiently recovered to go to slips he would have been drawn, leaving Sailing Away to be declared the winner, and when John Coke was seen to lead him from the kennel yard a fresh burst of cheering was set up. The betting, which had been 2 to 1 against him, dropped to nearly evens when it was seen how full of life and fire he was, and how the hearts of the crowd had been moved, was conclusively shown by the ringing cheers that went up as he dashed clean away from his opponent, the cheers being renewed again and again throughout the course as he each time showed in front.

It was truly an exciting scene, never to be forgotten by those who were present, and greater enthusiasm was perhaps never shown even at Waterloo, except in the days of the great M'Grath, when hundreds of Irishmen used to go almost frantic with wild delight.

This was not the last of Greentick's achievements, for he afterwards ran up to the flying Kangaroo for a Gosforth Gold Cup, being beaten in a final, in which speed was the great factor.

R. Robinson.

MISS GLENDYNE and BIT OF FASHION.
Cup Dividers in 1885, Miss Glendyne Winning in 1886.

FABULOUS FORTUNE, FEARLESS FOOTSTEPS, and FARNDON FERRY.
Waterloo Cup Winners, 1896, 1900-01-02.

CHAPTER XVII.

Waterloo, 1885.
Miss Glendyne and Bit of Fashion.

NATURALLY enough, the previous year's winner used to be elected to the position of favourite, when Waterloo Cup betting commenced, as it used to do, at this period shortly after the nominations were announced in November. And though not, in any sense of the word, a public idol, Mineral Water was accorded the honour upon the occasion now under review.

No big commissions, however, were this year worked beforehand, and it will suffice to say that on the night of the draw Mineral Water was favourite at 100 to 9, the runner-up to him (Greentick) being next in demand at 100 to 6, only a very slightly better favourite than Clamour. Tonic, Miss Glendyne, Ballymoney, and Gay City were all in request, but against Bit of Fashion, ultimate divider with Miss Glendyne, 1,000 to 15, after being taken, was still on offer.

It was touch and go with the weather all the week, snow being in evidence as well as frost, but the going was never seriously affected, and a couple of hours' delay on the last morning was the extent of inconvenience inflicted. The running was mostly on the severe side, genuine attributes often prevailing over superior speed, and amongst the upsets was the defeat of the favourite by Skittles, Mr. Stone's bitch running a longish course with rare cleverness and resolution.

The best performers of the day, however, were distinctly Miss Glendyne and Clamour, and this was truly reflected in the betting at night. The sensation of the day was the meeting of Greentick and Gay City. They went three times to slips, the last-named finally proving the victor, but they did not escape as Chloe did under a similar ordeal with Spider in 1863. The Yorkshire bitch proved still equal to winning the Cup, whilst Gay City and Greentick were both settled in running it off, so far as the week was concerned.

G

On the Wednesday evening Mr. Hamer Bass, M.P., presided, and I mention the fact particularly in order to record a little story in connection with the member of the great Burton-on-Trent firm. It was in the days when headquarters for the Border Union meeting were at the Graham Arms, Longtown, and Mr. Bass was in the chair after the first day's running. Upon these occasions the duty was imposed upon the chairman of carving a joint, and a goose was placed in front of Mr. Bass.

Now whilst there is no worse joint than a poor goose, there are few better than a really good one. Mr. Bass liked the juicy character of the bird, and dined well. About eight o'clock a message came upstairs that Mr. Bass's carriage was ready, but he sent back word to the coachman that he need not wait, as he didn't want the carriage.

That night Mr. Bass left the Graham Arms on foot for Carlisle, something after 9 o'clock, and after rather more than eight miles walk heard the midnight hour being struck by the church clocks as he descended Stanwix bank to Eden bridge, one of the most charming entrances to any city, though it has in recent years been somewhat blindfolded by stupid if not selfish obstruction of the view with trees. Next day Mr. Bass expressed his delight with his overnight courage, and said he was amply repaid with an undisturbed night's sleep.

Harking back to Waterloo, Clamour was now favourite at 9 to 2, Miss Glendyne pressing closely at 5 to 1. Bit of Fashion, too, advanced from the outside ranks to 10 to 1. False Standard and Skittles were most fancied of the remainder, though the Irish dog (Captain Archdale's) Anticipation was also well befriended, as he was going fast.

In the third round of the Cup the leading feature was Clamour's smart display in disposing of Reputation, 5 to 2 then being accepted about his winning outright. A twisting course in the next round, however, proved fatal. Mr. Crosse's dog went up well in front, but after the first few points the hare continued to break at very sharp angles, and Skittles, displaying all her previous quickness and determination, proved too nimble for him.

Miss Glendyne led and decisively beat Wingrave, and soon settled accounts against Clyde Wharf by leading and quickly killing. The other two courses in the fourth round were well contested, neither Bit of Fashion against R. Halliday nor Ballymoney against Petrarch having anything to spare.

In the semi-finals Miss Glendyne led Ballymoney three lengths, and in a fine trial gave him a severe licking, but Bit of Fashion only gained a slovenly victory over the tired Skittles with extra speed, the kennel companions then dividing. Masdeu, the property of Mr. C. Murless, who now breeds for sale, won the Purse, Danseuse running-up, and Mr. J. R. Marshall's Cocklaw Dene won the Plate, beating Mr. Crosse's Che Sara (by Cui Bono) in the final.

It is worthy of note that this year the severity of the running, coupled with withdrawals in view of future engagements, led to there being no fewer than 15 byes in the Purse and the Plate; but fortunately "Vindex's" simple suggestion of signalling by the use of blue and yellow flags had come into operation so that the old confusion was avoided.

Waterloo, 1886—Miss Glendyne Wins Outright.

THIS was quite a red letter one in the records of the Waterloo Cup. Amongst the croakers it was thought to be languishing in the face of the rich prizes to be won in the leading enclosures—Gosforth Park, Kempton Park, Haydock, etc.; and, of course, from some points of view Waterloo suffered by comparison. Despite all drawbacks, however, Waterloo weathered the storm of opposition, and giving her the same speech as Tennyson's Brook, she might proudly say—

> " They may come, and they may go,
>   But I go on for ever."

A great step in advance was made this year in connection with the protection extended to the public. The field stewards had for some years succeeded in maintaining a more orderly crowd, but thieving and welshing were still carried on. The new hon. secretary, Mr. Harold Brocklebank, however, did not confine his arduous labours to the secretaryship, pure and simple, but also took a broad view of what the public were entitled to, and reform in this direction was one of the happy features of a splendidly successful week. That I may not over-colour " sweet memories of the past," I append a few words of what I wrote at the time :—

" In many respects the anniversary of 1886 may be regarded as a red-letter year in the annals of the Waterloo Cup. After being marked by the same comparative tameness which had been conspicuous of late years in its earlier stages, an amount of enthusiasm was developed towards the finish which brought vividly to mind the glorious days of the past. This result was conduced to in many ways. Favourable meteorological accompaniments lent their powerful aid on each of the three days, the weather at the concluding stage being quite genial and springlike, whilst the sport itself was of a type that has never been surpassed in point of excellence on a Waterloo field.

" Every surrounding, too, was of the happiest description. The judging throughout was one of Mr. Hedley's greatest successes, being perfect even to the smallest fault, and Wilkinson's slipping almost surpassed the great treats his matchless skill had ofttimes previously afforded. The crowd on no previous occasion behaved better, nor, perhaps, even so well ; and never before were the whole of the arrangements either more admirably planned or more efficiently carried out.

" The secretary and committee this year placed the police arrangements entirely in the hands of Superintendent Jervis, of the Ormskirk division, and the way in which the welshers and thieves were summarily dealt with on Thursday will probably have the effect of ridding us altogether of these pests by another year. At any rate, I know that it is intended to make still greater provision for dealing with them."

Harking back to the beginning Sir Windham C. Anstruther occupied the chair at dinner, supported on his right by Lord Wodehouse and Sir Thomas Brocklebank, and on his left by the present, and the late, secretary, Mr. Harold Brocklebank, and Mr. T. D. Hornby.   Owing to a doubt about Miss Glendyne's condition, and the soundness of her autumn-injured toe, she was not made favourite, the honour resting with Mr. E. M. Crosse's Clamour at 100 to 12.

The Short Flatt bitch, however, was backed by the public at 10 to 1, Penelope being third favourite at 1,000 to 80, with Greater Scot next in demand at 100 to 7. It was thus quite the reverse of an outsider's year, Miss Glendyne and Penelope running first and second ; and the third and fourth favourites owing their defeats to the other two. Penelope beat Clamour in the third round and Miss Glendyne beat Greater Scot in the fourth.

These two courses were splendidly run, and that between Penelope and Clamour was grandly contested, though the " little 'un " (Penelope only weighed about 41lbs.) had always a bit the best of it.

It was quite a year of grandly-run courses, which conduced greatly to the inspiriting effect so conspicuous throughout the week, and the final for the Cup was one of the prettiest-run trials ever witnessed. It was not a course of rapid exchanges and thrills, like that between Master M'Grath and Bab at the Bowster, or even that between Hung Well and Tide Time, but for extreme cleverness on the scut, on the part of each, in turn. I have only seen it once excelled, in the many thousands of courses I have witnessed, and that was between Bab at the Bowster and Lobelia in the final for a Douglas Cup, at a Scottish National meeting.

A description of that course has been previously given, and this Waterloo final will be depicted in Miss Glendyne's career.

Recognising that Miss Glendyne had now established her great reputation, and as this Waterloo victory was her most famous performance, a sketch of her wonderful career will not be out of place here.

Miss Glendyne's Career.

She made her début at Gosforth Park in November, '84, and divided the St. Leger Stakes (68 runners) with Mr. Gladstone's Fisherman. I was unfortunately not present, as the meeting clashed with Newmarket, where her half-sister, Bit of Fashion, also divided, and in these recitals I am giving only my own impressions. Waterloo was the next scene of Miss Glendyne's operations, and she led off with a very smart display against Middleton, a son of Coomassie.

In the second round she made an example of Willoughby, in a polished performance, though a rare hare took her right across the Church House meadows before she pulled it down.

In the evening's betting the impression she had made was reflected by the fact that after starting at 20 to 1, she now disputed favouritism with Clamour, 5 to 1 being taken to hundreds of pounds.

Her next effort, on the middle day, was equally brilliant in the early stages of another course of good length, though, naturally enough, a good performer like Wingrave at last joined issue, and finished the task in which she had so narrowly failed. Against Clyde Wharf, who had led and beaten the good bitch, False Standard, in the previous round, she again showed her superior speed, and this time quickly succeeded in flooring her game.

The Cup was now reduced to four dogs, and the Short Flatt brace, steering clear of each other, it was Bit of Fashion against Skittles, and Miss Glendyne against Ballymoney. It was close betting between the first-named pair, but 7 to 4 was laid on Miss Glendyne, and she was also a pronounced favourite for the event. The correctness of this forecast was never in doubt, Miss Glendyne taking a strong lead, and, maintaining the splendid form she had shown throughout, won decisively. Bit of Fashion also easily defeated Skittles, whereupon a division was arranged. Short Flatt thus scored a double triumph, Mr. Dent being owner of one divider and trainer of both.

Her Second Waterloo.

Well as she had acquitted herself in her first Waterloo, it was in her second that Miss Glendyne was seen in greatest perfection. She was already a great public favourite, and as her home trial was four lengths in front of Lights of London (winner of 67 courses in public) she was heavily backed at 10 to 1. Mr. E. M. Crosse's Clamour, however, started first favourite at 100 to 12. Penelope was third in demand at 100 to 8, and Greater Scot (divider with Herschel the following year) fourth at 100 to 7.

Bit of Fashion, it is, perhaps, worthy of note, figured in the 1,000 to 15 division. Miss Glendyne led off with a bloodless victory, her moderate opponent, Wanganui, never scoring a point, and she had all her own way against Highland Fling for a long time, though she tired a bit at last, the black having the finish of the course and the kill. This was hardly a true reflex of Miss Glendyne's best style, and it transpired that she was short of a gallop, having had trouble with a toe.

On the Thursday she came out in her true colours, and it was great form, indeed, to smash up as she did two greyhounds like Ballangeich (winner of a Kempton Park £1,000) and Greater Scot. She led the Scotch dog nearly four lengths, and, though the hare came short round, she went up as far ahead for the second turn, this time keeping closer possession. Puss breaking sharply, Ballingeich was enabled to exchange a point, but the white collar soon took absolute command, and, handling her hare in great style, finished a brilliant performance with a fine kill. This display caused 5 to 2 to be laid on her against Greater Scot, but it did not look the odds in the run up.

It was a tremendous race, Miss Glendyne only securing the initial point by half a length. She was much the quicker, however, at the turn, as puss jerked back, going up well in front for the next. Showing great resolution, Greater Scot was not long in exchanging points, but Miss Glendyne would not be denied, and, though the black gave a game challenge, she soon took the hare from him, almost jumping over him in doing so. The finish was all in Miss Glendyne's favour, as she handled her hare in irresistible style, and finally effected a neat kill.

An Inspiriting Decider.

At the final stage it was Miss Glendyne against Luther, and Penelope against Pinkerton, our heroine being favourite for the event at 105 to 80 against. After running some distance Miss Glendyne had not drawn more than a length in front, but gaining, as usual, an advantage at the drain, she at last shot ahead between three and four lengths. The course was then quite one-sided, Luther only exchanging once in a trial of fair length, Miss Glendyne winding up another magnificent display with the death.

The final was almost thrilling, alike for its beauty and exciting character. Shooting from slips like a rocket, as she had been doing throughout, Penelope almost instantly showed a neck in front, but as soon as Miss Glendyne got into her raking stride she drew level, and then commenced one of the prettiest and gamest struggles ever seen. In clearing the drain, however, in her own inimitable style—whilst Penelope rose slightly in the air—Miss Glendyne got a clear advantage, and, dashing out at the finish, was nearly two lengths ahead when she forced her hare round.

Puss breaking by the right, Penelope, under the white flag, shot to the front like an arrow, and was wonderfully smart on the scut for several points. She also made a desperate attempt to retain her position as puss broke from her to the left. Miss Glendyne, however, spurting with equal determination, then wrested possession, and, lining her game beautifully, at once imparted a different complexion to the course.

Penelope, trying desperately all the time, shot in for half a point, but Miss Glendyne was never again fully displaced, her last three wrenches and kill being one of the most stylish finishes ever witnessed. It was a grandly-run course on the part of both, and had Miss Glendyne not been a greyhound of quite exceptionally high class she must have been beaten. Rather singularly, the same kennels had been in great opposition shortly before, Mr. Pilkington's Phœbus beating Gay City (Miss Glendyne's brother) in the final for the Kempton Park £1,000, so that Miss Glendyne's success was a sweet revenge.

Upon her third visit to Altcar Miss Glendyne carried the full confidence of her owner and trainer, her home trial being a length and a half in front of the speedy Huic Holloa, who had won the Kempton Park £1,000. Mr. Hibbert had no less than £2,000 on her, and Mr. Dent £400, as they thought she could not be beaten. A tragedy, however, was in store, and, though she vanquished her first two opponents, Mereworth and Hermes, easily enough, a rare hare took her and Hermes right across to Gore House Wood, under the shade of which the frost, which delayed the start until the Thursday, had not got out of the ground, the result being that Miss Glendyne was picked up with a broken, or seriously injured, toe.

Robert Hutton, the eminent London bone-setter, was immediately wired for, but through unlucky delay a special train from London enabled him to reach Altcar—just ten minutes too late ! Her next opponent, Longest Day, had meanwhile run a bye. After Dr. Hutton's magic touch Miss

Glendyne walked quite sound, but that her toe would have remained so had she run must be open to great doubt.

Every care and a long rest having had the desired effect, Miss Glendyne came out all right in the memorable year of 1888, marked by such tantalising delay. The meeting was finally run off on Saturday, March 3rd, and Monday and Tuesday, the 5th and 6th. Herschel was a hot favourite at 95 to 20, and Miss Glendyne and her brother, Gay City, were in strong request respectively at 8 and 9 to 1—rather a remarkable feature considering that they were fourth-season greyhounds.

They were also all strong favourites for their courses at the first draw, but a second one becoming necessary, we had the excitement of finding Herschel and Miss Glendyne drawn together, the betting being 6 to 4 on Herschel. The course was quite regarded as the tit-bit of the day, but unfortunately for Miss Glendyne and the spectators it was a poor trial. Herschel, however, proved that he possessed a little better speed than the bitch, and, though she took the second turn, he clinched accounts by shooting half round her to kill.

It would hardly be fair to Herschel to assume that, with his extra pace, he would not have been capable of beating her in a better trial, though few would advance the opinion that he was as great a stylist as the bitch. Upon being brought for inspection the hare was seen to have one of its forelegs little more than half the proper length. That this spoiled what ought to have been a great course which would have infused plenty of excitement in a good trial, was shown by the style in which Miss Glendyne polished off each of her five opponents in the Purse.

She made yet another visit to the classic ground, but greyhounds in their fifth season are in the " sere and yellow " stage, as was pointedly shown when Fullerton attempted to supplement his four great Waterloo successes with a fifth. Miss Glendyne did better than he, in winning three courses and beating the favourite for the stake in Happy Rondelle; but wonderfully well as she ran she only gave glimpses of the Miss Glendyne of old.

CHAPTER XVIII.

Waterloo, 1887.
Herschel and Greater Scot Divide.

OWING to a supposed dearth of superior puppies, amongst which Herschel shone as a bright particular star, together with age now telling amongst many of the good old ones, Mr. Harold Brocklebank had an extra preliminary task this year of transferring no fewer than thirteen returned nominations ; and it is worthy of note that the readjustment did not finally disturb the original allocation of 46 English, nine Scotch, and nine Irish nominations. It was a troublous year regarding weather, frost having interfered with training operations, and though it yielded at last, it still entailed a day's delay.

Even on the Thursday further delay was threatened, but a summer sun coming to the rescue, a start was made shortly after midday. The running (all of which was on Monks' Carr) did not compare favourably with that of the previous year, and the layers of odds were often " at sea," a sequence of nine non-favourites being successful.

Those backed at inside prices to win outright, however, mostly asserted themselves, Herschel, Greater Scot, Fluttering Fersen, and Huic Holloa, as well as the hot favourite, Miss Glendyne, being amongst the sixteen survivors of the day. Miss Glendyne was backed for all the money that could be got on, after the draw, at 7 to 2, and it was recalled after the ill-luck that led to her withdrawal, that it was the same fatal price at which Master M'Grath started when beaten by Lady Lyons.

Friday's running was a great improvement upon that of the previous day, the frost being now quite out of the ground, and the trials genuine. The only case of the odds being floored in the third round of the Cup was when Dorinda completely outworked the faster Huic Holloa. Clamour, Fluttering Fersen, Greater Scot, Herschel, Jenny Jones, and Dandaleur all winning easily ; Longest Day got a bye through the injury to Miss

Glendyne, previously referred to in the sketch of her career. In the fourth round the courses were well contested.

At night the betting was 11 to 8 against Herschel, 9 to 4 against Greater Scot, and 100 to 14 against Clamour and Jenny Jones.

It was a repetition of Sea Cove's year (1870) and of Misterton's (1879) when the Waterloo cavalcade set out for Altcar on a Saturday morning; but the situation in the meantime had materially altered. During the earlier periods a carriage and pair was the favoured mode of travel, though personally I generally preferred a hansom, to avoid waiting for friends in getting back.

The last day's running was over ground that became very familiar to old habitues—a round of the Plate and the Purse on the Rye Heyes, then an adjournment to the Withins to finish. The Cup semi-finals resulted as anticipated, though neither course was as one-sided as expected, and a final between two such clippers as Herschel and Greater Scot owned as they were by two of the best and most highly esteemed coursers of the period, was eagerly looked forward to.

Purely good nature on the part of the owners led to the undesirable division, on the importunities of the trainer, Archie Coke. Mr. Hornby afterwards regretted it, not only because it deprived his great greyhound of the honour of winning, and spoiled sport, but because it might set up a dangerous precedent. It further deprived the Waterloo crowd of giving Mr. Hornby a great ovation. There is no man to whom the coursing world owes more: it can safely be said that it was his personal endeavour that attached such a high tone to the Waterloo Cup, and thereby permeated the whole coursing system with that pure atmosphere which has ever since been so grandly maintained.

The Purse was won by Mr. G. J. Alexander's Alec Ruby, by Alec Halliday out of Rubia, Lord Wodehouse ns Mr. Steadman's Brixton, by Misterton out of Hertha, running-up.

The Plate was divided between Mr. M. G. Hale's Happy Omen, by Millington out of Radiant, and Mr. T. Graham's Harpstring, by Glenlivet out of Polly.

CHAPTER XIX.

Waterloo, 1888—Burnaby's Surprise Year.

THERE is little doubt but that the prolonged delay greatly affected results in this memorable year. An inauspicious outlook did not prevent the draw being duly held on Tuesday, February 21st, but there was no chance of coursing during the week, a fresh entry and draw taking place on the Monday following. This also looked like proving abortive, but luckily a change came at the eleventh hour, a start being made on the Saturday, and the meeting finished on Monday and Tuesday, March 5th and 6th.

The favourites for the event were Herschel at 95 to 20 ; Gay City, 800 to 100 ; Miss Glendyne, 1,000 to 120 ; 1,000 to 70, Forget-me-Not ; 1,000 to 50, Jenny Jones ; 1,000 and to 30 each Greater Scot, Marsden, Roxana, Glencotha, Galfride, and Hermes. 1,000 to 20 was laid against both the winner and runner-up, Burnaby and Duke M'Pherson.

Had all gone well, this ought to have proved an interesting year, but the fates were unpropitious, and several of the best trained greyhounds naturally enough went " off," with the long delay. The frost being quite out of the ground, there was nothing in that respect to interfere with the running, but a recent dressing of sand on Monks' Carr proved a further drawback, as it tended to make the going somewhat treacherous ; and there were many unexpected results.

Of the leading favourites only Herschel and Jenny Jones survived the opening day, and eventually four outsiders were left in. At this point Burnaby beat Dingwall, and Duke M'Pherson beat Caterham Apostle. In the final it was a third-season greyhound (Burnaby) against a puppy. In a long stretch down the Withins at a fast hare, the young one led for a long way, but Burnaby gradually collared him, and drew clean past before the hare was reached. Coming nicely round he held possession for a good start, but after an exchange of points, the Duke got well placed, and with a meritorious sequence placed the issue in the balance.

Further exchanges followed, Burnaby now running the stronger, and with a couple of wrenches and game kill close to the sough, he won Mr. Leonard Pilkington his first Waterloo Cup. Burnaby was bought out of a selling stake at Haydock Park for 30gs., and though he cannot claim to rank in the gallery of the higher class greyhounds, he gained his Blue Riband in very meritorious style.

The great feature of his victory was his defeat of Herschel in the fourth round : he was "running on" all the week, and the crack was clearly going off. Still, big odds were laid on Herschel for the course, this being one of the many knock-down blows received by backers during the meeting.

Herschel had previously led and beaten Miss Glendyne (at a three-legged hare), Mahonia, and the good Irish dog, Tullochgorum. The meeting of such a pair as Herschel and Miss Glendyne was, of course, the feature of the opening day, and it was quite in accordance with the ill-luck of the week, that they should have had such a poor trial. Mr. Hornby was not much addicted to joking, but upon one of Miss Glen-dyne's party attempting to belittle Herschel's victory with the remark " It was only a three-legged hare," he made the happy sally, " I suppose Miss Glendyne had all her four legs."

Other notable surprises of the week were the defeats or Gay City (with 4 to 1 on him) by Jock Scott, who also led to the hare, and that of Greater Scot (with 3 to 1 on him) by Caterham Apostle. The outsider again led to the hare, and won the course easily, running exceedingly well, though " the Scot " made a good finish when too late. Gay City's defeat was only a narrow one, and the trial was rather a scramble, both dogs slipping about. Gay City did not run in the Purse, but Miss Glendyne did, and she polished off all her five opponents in her own great style.

CHAPTER XX.

Waterloo, 1889~90~91~92—The Fullerton Era.

THERE will not be very many left who witnessed the
doughty deeds of Master M'Grath ; and those who
are, would little dream of ever seeing his great feat of
winning three Waterloo Cups repeated, let alone
eclipsed ! But wonder of wonders, an even greater halo of
Waterloo glory now surrounds the fame of Fullerton. He was
at the end of four Waterloo Cups, and the son of Greentick
was so imbued with vitality through the blood of Bab at the
Bowster and Bed of Stone that he even essayed a fifth triumph.
Nature, however, had already reached the high-water mark,
and perhaps rebelled against the further strain of training.
Who can tell ? At any rate, Fullerton was not only beaten,
but proved incapable of perpetuating his splendid powers.

He was not favourite for the Cup in his first year, for he had
previously got such a battering at Haydock over ground as
hard as a turnpike road, that there were great doubts whether
the ordeal might not have left its mark. His excellence,
however, had been so striking—I remember well, writing at the
time, that he was the best I had seen since Master M'Grath—
that he was well backed at 10 to 1, his closing price being
100 to 11.

Calculations were often upset at the opening stage, but
the four best favourites all survived the day. Herschel,
Burnaby, Troughend and Miss Glendyne were amongst the
best performers, but Fullerton's form was clearly the most
striking.

Fullerton had a narrow escape on Thursday morning in
the third round against Barbican II., but it was entirely
accidental. The course was run on the flat close to Hill House
Wood, known as Rye Heyes, where the hares always twisted
a good deal, and Bootiman had run out to several, at which
he was unable to get a satisfactory slip. This upset Fullerton
more than it did his older opponent, and he was very slow from
slips when they were at last delivered. Still he would have

been first to the hare, had she not at last bent in Barbican's favour ; as it was, the white got both the first and second turns. Fullerton dashed to the front immediately the hare broke clear, and had the best of what followed in a short scrambling trial, the hare at last jumping high in the air to evade her pursuers, now on each side of her, and being nailed by Barbican as she dropped. More than a murmur of disapprobation went up from the big crowd on the bank as undecided was signalled.

Next time Fullerton showed considerable superiority, both in speed and at all points. At the end of the round Colonel North had no fewer than four standing in the last eight, but as there is no guarding at Waterloo (all being single nominations) they twice over had to oppose each other. Fullerton easily disposed of Sorais, and Troughend proved too fast and good for Miss Glendyne, now in her fifth season. The final four were now Fullerton to meet Herschel, and Troughend to meet Danger Signal.

It would have been a battle royal between Fullerton and Herschel had they met on equal terms, but Mr. Hornby's grand dog had been terribly gruelled on Thursday in the fourth round. After a one-sided victory over Sloane Square, and after his opponent had had enough, a demon hare took him right away to Gore House Wood, and as if this were not enough, he struck a fresh hare on his way back. Consequently 3 to 1 was laid on the course, and Fullerton justified the odds, by leading up fully four lengths, and winning in a canter for some time. Herschel, however, at last warming up, gave a great challenge, dusting his hare with such wonderful resolution that it almost looked as though he might yet have won, had he deferred his game kill. It was a great race to the hare between Troughend and Danger Signal, but in another fine trial Troughend was infinitely the better. Colonel North's pair then divided, this being the first time, since Selby and Clive's division in 1859, that the same owner ran first and second.

The Purse and Plate were both run out, the former being won by the Earl of Sefton ns Mr. Huntingdon's Highness, with Mr. A. Brisco ns Mr. Pilkington's good bitch Pins and Needles second. In the Plate Sir R. Jardine's Glenogle beat Captain McCalmont ns Colonel North's Dingwall.

Waterloo, 1890.

IN Fullerton's second year, he may truthfully be said to have dominated the situation from start to finish. He was freely backed at 9 to 2 in hundreds on the night of the draw, and after the first day's running, with, of course, four courses yet to win, his admirers accepted 65 to 40 freely, the bookmakers' offers dropping to 6 to 4. At the outset the only other backed at less than 20 to 1 was Mr. Pilkington's Pins and Needles, about which 1,000 to 70 was taken and wanted. On the second night she was again second favourite at 100 to 12, long prices ruling against the others. Thursday, however, brought about her dismissal. She vanquished Dolon easily enough, but then fell away in her form, and went down before Donald O'Kane.

Fullerton, on the contrary, kept rejoicing his backers with easy victories over Monkside (who gave one good challenge) and Gladiola ; and at the final stage neither Mr. Gladstone's Green Fern, nor Mr. N. Dunn's Downpour (runner-up) stood the least chance with him. It was a splendid victory, by a great greyhound, and Downpour performed very meritoriously in taking second honours. Ireland won the Purse, with Mr. Swinburne's Knockninny Boy. Fullerton's half-brother, Troughend, running-up. Mr. T. Graham's Jim o' the Hill won the Plate ; Mr. Crosse's Coca Water running-up.

Waterloo, 1891.

THIS was the most interesting point of Fullerton's great career, for he was attempting a task in which both Master M'Grath and Miss Glendyne had failed, viz : to gain three consecutive Waterloo triumphs. That he not only succeeded, but added yet a fourth victory to his triple crown, is, of course, now ancient history. I am at present referring only to his third success. His starting price was 7 to 2, and, rather remarkably, Faster and Faster was a pronounced second favourite at 1,000 to 80, the two running first and second. In the first round Fullerton met his younger brother Simonian (betting 3 to 1 on Fullerton), and was for the only time led to the hare. Being a third season

John Worsnop.

FULLERTON, Winner of Waterloo Cup, 1889-90-91-92.

KING COB.

greyhound he did not jump off like the puppy, but he was going the faster at the finish, though he could not quite get up for the first turn.

He squeezed up so closely, however, that the young one had to put on high pressure to get first up. This caused him to run out, and Fullerton coming round in possession had always the course won afterwards. Simonian, trying hard for possession, dashed up on the outside, and repeated this a second time, giving a false impression to the distant view of the crowd, who had not got sufficiently forward—the course was run in the vicinity of Gore House Wood, just after a longish move—but Fullerton was, all the time, true on his hare, and had won well when he killed, though to this day I sometimes meet an old courser who thinks Simonian beat him.

An abrupt termination to the first day's sport was brought about by fog, which had delayed the start, again closing in ; and the stewards were fortunate in being able to break off at the point of half-way down the card. Fullerton was virtually at his previous night's odds at the calling over of the card, and Real Lace was a decided second favourite at 100 to 12. Faster and Faster, and the remainder of the bottom 32 that had not run, were not called over.

All turned out well on Thursday. The fog was still in evidence when Hill House was reached, but a glorious sun came to the rescue. The order of running being, of course, only to complete the first day's programme, Fullerton again ran only one course in which he beat Rhymes pointless. He did not lead far—barely two lengths—but he came round beautifully at the turn, and held close possession for a few strong wrenches before giving the *coup de grace.*

In the betting at night Fullerton was freely supported at 9 to 4 (he had four courses yet to win) and then 200 to 100 was taken several times, but the bookmakers still offered these odds. On figures, too, they were amply justified.

On Friday the fog demon still pursued us, and there had been, in addition, a touch of frost ; but after some delay at the Hill House meet, the order was given for the Withins, the

H

going there having been found all right. Before midday Mr.
Hedley's and Tom Bootiman's scarlet shone in the sunlight.
The great course of the day was rightly regarded as that
between Fullerton and one of the best puppies of the season,
Real Lace   Betting was 7 to 4 on Fullerton. It was a grand
tussle for some distance, but Fullerton, as all along, increasing
his speed, was three lengths in front when he forced his hare
round.   Puss, breaking very sharply, gave Real Lace an
opening, which she instantly took, and reaching her game well
in front for the second point, swept beautifully on the scut for
the third. Puss then breaking clear, they got together for a
stretch, in which Fullerton showed in advance and got the
next point.

An exchange followed before Real Lace again got nicely
placed, the issue then hanging in the balance ; but Fullerton
having now warmed grandly to his work, drew to the front as
the hare again broke clear, and with a splendid finish and
brilliant kill won well. Against Meols Major it was 8 to 1 on
Fullerton, and, as the odds suggested, it was a one-sided
victory ; also a grandly run course, finished with a fine kill.
The Short Flatt puppy Not Out (Greentick out of Miss Glendyne) had done well in winning three courses, but Faster and
Faster was too good for him in the fourth round. The four
now left in were Fullerton against Button Park (runner-up two
years later to Character) and Faster and Faster against Bovril.
Very long odds were laid on each result—10 to 1 on Fullerton
and 7 to 1 on Faster and Faster—and each course was well
won, though not in the one-sided fashion suggested by the odds.

In the final it was 5 to 2 on Fullerton. After rejecting
several hares as not good enough, Bootiman effected a perfect
slip, and it was a close race for some distance. The crack then
drew in front, being two lengths ahead as he cleared the drain
in grand style, and increasing his advantage to three lengths
for first turn. He flew a bit wide as puss broke short round,
the blue now going up well in advance and apparently being
well placed. She only scored twice, however, before puss also
threw her out, and Fullerton, going up well in front, this time
held strong possession. He lined his hare with splendid force
and truth for several strong wrenches towards the edge of the

drain, and before puss could essay the jump, he struck her into it. This was not as grand a final performance as his previous one, nor even as the one with which he followed, in his fourth season, but it was a decisive victory over a good greyhound, by a better one.

Waterloo, 1892—Fullerton's Fourth Success.

AS in Meg's year, 1865, and in Burnaby's, 1888, adverse weather necessitated a fresh entry and draw; but, happily, the end of disappointment had this time already been reached, a start being made on Tuesday, February 23rd, and the meeting finished on Thursday, the 25th. At the first draw it was made known that in the event of any of his other three coming against Fullerton, there would be a withdrawal in the old champion's favour. This announcement was not well received, and in the meantime wiser counsels prevailed, Mr. Alfred Brisco announcing from the chair that Colonel North had authorised him to state that all his dogs would be run out upon their merits.

Fullerton's approach to " the sere and yellow " did not shake the public confidence in the popular idol, 100 to 30 being freely taken; Mr. Russel's Race Course was second favourite at 1,000 to 90 and Woodcote Green third favourite at 1,000 to 60.

The opening day's sport was an excellent one, and there were several courses particularly well run, but Fullerton quite overshadowed everything with his two clipping displays, and at the night's betting 65 to 40 was the best price obtainable, Race Course being again a good second favourite, at 100 to 15.

Fullerton was not able to polish off his third opponent as he did the previous two, Rhymes giving a couple of stout challenges that caused plenty of excitement. The champion, however, after going up between two and three lengths in front made a good start, and, finishing the spin with fine resolution, was an easy winner when he killed. Odds of 6 to 1 were laid on Fullerton for the course, but the fielders took 7 to 2 freely when he met Patrick Blue in the fourth round. A great shout went up when the non-favourite was seen to draw slightly in advance, and after a fine tussle for seventy or eighty yards, Patrick was a neck in front.

Fullerton, however, shot past him at the drain (like Miss Glendyne, he was a wonder in this respect) and was well clear when he brought his hare round by the left. This was carrying her away from his opponent, but Patrick, with great dexterity, crossed behind, and made a fine shoot forward. Fullerton, however, splendidly on his mettle, also spurted grandly, never quite losing possession, and he finished the spin brilliantly by forging half-round his opponent for a fine kill.

The four left in were now Fullerton against Race Course and Fitz Fife against Roman Oak. The last named was the only puppy. Race Course and Fitz Fife were both second season, the best point of a greyhound's life. All three were Border Union performers, Race Course having divided the Netherby Cup the previous October, and Roman Oak the Border Union Stakes ; Fitz Fife divided the latter event the previous year.

Semi-Finals.

Fullerton beat Race Course. Betting, 8 to 1 on Fullerton, After they had run a short distance together Fullerton gradually drew ahead, being between two and three lengths in front as puss after clearing the drain broke short to the left. This was to the black's side, but Fullerton sweeping grandly on the line of hare never lost an inch of ground, and moved strongly on the scut two or three times before puss threw him off with a sharp double and recrossed the drain. He was after her like a flash and killed before puss could again get into her swing.

Fitz Fife beat Roman Oak. Betting, 2 to 1 on Roman Oak. It looked for seventy or eighty yards as though Roman Oak would lead, but in a good stretch Fitz Fife at last shook him off, and gaining an advantage at the drain he was nearly three lengths in front as he made the turn. Swinging grandly with his hare, he held close possession for three points before making a vicious attempt to kill. Blundering in making it, Roman Oak now took a good position, but Fitz Fife soon again joined issue, and although the blue had a bit the best of what followed in a fine trial and finished with a good kill, there was a clear balance against him.

Deciding Course.

Fullerton beat Fitz Fife (1). Betting, 9 to 2 on Fullerton. After a short undecided in which Fullerton led, and Fitz Fife killed, the crack led nearly three lengths and made a brilliant beginning. A ding-dong trial followed, Fitz Fife at one point making a bold show, but the champion was a good winner when he pulled down the rare hare.

Colonel North, as in the previous year, also won one of the minor events, Simonian following up his Purse victory by winning the Plate, Mr. J. B. Thompson's Lecturer running-up. Mr. J. Russel, made a good show by reaching the semi-finals for the Cup with Race Course, and winning the Purse with Red River, Sir Sankey being second. Four of Greentick's sons thus figured in the finals—Simonian, Sir Sankey, and Lecturer— in addition to Fullerton claiming his parentage. As showing his popularity at this time, it is worthy of mention that no fewer than 25 sons and daughters were embraced in the 64. In stud fees, and winnings, Greentick earned between £6,000 and £7,000.

Fullerton's Record.

In making the record of four Waterloo successes, Fullerton's triumph as a fourth-season greyhound was not unique, for Master M'Grath's third victory was gained at the same age. In his case, however, it was clearly not the great M'Grath of old that won, whilst Fullerton's powers were seemingly but little impaired.

CHAPTER XXI.

Waterloo, 1893—Character's Year.

LIKE many other champions, in other spheres, Fullerton did not retire in time. The fascination he still held over the public mind, however, was exemplified in the extraordinary fact that 4 to 1 was taken in hundreds about a fifth season greyhound winning a Waterloo Cup ! The second favourite was Fine Night, at 10 to 1, her form in dividing the Newmarket Champion Puppy Stake having been exceedingly smart. The previous year's runner-up, Fitz Fife, and Dillon, that had shown fine speed at Haydock, were also in good demand at 1,000 to 70. None of these got near the end. The winner started at 1,000 to 15, and the runner-up, Button Park, at 1,000 to 10.

Fullerton was in the first course of the meeting and, with 7 to 1 on him, he very easily disposed of Castlemartin, though he was a longish time in pulling his hare down. Odds of 3 to 1 were laid on him in the next round, but his great powers at last gave out. The Irish dog, Full Captain, led him a couple of lengths, and always had him beaten. The old champion made a gallant fight, and even after slipping into the drain, quickly rejoined, and gave another game challenge. But the fawn was running with considerable fire, and Fullerton making a second mistake, the die was cast, the Captain having the best of the finish, and being an easy winner as Fullerton knocked puss off her legs for the fawn to kill. A few farewell words, written on the day of Fullerton's defeat, may appropriately be added.

" Two striking features will serve to make the first day of this year's Waterloo a memorable one, viz., the defeat of Fullerton, and the stoutness with which the hares ran. Even on the Carrs, which we had been accustomed to villify so much, it often happens that the first hare from a beat is a bold and stout one, so that it was nothing in the crack's favour that he should have been one of the first pair drawn on Tuesday night, and, true to tradition, puss proved a trimmer. Fullerton won

Lafayette.

Mr. H. HARDY,
Owner of Wild Night and Hoprend.

Elliott & Fry.

Mr. J. EDGAR DENNIS,
Joint Owner of Dendraspis and Dilwyn.

Bullingham.

Mr. E. DENT,
Trainer of Fullerton and Miss Glendyne.

Sport & General.

Mr. J. COKE,
Owner of Character.

his course, it is true, but the result may be said to have sealed his fate, so far as winning the Cup was concerned, and, as it turned out, it even prevented his raising a second flag. Curiously enough, he ran over the same ground that was fatal to another great Short Flatt celebrity in Miss Glendyne when slipped with Hermes, the hare to-day, as upon the previous memorable occasion, making right away for Gore House Wood. Miss Glendyne, I need hardly remind my readers, was successful just as Fullerton was to-day, but she broke a toe, which incapacitated her from going to slips in the succeeding round, whilst Fullerton's strong dose, without preventing his going to slips a second time, evidently stiffened his muscles and took away his pace.

"Never was a more gallant effort made by the loser of a great fight, and the crowd evidently had a strongly sympathetic feeling from the cheers with which they greeted the fallen champion as he was led back. It was a case of the same old natural law asserting itself, and it will probably be many years before we again have a fifth-season greyhound attempting to win a Waterloo Cup."

Stripped of Fullerton's defeat the opening stage of Character's year produced no striking feature except that the hares ran with exceptional stoutness, several of the courses being unduly severe. Fitz Fife, Character, Patrick Blue, Texture, and old Button Park, were amongst the best performers, and they were all lucky enough to get lightly off. At night Fitz Fife was a pronounced favourite at 5 to 2, Character and Texture being in next request at 7 to 1 ; 10 to 1 being also taken about Patrick Blue, Red River, and Full Captain.

Fullerton's victor did not get any further. It was a great struggle to the hare between him and Character, but afterwards the ultimate winner was much the smarter and fully justified the odds of 7 to 4. He was a better favourite next time at 2 to 1 against the handicapped War Lad, who never scored a point, Character giving a clipping display. Patrick Blue's defeats of Bodisco and Hendersyde were also marked by particularly smart running, and old Button Park again performed exceedingly well, though his defeat of Fitz Fife was discounted by the fact that Messrs. Fawcett's dog had been very hard run in his defeat of Hornet in the previous round. Texture, like the other three survivors of the second day, ran her courses well, easily vanquishing two handicapped opponents in Torrance and Hooks and Eyes ; but she in turn now caught it hot, her course with the last-named being a stinger.

The betting at night was 7 to 4 against Patrick Blue, 5 to 2 Button Park, 3 to 1 Character, and 4 to 1 Texture. In the semi-finals Character led and cleverly beat Patrick Blue, and Button Park easily disposed of Texture.

Final Course.

" Character beat Button Park. Betting, 3 to 1 on Character. The unique spectacle was seen of one trainer taking both dogs to slips for a Waterloo final, and John Coke must have felt a proud satisfaction at the splendid tribute the loud cheers of the crowd conveyed. It was not long before a hare came forward, and the favourite in a good stretch drew out between three and four lengths. Then driving away on the scut in fine style he held a winning position for some time. Button Park at last seeing an opening, spurted gamely to the front for a couple of points, but he lost his place as puss broke round, and the white, finishing the course in grand style, was the easiest of winners when he killed."

The Purse was won in good style by Sir Sankey, who thus improved upon his second the previous year, Ivan the Great running-up. The Plate was divided between Annihilator and Tasmania, the latter being the only puppy that took honours at the meeting.

Character's owner, Mr. John Coke, I may mention, was quite in luck's way. Wishing to catch the last train back to his Southport home, and Character not having yet been called, he left a commission with a friend to back him to win a thousand. Through mistake, his friend backed him to win £2,000. Not having seen his commissioner before Character had to go to slips, John, to make sure of being on, also took £1,000 to 15 on the ground, and at the finish had the pleasure of winning £3,000 instead of £1,000, less a little hedging.

CHAPTER XXII.

Waterloo, 1894.
Texture's Year—A Day's Delay.

THIS year was specially signalised by the winner being owned by a foreigner—the Russian nobleman, Count Stroganoff. There were also preliminary features that demand a few words. The entry, dinner and draw were duly held at the Adelphi Hotel, with that fine old sportsman, Sir Windham Anstruther, in the chair, although it was already known that there would be no coursing before Thursday. After the usual loyal toasts, the health of the Earl of Sefton was even exceptionally well received, but that of Mr. Harold Brocklebank, when he rose to respond, elicited still louder cheers. It was well known that he was retiring from his official position after this year, and arduous as the duties of Waterloo secretary must always be, they had been quite exceptionally so during his tenure of office. Upon two occasions a fresh entry and draw had become necessary, in addition to other delays and difficulties, and to always do the right thing, in the right way, is a great trial; but Mr. Brocklebank never failed. He successfully maintained the tradition that the Waterloo Cup was a sport for gentlemen, to be pursued by gentlemen; and he also extended a helping hand to the general public.

Mr. Brocklebank's predecessor, Mr. T. D. Hornby (*facile princeps* of secretaries in his day) taxed himself very heavily in attaching and maintaining a high tone, but was rather inclined to blame the public themselves who fell a prey to the thieves and welshers. Mr. Brocklebank took a broader view, and enlisting the energetic services of Superintendent Jervis, of the Ormskirk division, soon made Waterloo not only a less dangerous, but a much more enjoyable field for those who came to Altcar " on pleasure bent."

It was expected to be good odds on the field this year, but quite a hot favourite was found in Falconer—a puppy that had only been once in public, when he shared in a four-cornered division of the all-aged Netherby Cup. His price was 100 to 15 taken freely, and his kennel companion and sister, Free Kick, held the position of second favourite at 100 to 9. They were two of the afterwards famous Herschel and Fine Sport litter. Follow Faster and Patrick Blue were each well backed at 1,000 to 60, and of the remainder War Lad and Joss Bones were in best request.

A change in the weather taking place on Wednesday afternoon, it was announced that the meet would be at Hill House at 10 o'clock on Thursday morning. Ill-luck again came in the way, for though the frost had gone, fog supervened, and it was 2 o'clock before a start could be made. It was hoped to get once down the card, but when darkness declared a veto at 6 o'clock we were a few courses short. The leading favourites, however, were all slipped, and they not only all won, but acquitted themselves well. Falconer cut his course short with a pretty stroke, and Patrick Blue ran a shortish spin very smartly.

On the Friday, in addition to the courses left over, the second and third rounds were run through, this still leaving eight in for the Saturday finish. This, as it turned out, was very unfortunate for Falconer, as his extra undecided in the semi-finals with Follow Faster made the final course his fourth effort during the day, and he was a dog puppy. Texture, on the contrary, was a ripe third-season bitch, and also much the fresher greyhound. It was a well-contested final, but Texture, after leading a length for the initial point, was always showing more fire than the puppy. Falconer made one very game challenge, but could not sustain it long enough, and Texture having the finish as well as the beginning, won well.

Mr. M. G. Hale's Happy Relic and Mr. L. Pilkington's Pennegant divided the Purse ; and the Plate (only commenced on the last day) was divided between Mr. W. Thompson's Tasmania and Mr. M. Fletcher's Free Kick. It was quite a Herschel year, Texture, Falconer, Happy Relic, and Free Kick all claiming him as sire.

THOUGHTLESS BEAUTY, Winner of Waterloo Cup, 1895.

From Painting by Mr. J. Armstrong, Aglionby, Carlisle.

HONEYWOOD, Winner of Waterloo Cup, 1880

CHAPTER XXIII.

Waterloo, 1895—Thoughtless Beauty's Year.

FROST and snow were terribly in the ascendent this year. So severe was (and had been for a month or more) the weather, that a week's postponement was announced several days beforehand, and in what ought to have been the running week, a further postponement of seven days was decided upon, the entry and draw then standing fixed for March 5th. But the end of the trouble was not yet. There was yet another week's delay, the meeting being run off on Wednesday, Thursday and Friday, March 13, 14th and 15th.

Though beaten in the final the year before, Falconer, as upon that occasion, was made a strong favourite, the short price of 1,100 to 200 being taken and wanted.

In face of the unwritten law, now rigidly observed, that no owner ought to run more than two, it will read rather strange that both Messrs. Fawcett and Mr. Matthew Fletcher ran no fewer than five. The form of the Saughall team was the great feature of the day, for not only did four of the quintette survive the two opening rounds, three of them, viz., Fair Floralie, Fabulous Fortune and Fortuna Favente (of the famous Herschel—Fair Future litter), also carried off the honours with brilliant running. Mr. Fletcher's lot on the contrary figured amongst the early slain, Falconer alone excepted. He, however, may be said to have redeemed the situation, for he ran both courses in irreproachable style and with great fire. Thoughtless Beauty also gave two brilliant displays, and the betting on Wednesday night was strongly in favour of those mentioned.

On Thursday all the five leading favourites vanquished their first opponents in great style, the next round being full of interest.

Falconer beat Ivan the Great. Betting, 4 to 1 on Falconer. The favourite, much quicker on his pins than his handicapped opponent, drew clear in the first few strides, and eventually finished a nailing good performance with a fine kill.

Fortuna Favente beat Fair Floralie.   Betting, 11 to 8 on
Fair Floralie.   In a fine stretch the non-favourite gradually
drew out nearly two lengths, but Fair Floralie flying the drain
as they neared the hare in brilliant style, whilst the dog jumped,
the bitch closed the gap, and it was only with a grand effort
that Fortuna Favente gained the turn on an outside.   Puss
breaking further to the left Fair Floralie shot up for the second
point, but the red collar returning her spurt with equal determination dashed up for the third as puss came to the right.
Then, as she broke again to the left, the bitch with another
fine effort took the fourth, but the dog instantly forged up to
her, and, after a momentary exchange, they ran into the hare
together.

Thoughtless Beauty beat Fabulous Fortune.   Betting,
13 to 8 on Fabulous Fortune.   It was a tremendous struggle in
the run up, and until they neared the drain it looked as if
Fabulous Fortune would lead, for he had about half-a-length
the best of it.   The bitch, however, fairly shot him in the jump,
and continued to have the best of it, being a decisive winner
as she drove the hare quite clear for a fine kill.

Gallant beat Mellor Moor.   Betting, 7 to 4 on Mellor Moor.
For some distance it looked as if the favourite would lead, but
in a good stretch Gallant at last drew out fully two lengths,
and sweeping well with his hare he added the second and third
points.

Semi-Finals.

Fortuna Favente beat Falconer.   Betting, 15 to 8 on
Falconer.   Fortuna Favente gradually forged ahead, and
at the end of a fair stretch was two lengths in front as he
got on terms with his hare.   Puss coming round strongly to the
right Falconer saw an opening, and crossing behind to the
inside dashed up with considerable fire, and drove at his hare.
Puss breaking sharp round to avoid his stroke Fortuna Favente
came cleverly with her, finishing a decisive victory with a
good kill.

Thoughtless Beauty beat Gallant.   Betting, 2 to 1 on
Thoughtless Beauty.   In another beautiful stretch Thoughtless
Beauty quickly showed in front, and had drawn well clear in
the first hundred yards.   Gallant then, after holding his own

for a short distance, gradually forged up and had drawn all but level when they got on terms. Puss breaking short to the bitch's side she shot away in smart possession, and "Thoughtless" won easily.

Deciding Course.

Thoughtless Beauty beat Fortuna Favente. Betting, 2 to 1 on Fortuna Favente. In a splendid race down the Withins Fortuna Favente gradually forged half a length in front, but pecking just the slightest upon landing over the drain, whilst the bitch shot it like a snake, the lead was instantly reversed. Thoughtless Beauty in the last few strides also went the faster, scoring the first turn by a length and a half. She ran out just the least bit as puss came round, and the red taking strong possession at once raised the hopes of his friends. As puss broke from him, however, the bitch dashed up for the third point, a decisive victory being hers when she finished with a fine kill.

The Purse was divided between Mr. F. Watson's Word of Honour, by Herschel out of Watchful Duchess, and Mr. A. F. Pope ns Messrs. Fawcett's Fertile Field, by Townend out of Honey Dear.

The Plate was won by Mr. Gilbody ns Mr. M. Fletcher's Forum, by Herschel out of Fine Sport, Mr. Marfleet ns Mr. M'Callum's Ruby Red running-up.

Thoughtless Beauty did not do a great amount of running, but she was a grand bitch, and ran into the last four for the Cup the following year: her full performance was winning 25 courses and losing three.

"Thoughtless" never threw a Waterloo Cup winner, but two of her sons—Paracelsus and Prince Plausible—ran-up, and her son Pateley Bridge produced two winners in Long Span and Hallow Eve. Being a daughter of Herschel, and a grand-daughter of Greentick shew as difficult to mate satisfactorily, but a great hit was made in sending her to Mellor Moor, by Monkside, by Jester, one of the famous Ptarmigan—Gallant Foe family.

Her first visit in 1898 resulted in producing Pensive Beauty, Peerless Beauty, Pikelaw and Pateley Bridge, and from a second in 1900, came Pretty Lassie, Priestlaw and Prince Charming.

CHAPTER XXIV.

Waterloo, 1896—Fabulous Fortune's Year.

THIS year was made memorable at the outset by two greyhounds being each backed at very short odds. Thoughtless Beauty, previous year's winner, was favourite at 9 to 2, and Fabulous Fortune was supported freely at 5 to 1.

Good coursing and pleasant weather marked the opening day's sport, but the performances all round were hardly suggestive of a high-class 64. Fabulous Fortune's two displays stood out boldly, and truthfully foreshadowed the final result.

Utopia was distinctly amongst those that acquitted themselves best, and so were the Irish pair, Wolf Hill and Weatherwise ; but the latter was very hard run in his defeat of Fair Floralie.

On Wednesday night the betting was 2 to 1 against Fabulous Fortune, 4 to 1 Fortuna Favente, 5 to 1 Thoughtless Beauty, and 10 to 1 each against Utopia and Weatherwise.

In the eight courses in third round the odds of 7 to 4 on What's the Odds against Juggernaut, 9 to 4 on Guiding Star against Mellor Moor, 6 to 4 on Grey Moor *versus* Wolf Hill, and 3 to 1 on Fortuna Favente against Weatherwise, were all floored.

The feature of the second day's running was the grandly-sustained form of the overnight favourite, Fabulous Fortune, and the great improvement shown by Thoughtless Beauty upon her earlier displays. At night the betting was 5 to 4 against Fabulous Fortune, 13 to 8 against Thoughtless Beauty, 11 to 2 against Utopia, and 100 to 8 against Wolf Hill.

At the final stage Fabulous Fortune proved too fast for Utopia, but Wolf Hill floored the big odds laid on Thoughtless Beauty, and after just leading beat her fairly.

Deciding Course.

Fabulous Fortune beat Wolf Hill. Betting, 7 to 2 on Fabulous Fortune. The delivery taking place close to the cross drain where Townfield and Green Nut came to grief in the first round of the Cup, they had only gone four or five strides when Wolf Hill blundered badly through landing with his hind legs barely clear. Fabulous Fortune thereupon drew out over half a dozen lengths for the first turn, at which he swept round in grand style and maintaining a splendid style throughout a trial of good length, finally ran into his hare without allowing the Irish dog to score.

Waterloo Cup : Mr. G. F. Fawcett's r d Fabulous Fortune, by Herschel out of Fair Future, won ; Mr. W. H. Smith ns Mr. W. Smyrl's f d Wolf Hill, by Carr's Green out of The Pug, ran up.

The Purse was won by Mr. Harold Brocklebank ns Sir T. Brocklebank's w f d p Biere, by Branston out of Barbon ; Mr. C. Murless's bk w d p Brummagem Man, by Birmingham out of Mischievous, running-up.

The Plate was won by Mr. J. Russel's good bitch Reception, by Restorer—Real Lace, Mr. T. Holmes's Gallant (the following year's Cup winner) running-up.

It was a pity that the final for the Cup was not invested with a fair and square run-up, but the issue could hardly have been different. The winner must have led without the advantage he gained, and he was running in irresistible form ; he was " the Hamlet " of the play all the week, from start to finish. I heard complaints about the slip, but it was not in the least Bootiman's fault. Through the hare coming wide he had to run an extra distance to get dead behind, which took him perhaps dangerously near the drain, but he delivered them beautifully together, and they were neck and neck when Wolf Hill jumped slightly short.

Of full size and beautiful mould, Fabulous Fortune was a splendid specimen of a greyhound, and at his best he was as good as he was good-looking. At the stud he was almost as great a success as his sire, Herschel. He sired the double winner Fearless Footsteps as well as another Cup winner in Homfray.

CHAPTER XXV.

Waterloo 1897—Gallant's Year.

THIS was a puppies' year in point of numbers, 38 first-season greyhounds being entered against 28 seniors. The latter, however, embraced the previous year's winner and runner-up, as well as others of note, and there was not a puppy left in the last four of the Cup. Fabulous Fortune was distinctly favourite, but at the official calling over bookmakers only offered 4 to 1, and there were no takers. £1,100 to £100 was accepted several times about Five by Tricks (who ran-up), but it was still offered. £1,000 to 90 was taken freely about Fair Floralie, and the third Saughall representative, Faber Fortuna, was supported at 1,000 to 60.

The opening day was marked by grand coursing, favourable weather, and a big crowd, every card being sold early. The running, however, was singularly free from impressive displays. Even Fabulous Fortune did not show to advantage, and the second favourite, Five by Tricks, gave openings. Black Veil and Gallant were two exceptions that in both successes showed marked cleverness and fire. Laurel Crown showed fine speed down the Withins in leading Guiding Star so far.

On Wednesday night the betting was 90 to 40 against Fabulous Fortune, 5 to 1 Faber Fortunæ, 6 to 1 Five by Tricks, 7 to 1 Black Veil, 100 to 11 Laurel Crown, and 10 to 1 Gallant, these being the only six in much request, and they embodied the final four.

There were a bigger proportion of meritorious performances on Thursday than at the opening stage, and the Lydiate hares never ran better. Fabulous Fortune improved upon his earlier form, though still not seen at his best, but Five by Tricks and Gallant were evidently "running on." The unlucky dog of the day was Laurel Crown the short squirt between him and Black Veil after the fawn's outside lead might well have been undecided.

On Thursday night the betting was 50 to 40 against Fabulous Fortune 3 to 1 against Gallant, 75 to 20 against Five by Tricks, and 6 to 1 against Black Veil.

After a grand race Five by Tricks gained the turn by a length and a half, and held strong possession for a fine innings. Fabulous Fortune then made a gallant effort, but was well beaten. Black Veil led up two lengths, but Gallant shot in as puss broke round, and sticking closely to the scut was a clear winner when he killed.

Deciding Course.

Gallant beat Five by Tricks. Betting, 6 to 4 on Five by Tricks. The favourite looked like leading for a few strides as they split slightly, but in a very short distance Gallant showed in front, and clearing the drain in good style then went faster every yard of the way, being two lengths in front as he approached his hare. Five by Tricks made a game rush up and cut to kill, but the movement only served to entirely destroy his chance, for Gallant swept round grandly with his hare as she broke to the left, used her strongly twice more, and killed in great style. It was only a poor trial to decide a Waterloo Cup, but the win was clear and decisive.

Waterloo Cup: Mr. T. P. Hale ns Mr. T. Holmes's bd d Gallant, by Young Fullerton out of Sally Milburn, won ; Mr. H. Hardy's f d Five by Tricks, by Freshman out of Full Hand, ran up.

The Purse was won by Mr. M. G. Hale's bk d p Happy Sight, Mr. Gladstone's f b p Gauge, by Herschel out of Myrtle Green, running-up.

Mr. T. Graham's Under the Globe won the Plate, the Marquis of Anglesey ns the Duke of Leeds's bk b p Laurel Leaves (sister to Laurel Crown) running-up.

Gallant was grandly-bred, and strained to Bab at the Bowster on both sides. Through his sire Young Fullerton (the great Fullerton's younger brother), by Greentick out of Bit of Fashion, he also inherited Bed of Stone's blood, and that of the great Ptarmigan—Gallant Foe cross. He also strained to Canaradzo on both sides, and through his dam Sally Milburn (who bred many winners) to both Fusilier and David. Gallant's victory was a great tribute to Mr. Tom Graham's skill in management and training.

J

CHAPTER XXVI.

Waterloo, 1898—Wild Night's Year.

NOTABLE changes marked this anniversary. That fine old courser, Sir W. C. Anstruther (patron of the popular Carmichael meetings), who had presided at Waterloo for several years, had passed away, the void being now filled by another member of the Committee, Mr. Alfred Brisco ; and Mr. Hedley, after his great record of judging 24 Waterloo Cups, was succeeded in office by Mr. R. A. Brice, destined also to wear the Waterloo scarlet for a long stretch of years.

In the absence of any great greyhound, or any " standing-out " performance during the season, favouritism was uncertain during the day, but when the list was called over after dinner the honour fell upon Faber Fortunæ, who was backed down to 100 to 12. Peregrine Pickle, Wet Day and Wilful Maid were all strongly supported at 1,000 to 70 ; and Black Veil at 100 to 6.

The opening stage was productive of a fine day's sport, hares running well, both on Rye Heys and the Withins, and the driving was so successful that the 48 courses were disposed of shortly after three o'clock. Many of them, too, were of an inspiriting character, a great proportion of the trials being well run.

Peregrine Pickle was the star performer. Getting a second hare after his first brilliant success, he was handicapped against Gallant, but still proved too fast and good for the previous year's winner, and it was hard luck for Mr. Pilkington that he then had to be drawn through injury.

At night the betting was 4 to 1 against Faber Fortunæ, 5 to 1 Wet Day, 10 to 1 each Wilful Maid, Under the Globe and Wild Night, and 100 to 8 each Chuck and Lang Syne.

There was quite a " slaughter of innocents " on the second day, all the remaining original favourites being bowled out, and four outsiders finally left in—Ryde (50 to 1), Lang Syne (100 to 1), Chock (1,000 to 15), Wild Night (1,000 to 30).

The closing scene was on the Withins, and the famous battleground yielded quite an inspiriting wind-up, despite there being no public favourite left in.   Lang Syne, with odds against him, always went too fast for Ryde, and Wild Night, after squeezing up in front of Chock, polished him off in good style.   For the final Lang Syne's lameness was now very manifest and the odds went up from 5 to 4 to 6 to 4 against him.   Not feeling his feet quickly he dropped well behind in the first eighty yards, but he stretched clean past before the hare was reached.   Wild Night, however, took smart possession as puss broke short round, and in a circling course quite out-matched her opponent, being an easy winner when she finished a clipping display with a smart kill.

Waterloo Cup : Mr. J. Trevor ns Mr. H. Hardy's f w b Wild Night, by Freshman out of Fine Night, won ; Duke of Leeds's bk d Lang Syne, by Boss o' the Shanty out of Belle of Soham, ran up.

The Purse was divided between Mr. J. Russel's Real Turk, by Falconer out of Real Lace, and Mr. J. Coke's Cissy Smith, by Falconer out of Mrs. Mack.

The Plate was won by Mr. Baxter ns Mr. D. Graham's Genetive ; Silver Lace (late Roscommon), by Restorer out of Real Lace, running-up.

Wild Night cannot be classed against some of the Waterloo winners of her own sex, especially such as Miss Glendyne, Bed of Stone, Coomassie, Thoughtless Beauty and Fearless Footsteps, but her victory was, nevertheless, an exceedingly meritorious one.   Wild Night was one of the quartette for which Mr. Hardy gave Mr. Waters £800 the previous season.

Glancing at her courses, Wild Night's defeat of Cissy Smith was enhanced by the latter's division of the Purse, and it was a distinctly good performance to beat Faber Fortunæ.   Wild Night improved every course she ran, her displays against Under the Globe, Chock, and Lang Syne all being without blemish.   She was well backed, and her popular owner, Mr. H. Hardy, landed a good stake.   And so did her nominator, Mr. J. Trevor, who had " Vindex " to thank for finding him his representative.

CHAPTER XXVII.

Waterloo 1899—Black Fury's Unexpected Win.

HAD all gone well with Peregrine Pickle, he would probably have been a pronounced favourite, 5 to 1 being his price in the preliminary betting, which had not yet quite died out. But it became known that the injured toe which caused his withdrawal after winning two courses the previous year had partially given way. Even as it was he was well supported at 100 to 8, Faber Fortunæ and Real Emperor being joint favourites at 100 to 12.

Messrs. Fawcett this year made the mistake of running Fire Flash, in preference to the puppy Fearless Footsteps, subsequent winner in 1900 and 1901. She and the Duke of Leeds's Lapal had both shown brilliant form in dividing the South Lancashire Stakes at the first Ridgway Club meeting, but in a Waterloo trial at Lytham, Fearless Footsteps was led and beaten by Fire Flash.

All the leading favourites survived their first day's ordeals except Wild Night, who was slightly led and smartly out-pointed by the puppy George Tincler.

In the third round Black Fury upset big odds by luckily beating Faber Fortunæ in a short spin. "Faber's" kennel companion, Father o' Fire, also went down before Lapal, her brilliant early points, and kill at last, more than balancing the Father's strong sequence of driving points in the middle. Lapal gave a clipping performance in the fourth round in beating Genetive under difficulties, and Black Fury gave a smart display against Circus Clown, again getting off lightly. Weatherwise being drawn injured, Hesper ran a short bye with Fearless Footsteps, and was led and beaten. George Tincler led his brother and kennel companion, Dick Burge, a couple of lengths, and at once floored his hare with a capital stroke.

Semi-Finals.

Lapal beat Hesper. Betting, 2 to 1 on Lapal. The favourite after leading a couple of lengths momentarily lost position as puss broke short round, but she soon shot to the front, and, as soon as she got a clear run, floored her hare.

Black Fury beat George Tincler. Betting, 55 to 40 on George Tincler. This was a one-sided win for the non-favourite.·

Final Course.

Black Fury beat Lapal. Betting, 2 to 1 on Black Fury. After a smooth delivery it was a tight race to the filled-in cross drain, which had sunk a little and was rather soft. Lapal was unlucky enough to strike into it, whilst Black Fury cleared it in his stride and instantly gained an advantage of a length and a half.

In these positions they reached a weak hare, which the black commanded with plenty of force. Lapal pressed close up, but got no chance of wresting possession until Black Fury had wrenched five or six times, when with a fine spurt she shot past and killed. It was a poor trial to decide a Waterloo Cup, but a clear win. The Duke of Leeds thus repeated his second of the previous year with Lang Syne. It was the first Waterloo attempt of Mr. E. Rogers, owner of Black Fury, just as it was that of Mr. S. W. Beer with Fighting Force, and of Lord Dewar with Winning Number, some years later.

Black Fury cannot in truth be designated a worthy type of a Waterloo winner, though never being called upon to run a genuine Waterloo trial, he gained his honours meritoriously enough, showing good speed in all his courses, with plenty of dash.

Waterloo Cup: Mr. J. B. Thompson ns Mr. E. Rogers's bk d Black Fury, by Mad Fury out of Mischief X., won ; Col. J. M. M'Calmont ns The Duke of Leeds's bd b p Lapal, by Fortune's Favourite out of Nopal, ran up.

The Purse was divided between Mr. T. Quihampton's Quite Bright, by Falconer out of Fine Night, and Mr. W. H. Smith's (k) Countess of Udston, by Ruby Red out of Maroon.

The Plate was won by Sir W. Ingram ns Mr. J. Wilson's Wild Oats, by Sir Sankey out of Bessie Mountford ; Mr. J. Coke ns Mr. L. Pilkington's Prescot running-up.

CHAPTER XXVIII.

Waterloo, 1900-01—Fearless Footsteps' Double.

THE first Waterloo of the present century was variously signalised. After a wintry visitation that betokened much trouble, a week's delay was followed by a swift change giving a happy release ; but Liverpool was no sooner reached than the word went round that the draw would take place, but there would be no dinner, nor calling over of the card.

Long odds betting took place at Hill House on Wednesday morning, Mister O'Shea and Black Fury being well backed at 100 to 8, until 10 to 1 became the best offer against each. Father o' Fire, Peregrine Pickle, and Dick Burge were next best favourites at about 100 to 7, with Pikelaw close up, and Lavishly Clothed, Genetive, Winter Pasture, and Prescot in next best request. The only one of this lot to survive the day was Lavishly Clothed, and the course betting in both rounds was also greatly in favour of the " bookies."

A few of the biggest upsets were the defeats of George Tincler (7 to 2 on) by New Melody, of Black Fury (3 to 1 on) by Rare Luck, of Prescot (3 to 1 on) by Prince Falcon, of Whitacre (11 to 4 on) by Dear Westwood, of Money Bay (11 to 4 on) by Hillyjimitit, of Peregrine Pickle (5 to 2 on) by Cherry Whiskey, of Pikelaw (2 to 1 on) by Anstrude, and of Happy Laird (2 to 1 on) by Gimcrack. A striking feature, too, was the fact that not one of the final four in the previous year's Cup—Black Fury, Lapal, George Tincler and Hesper—succeeded in raising a flag.

Lavishly Clothed's opening effort against Copper Cash was as fine as anything in the first round, 1,000 to 80 being then accepted about her winning.

In the third round, backers were at fault in laying 7 to 4 on the young Castle Milk bitch, Mrs. Grundy. She squeezed up in front, and made a pretty start, but Cherry Whiskey finished with rare resolution, and had won nicely when he killed. He was decisively beaten next time by Hawthorn VI., and of the other three survivers of the day, Lavishly Clothed and Fearless Footsteps again showed splendid form.

There was quite a great wind-up on the Withins and a grandly-contested exciting final in the Cup. Lavishly Clothed gave Hawthorn VI. a good licking in a ding-dong trial well run by both. Fearless Footsteps, with 9 to 4 on her, went too fast for Prince Falcon, and quickly floored her hare.

Deciding Course.

Fearless Footsteps beat Lavishly Clothed. Betting, 9 to 4 on Fearless Footsteps. From a splendid delivery to a trimming hare they raced neck and neck for eighty or ninety yards, when the favourite shook off her opponent and gained the turn by a length and a half. Commanding her hare beautifully, she made a fine start, but Lavishly Clothed took possession at the first opening and quickly gave a different aspect to the course. So grandly did the fawn sweep with her game that she had the trial well won at one point. She failed, however, to finish it, though she got some fur, whereupon Fearless Footsteps shot to the front and scored thrice before giving the *coup de grace*. It was a grand trial for a final and closely balanced.

Waterloo Cup: Mr. Hartley Bibby ns Messrs. Fawcett's bk tk b Fearless Footsteps, by Fabulous Fortune out of Fille de Feu, won; Duke of Leeds's f b Lavishly Clothed, by Fabulous Fortune out of Irish Queen, ran-up.

The Purse was divided between Mr. A. Brisco ns Mr. T. Graham's bd b p Gutta Percha, and Mr. R. W. B. Jardine ns Sir Robert Jardine's f b p Long Glass.

The Plate was won by Mr. J. B. Thompson's r d p Red Fury; Sir T. Brocklebank's bk d Border Song running-up.

Memorable as it must be in many ways, the Waterloo Cup of the year 1900 will certainly be remembered for filling the Duke of Leeds's cup of misfortune to the brim.

In his first year, 1897, the Duke ran Laurel Crown, and this dog, after showing immense speed and fine form, was simply fluked out by Black Veil in the fourth round, and, taking the direct line through Sir Thomas Brocklebank's bitch, Laurel

Crown would have led Gallant, the winner, four lengths up the Withins. In 1898 the final course was, as it were, made to suit Lang Syne's victress, Wild Night, and in 1899, when Lapal was running so well, and killed all her six hares, the final course was made to order for Black Fury.

It was a great year for Fabulous Fortune, two daughters running off for the Cup, and a son carrying off the Plate, so that Messrs. Fawcett took additional honours through their Waterloo winner of 1896. Whilst the Duke of Leeds's feat of running second three times consecutively was unique ; there was a fourth yet to follow, Leucoryx running-up to Dilwyn in 1914.

Years in which Bitches were First and Second.

The fact of two bitches going to slips for the final was strong testimony as to the all-round character of the running, for the days of long slips—too long in my opinion—had already arrived, giving the longer striding dogs an unmistakable advantage : it was fourteen years since a similar occurrence.

In the fourth year of the Cup, being a 64 dog stake (1860), Blackstock's Maid of the Mill and Lord Sefton's Sampler were first and second ; in '62 Gregson's Roaring Meg and Brocklebank's Bowfell filled the positions, to be immediately followed by Chloe and Rebe in '63. In 1867 Lobelia and Royal Seal fought it out, and then there was a gap of ten years before the sex was again in the ascendant.

In Coomassie's two victories she disposed of Braw Lass in '77 and Zazel in '78. In 1883 we had Wild Mint's and Snowflight's sensational final, and in '85 Miss Glendyne and Bit of Fashion divided, Miss Glendyne and Penelope II. giving a great treat with a beautifully-run course the following year.

Continuing the ladies' record up to date, the Croxteth bitch Shortcoming, running in the Countess of Sefton's nomination, and Sir R. W. Buchanan Jardine's Jassiona meritoriously attained the leading positions last year (1921) ; but the finalists in 1908, Mr. (now Sir Edward) Hulton's Hallow Eve and the Earl of Sefton's Silhouette, were served by good luck as well as by genuine trials.

Fearless Footsteps' Second Win.

A REPETITION of the previous year's delay was strongly threatened the week before the fixture, the announcement being made that the Committee would meet early on Monday, February 18, to decide as to a postponement. Even then the danger was not past, but the outlook had improved, and the decision to adhere to the original fixture proved a happy one.

The betting on many of the individual courses this year was closer than it often is, and at the long odds there was the remarkable feature of Messrs. Fawcett supplying the three leading favourites. Farndon Ferry held the position of honour at 9 to 1, Fearless Footsteps pressing closely at 10 to 1, with Father o' Fire also near at 100 to 11.

Farndon Ferry and Fearless Footsteps came triumphantly through their ordeals on the opening day, but Father o' Fire was beaten in the second round by Lady Husheen.

On Thursday Farndon Ferry came out in great form, despite his hard opening course with Woolpit, and another fairly stiff one with Pincher, and polished off both Public Life and Dear Cardigan in splendid style. Fearless Footsteps, too, was clearly "running on." In her second course on Wednesday, against Brokerage, she had palpably hung fire during the middle points. She was nearly held for speed by Guid Wife, but the latter kept running in spurts, whilst Fearless handled her hare in polished style.

She even did better against Rare Luck, and finished a sparkling performance with a good kill. Lady Husheen in both courses again ran cleverly and well; but after easily beating the lame Hazleton Lass, it was only his extra pace that enabled Cleughbrae to dispose of Garbitas.

The final stage, so far as concerned the Cup, was singularly unfortunate and disappointing. The trial between the two outsiders was very interesting up to a certain point. Cleughbrae was a little the faster, but Lady Husheen was the smarter, and the issue hung in the balance for some time.

A demon hare, after breaking back down the Withins, took them into the country, and though Cleughbrae won easily at last, through staying the longer, his chance of winning the final was clearly gone.

For the kennel companions an apparently good hare came bounding along, but she proved a gay deceiver, and quickly died. Farndon Ferry, with 9 to 4 on him, was clearly going the faster, but puss bearing to the right, towards the crowd, he had to struggle hard on the outside to just gain the turn. The hare breaking short round, still in favour of the black, she shot away well in front, and Farndon never got another chance, Fearless moving on the scut with great fire.

Deciding Course.

Betting, 11 to 2 on Fearless Footsteps. In a good stretch down the Withins the favourite drew ahead between three and four lengths, and commanding her hare in fine style soon ran up a winning sequence. Cleughbrae seizing an opening, made a game effort, but Fearless was a one-sided winner as puss reached the sough in the bank.

Waterloo Cup : Mr. Hartley Bibby ns Messrs. Fawcett's Fearless Footsteps, by Fabulous Fortune out of Fille de Feu, won ; Mr. F. Watson ns Mr. P. Clark's bk d p Cleughbrae, by Under the Globe out of Tiny Polly, ran-up.

The Purse was won in dashing style by Mr. W. Osborne ns Messrs. Aston & Spruce's Agile Spurt, Mr. Newbold's New Tripper running-up.

The Plate was divided between Mr. R. Anderton ns Messrs. Fawcett's Father o' Fire and Mr. J. Coke's Cousin Mary.

In running second for the Cup, Cleughbrae made a record for a dark puppy, and the youngsters on the whole acquitted themselves well. Three of the last four in the Cup—Farndon Ferry and Lady Husheen, as well as Cleughbrae—being in their first seasons, and also Agile Spurt and New Tripper—winner and runner-up for the Purse.

The year was signalised by the appointment, for the first time, of a professional flag steward. Since the retirement of Mr. Nathan Slater, the often arduous duties had been carried out in the same honorary and efficient way by Mr. Harold Brocklebank, Mr. C. H. Brocklebank (Mr. Charles), Mr. A. Brisco, Capt. Bayley, Mr. J. Hutchison, Mr. T. Stone, and Mr. Hartley Bibby ; and the task must sometimes have been a great tax upon the kindness of these gentlemen. The engagement of Ellis Jolly was quite a success, the winner always being correctly signalled as heretofore.

CHAPTER XXIX.

Waterloo 1902—Farndon Ferry's Year.

OMINOUS conditions raised visions of Burnaby's year in the week before this season's fixture, the Altcar country, under at least three inches of frozen snow, being more like a picture of the Arctic regions than of a coursing arena. Happily, however, one of the swift changes for which our climate is so famous—or notorious—came to the rescue, a week's postponement being all that had to be endured. The entry, dinner and draw took place on Tuesday, February 25th, and a graceful touch was imparted to the important function with the Duke of Leeds in the chair.

The entry was rather a striking one, with no fewer than seventeen of the previous year's runners engaged, viz: Farndon Ferry, Lady Husheen, Garbitas, Glenstrae, Attorney, Dutiful Daughter, Brokerage, Glenbervie, New Tripper, Loving Cup, Sea Fog, Goosey, Spytfontein, Hazleton Lass, Gelatine, Blackheath and Rale.

The betting on the individual courses was unusually close, big odds seldom being asked for ; and at the long odds quite an exceptional number were supported at what may be termed inside prices. This, of course, was the natural result of there being no hot favourites. Farndon Ferry was out by himself at 1,000 to 100 taken freely, the next shortest price taken being 1,000 to 70 Lady Husheen, and 1,000 to 60 Cheers.

Spytfontein was supported freely at 1,000 to 50, and Loving Cup, Blackheath, and Croix were on the same mark.

A feature of the opening day was the downfall of the puppies, Wartnaby and the outsiders High Crawler and Little Maiden being the only three survivors. The last-named outpaced both Mr. Gladstone's Millions and Mr. Crosse's Croix—to the delight of her veteran owner, Lord Masham, who in his 88th year was present to see her run. Farndon Ferry ran both his courses in superb style, and got off lightly each time.

Glenbervie (his next opponent), on the contrary, got a gruelling in the opening round against the faster Bridge of

Arta, but " came again " wonderfully and finished her course against Moriarty in beautiful style, after being again beaten for the early points. Brokerage and Dutiful Daughter ran their first courses beautifully, and it was unfortunate that such a scuffling sort of trial should have decided what promised to be an interesting issue between them. Sea Fog performed as well as anything during the day except Farndon Ferry, and Blackheath earned a similar encomium, the speed and fire he displayed against Marauder being quite striking.

On Wednesday night the final issue was pretty well fore-shadowed, Farndon Ferry being backed at 5 to 2. Blackheath, who won two more courses, was second favourite at 100 to 15, and Wartnaby (runner-up) was third favourite at 100 to 12.

A delightful day's coursing was witnessed at the second stage, in spring-like weather, the uniformity as well as the excellence of the trials being most marked. The going on the big Lydiate flat was perfect, and a fine performance was achieved by Flatman, the head-keeper, in bringing sufficient hares, for the whole of the running, from the Sefton Church end, at the left of the crowd. Farndon Ferry was quite the star performer both in his defeat of the handicapped Glenbervie, and in his bye through the withdrawal of the unlucky Handsome John, though the other three survivors of the day—Wartnaby, Blackheath and Grafter—each attained his position meritoriously.

On Thursday night slight odds were laid on Farndon Ferry, 11 to 4 against Blackheath, 4 to 1 against Wartnaby, and 100 to 8 against Grafter.

The final stage was marred in a most unusual way. Farndon Ferry's easy defeat of Grafter was unattended by extraneous incident, but with Wartnaby and Blackheath in slips it was quite the reverse. Hares kept coming forward in pairs, and batches, and when one came singly, and Wilkinson ran out, he had to pull up his dogs and return to the screen, some hares not being good enough, and others declining to go straight. It was a terribly perplexing time for so young a slipper, and, of course, the dogs got greatly excited, and barked furiously, especially Blackheath. They were got away well together at the finish, and after a fine tussle Wartnaby drew clear of his opponents and quickly floored his hare.

Deciding Course.

Farndon Ferry beat Wartnaby. Betting, 2 to 1 on Farndon Ferry. The favourite, much the quicker on his pins, almost instantly showed in advance, and going much the faster in the first hundred yards was fully a length and a half in front. The puppy then fairly held him for a short distance, and at last began to reduce the gap; in fact, he was closing up rapidly at the finish, and it looked for all the world as if he would have gone by had the hare been able to race. As it was, Farndon Ferry gained the turn by a good half-length, and being much the smarter as puss broke to the left he shot well clear for the second point. He again came beautifully around in close possession for the third, and after wrenching strongly made a good attempt to kill, stumbling in the effort. Wartnaby then instantly dashed to the front, driving his hare in fine style, Farndon Ferry meanwhile dropped further behind as if done with the course. A great shout of excitement rent the air. Just at the moment, however, when Wartnaby's chance began to look so rosy, two men in the field (trainers, or pickers up) interfered with the hare, causing her to break round by the left, Farndon Ferry instantly nailing her.

Waterloo Cup. Mr. G. F. Fawcett's bd w d Farndon Ferry, by Fiery Furnace out of Fair Florence, won; Mr. W. Ward's r d p Wartnaby, by Mellor Moor out of Tiny Polly, ran-up.

Waterloo Purse. Colonel Bruce ns Mr. W. Smyrl's f d Star of Antrim, by Wolf Hill out of Sweet Merrie, won; Mr. R. F. Gladstone's w d Millions, by Fabulous Fortune out of Melpomene, ran-up.

Waterloo Plate. Mr. H. Brocklebank's bk b Brokerage, by First Fortune out of Follow Me, and Sir R. Jardine's r w d Vindicator, divided.

This year's winner, like Fearless Footsteps, was home-bred on both sides, and, like her, was produced by the Greentick—Herschel combination, only instead of being by a Herschel dog from a Greentick bitch, his parentage was the reverse way.

His attributes in running were such as at once commended him to the courser's heart, for after leading to the hare, which he invariably did, he rarely, if ever, failed to go round in possession for the second point. And this is one of the great marks of excellence in the greyhound, and is also—or, at any rate, ought to be—one of the great factors in deciding a course.

CHAPTER XXX.

Waterloo 1903—Father Flint's Year.

FARNDON FERRY a third time threw down the gauntlet, and again had the honour of heading the quotations; but as in 1901, he suffered defeat in the semi-finals from a kennel companion. The present Earl of Sefton presided this year, for the first time as Lord of the Soil, and amongst his near supporters were the Duke of Leeds, Earl of Enniskillen, Mr. Hervey Talbot, Mr. L. Pilkington, Sir R. W. Buchanan Jardine, Mr. H. Brocklebank, Mr. M. G. Hale, Mr. J. Mugliston, and Mr. Hartley Bibby—all still happily with us.

After " the King " had been honoured, the Duke of Leeds proposed the health of " the Lord of the Manor," cheers greeting the announcement that the Earl of Sefton, in addition to giving permission for the public to enjoy coursing over his unrivalled grounds, had decided to present a hundred guinea cup, so that the winner would have something to hand down to posterity. Lord Sefton made a felicitous reply, and in connection with permission to course over Altcar, said it would always be given so long as he lived, and he hoped for many generations after him.

The opening day was not suggestive of outsiders having much to do with the finish, Farndon Ferry, Father Flint, and Paracelsus clearly standing out as the best performers. At night Farndon Ferry was all the rage, as little as 2 to 1 being finally taken. Paracelsus was in next request at 7 to 2, and Father Flint was well supported at 110 to 20. 100 to 9 was taken about Limetta, though she was clearly not in her Ridgway sparkling form; and Handsome Creole and China Craze, both of which had run well, were each supported at 100 to 5.

Mr. R. W. Buchanan Jardine presided at night, and as on the corresponding evening the previous year, slight odds were laid on Farndon Ferry, 7 to 2 against Paracelsus, 4 to 1 Father Flint, and 100 to 9 Handsome Creole.

A grand wind-up was enjoyed by a large crowd, the weather being delightful and the trials all that could be wished. In the semi-finals Paracelsus drew well away from Handsome Creole for first turn, but the bitch put in a clever and stout resistance, the issue being very close. Father Flint, with 3 to 1 against him, fairly had the foot of Farndon Ferry, and running a short spin with great fire, killed without allowing the favourite a point.

Deciding Course.

Father Flint beat Paracelsus. Betting, 11 to 4 on Father Flint. After a fine delivery, a desperate neck-and-neck race was witnessed, Paracelsus for a considerable distance having the advantage of a few inches. As they crossed the broken ground at the filled-in drain, Father Flint obtained a slight advantage, and puss at the same moment bearing to the right (Father Flint's side) he drew out well clear for the first point. The hare then breaking sharply in the same direction, he shot away quite brilliantly for the second point, and came nicely round in possession for a third. An opening then presented itself, which Paracelsus instantly took, and he at once covered the scut in fine style, but his couple of wrenches and the kill left Father Flint a clear winner.

Waterloo Cup : Mr. J. Hartley Bibby ns Messrs. Fawcett's bd d Father Flint, by Fiery Furnace out of Fanny Faithful, beat Mr. A. F. Pope ns Mr. L. Pilkington's bk d p Paracelsus, by Under the Globe out of Thoughtless Beauty.

Waterloo Purse : Mr. W. S. Simpson's f d Strange Mystery, by Under the Globe out of Whitacre, beat Mr. Glover's bk d Bonnie Bairn, by Under the Globe out of Fear to Fall.

Waterloo Plate : Duke of Leeds's bd b p Lonely Star, by Fiery Furnace out of Lapal, and Mr. Newbold's Mallory, by Fabulous Fortune out of Elaine, divided.

This was Messrs. Fawcett's fourth Waterloo Cup consecutively, equalling Col. North's great feat, and their success in 1896 with Fabulous Fortune added takes them a rung higher in the ladder of Waterloo fame, just as Col. North's four successes eclipsed Lord Lurgan's three. This, however, applies exclusively to the owners and not to the greyhounds.

CHAPTER XXXI.

Waterloo 1904—Homfray's Surprise Year.

BLUE riband honours have been associated with many unexpected results, but Homfray's success was almost the " surprise of surprises ": he started at 1,000 to 5, taken and offered, yet there was no solid reason for his being so utterly despised. He gave quite fair promise in the Border Union Derby by the style in which he disposed of two opponents, and when beaten he had all the best of the early points. He afterwards ran second at both Plumpton and Eye, and in the latter case was handicapped by having run four courses (two being extras) the previous day.

Paracelsus, the previous year's runner-up, was made a strong favourite, closing at 85 to 20, and as little as 9 to 1 was taken about Lonely Star. Strange Mystery and Prince Plausible were both in good request at 1,000 to 70, and so was Wartnaby at 1,000 to 60.

Perhaps the running partook rather much of a slogging character, the somewhat soft and slippery state of the Withins proving to be all in favour of the hares. The surface of the Rye Heys, however, was in perfect trim, and the majority of the thirteen courses obtained there were beautifully run. Lonely Star's one-sided defeat of Priestlaw here was a superb display, and fairly transfixed Joe Wright to the ground, reminding me of a similar effect produced upon Doctor Eltringham when Coomassie served Master Sam in an almost similar way.

One of the prettiest races to the hare ever seen, took place between Paracelsus and Klip. They ran head and head, as though locked together, until within striking distance, and the black just anticipating the bitch, made his successful shot a few inches in front.

The majority of those fancied at long odds failed to survive the opening day, but on the individual course betting backers had the best of it, in the first round, and made a capital start by hitting the mark in each of the first six courses. They had two nasty knocks, however, in the defeats of Fearsome Fight, with 4 to 1 on, by White Ruffle, and of Strange Mystery, with 5 to 2 on, by Gallant Graham.

Disaster soon came in the second round when Prince Charming, with 5 to 2 on, went down before Homfray, and 9 to 4 were floored when Fecht Fair put out Lonely Star. White Ruffle upset a 2 to 1 favourite in Pistol II., and Prince Plausible, Militant and Goldsmith were all beaten.

On Wednesday night Paracelsus had strengthened his position, as little as 2 to 1 being accepted.

Limonum, whose price at the start was 1,000 to 35, advanced to the position of second favourite at 6 to 1, Minchmuir (at 1,000 to 15 on the previous night) being now backed at 100 to 14.

Thursday's running at Lydiate was very eventful. The same destiny that has ever prevented a previous runner-up attaining higher Waterloo honours again cast its fatal spell, Paracelsus and Wartnaby, the respective runners-up the previous year and in 1902, both being beaten. All round, the second stage was full of startling denouement. In the third round of the Cup the tide of events worked smoothly, much to the delight of the ardent spirits who overnight took 100's to 5's about naming the last four.

At the subsequent stage everything went seriously wrong. The outsider, Homfray, led off the surprises by giving a severe licking to Loran Leader, even after losing the turn, and Paracelsus and Limonum both bit the dust, the only favourite in the round to bring a crumb of comfort to the layers of odds being Minchmuir.

At night Fecht Fair was favourite at 11 to 8, Minchmuir being a good second favourite at 7 to 4. 100 to 14 was laid against Homfray and 100 to 12 against Haughton Ferry.

Continuing its sensational character, the final stage brought about the unexpected defeat of Fecht Fair by Homfray, who was " running on " with considerable fire ; and Minchmuir led and polished off Haughton Ferry in great style. Unluckily it was a demon hare that would not be killed, and poor Minchmuir was heavily handicapped for the final. Homfray consequently led up a long way, and though Minchmuir after

K

getting luckily placed made a marvellously game effort, and had won if she had succeeded in her attempt to kill, it was her expiring effort, Homfray winning easily at last.

Waterloo Cup: Mr. G. Darlinson ns Mr. E. Herbert's r d p Homfray, by Fabulous Fortune out of Kilmode, beat Mr. Whitworth ns Mr. H. T. Michels's bk b p Minchmuir, by Wet Day out of Kaffir Queen.

Waterloo Purse: Mr. A. F. Pope ns Mr. L. Pilkington's r d Priestlaw, by Mellor Moor out of Thoughtless Beauty, and Mr. Newbold's r d Mallory, divided.

Waterloo Plate: Duke of Leeds's bd b Lonely Star, by Fiery Furnace out of Lapal, and Mr. L. Pilkington's r d p Prince Plausible, by Boswell out of Thoughtless Beauty, divided.

In the past there had been not a few little expected Waterloo Cup results, but I don't think any previous winner had started at such extreme odds as 1,000 to 5. Homfray's success came at a very opportune time in one respect, especially with Minchmuir running-up. Messrs. Fawcett's and Mr. L. Pilkington's kennels were about this time sweeping all before them to such an extent that a wearisome feeling was growing as to the futility of trying to stop their triumphant careers, but there were golden days yet in store for the lesser lights : Pistol II. vanquished Mr. L. Pilkington's Prince Plausible in the final the very next year.

Homfray, like a few other winners, found his way into the select 64 quite accidentally. His owner, Mr. Margetts (Herbert was his assumed name), had no thought of running him a few weeks previously, but whilst sitting together at Mr. Darlinson's luncheon during the Wappenbury January meeting I happened to ask if he was running anything at Waterloo.

The reply was, " No ; unfortunately I have nothing good enough." I at once rejoined, " Yes, you have ; you have a nice puppy in Homfray, that would beat more than would beat him." Mr. Margetts then replied, " If you say that, I will apply for a returned nomination," and, oddly enough, he was awarded that of the patron of the meeting we were then attending. As a souvenir of that conversation, I still have a handsome gold-mounted pocket-book that seems impervious to wear.

CHAPTER XXXII.

Waterloo, 1905—Success of Pistol II.

THE extraordinary predominance of Messrs. Fawcett and Mr. Leonard Pilkington had not yet expired, the whole of the five leading favourites on the night of the draw being furnished by the two kennels.

There was some lively betting this year on the individual courses, big odds being laid on several of the leading favourites. At the long odds Paracelsus, as in the previous year, was a hot favourite, as little as 9 to 1 being accepted, and his kennel companion, Prince Plausible, was freely supported at 100 to 9. Of Messrs. Fawcett's three, Free Ferry was in strongest request at 1,000 to 100, Fecht Fair's price being 1,000 to 90 and Firth of Forth's 1,000 to 80.

Paracelsus carried off the honours with two grand displays, and his kennel companion, Prince Plausible, ran both his courses well, though the Irish bitch, White Collar II., would probably have beaten him in the opening round but for stumbling at a critical point. It was a day of many surprises, two of which were effected by Mr. Charles's Tight Rope in her clever defeats of Fecht Fair and Joyous Guest, with 9 to 2 against her in the first, and 11 to 4 in the second instance. Other conspicuous upsets were those of Hoprend (by Dividend Deferred), Henry the First (by Foggy Belle), Greenbrae (by Ballyjimmie), Pegasus (with 4 to 1 on) (by Pistol II.), Aladdin (by Blouse), Earl's Court (by Helen), and Submarine (by Handsome Cup). The Saughall trio all failed to survive the opening day. Fecht Fair fell in the first round ; in the second Free Ferry was beaten by Mallory, and Firth of Forth by Prince Plausible.

Excellent as had been the sport at the outset, it was quite eclipsed at the middle stage, from every point of view, and I don't think a finer day's coursing was ever seen on the Lydiate ground. The trials, too, were brimful of interest, and not void of features, chief amongst these being the overthrow of Paracelsus with 6 to 1 on him, by the Duke of Leeds's puppy Love's Reward, who both led to the hare and stayed the longer.

Oddly enough they were beaten in the fourth round by Mr. Michels's pair, Mandini and Minchmuir, both of which were going uncommonly well; the other two left in being Pistol II., who had gained a lucky victory over Foggy Belle, and Prince Plausible, who had easily disposed of Helen and Handsome Cup.

Just as Paracelsus commanded overweening confidence after the first day's running, Prince Plausible was now regarded as the very probable winner. He was a decided favourite at 5 to 4, 9 to 4 being laid against Minchmuir, 6 to 1 Mandini, and 100 to 7 Pistol II.

At the final stage, a continuance of the previous splendid sport prevailed, but the Cup anticipations were rudely shattered. Pistol II. first easily upset the odds laid on Mandini, and though Prince Plausible pulled through in a well-contested course with Minchmuir, he had to knock under in the final with 5 to 2 on him.

The decider provided an extraordinary exhibition on the part of both, each having evidently been strongly stimulated. They were in collision three times, Prince Plausible being the first and worst offender with a deliberate cross-cannon, which sent Pistol spinning. The latter got the best of the second meleé, but after the third brush, they were both sprawling on the sward together. It was a terrible sight, especially in the final of a Waterloo Cup, and Mr. Brice was not to be envied in having to judge such a course. Luckily for him, Pistol, who had led two lengths for first turn, showed a touch of superiority again at the finish by racing past and wrenching twice before they disappeared over the Withins bank.

Waterloo Cup: Mr. W. H. Pawson's bd d Pistol II., by Fighting Fire out of Thessaly, beat Mr. A. F. Pope ns Mr. L. Pilkington's r d Prince Plausible, by Boswell out of Thoughtless Beauty.

Waterloo Purse: Mr. E. M. Crosse ns Mr. Dudley Ward's f d p The Lion, by Pateley Bridge out of Forest Fairy, and Mr. G. F. Fawcett's r w d Fecht Fair, by Fiery Furnace out of Fearless Footsteps, divided.

Waterloo Plate: Mr. S. S. Death's w bk d p Dividend Deferred, by Grampus out of Dark Dame, and Mr. W. H. Smith ns Mr. R. Dunn's f d p Cockluie, by Blackheath out of Countess Udston, divided.

Bowden Brothers.

HOPREND, Winner of Waterloo Cup, 1906.

Tassell, Carlisle.

LONG SPAN, Winner of Waterloo Cup, 1907.

CHAPTER XXXIII.

Waterloo, 1906—Hoprend's Year.

A FINE Waterloo tip was given this year at the Altcar Club January meeting, for Hoprend ran through the Members' Plate in great style ; yet he did not start favourite for the premier event. This honour was once more conferred upon a Saughall representative—Firth of Forth, who had run-up to Hoprend the previous month, the odds against him being 100 to 14. Mr. Hardy's dog, however, disputed the position of second favourite with the Croxteth representative, Submarine (who had won the Netherby Cup the October previous), each being supported at 100 to 11.

A great day's sport was enjoyed at the outset, and a record was made in the Cup being run once through on Rye Heys before the move to the Withins. Hares ran " like stags " from start to finish, putting every attribute fully to the test, and the weather enhanced the enjoyment, a misty morning giving way to bright sunshine which lasted throughout. The beautifully-clear atmosphere also gave a good view of the running. Results were somewhat disastrous to " the talent," no fewer than fourteen favourites going down in the first round, and big odds were several times floored—Firth of Forth, with 9 to 2 on, was beaten by the Norfolk dog, Staff Surgeon ; Buckenham Ferry, with 9 to 4 on, by Parson Parkes ; Prince Plausible, with 5 to 2 on, by Cost Price ; White Collar II., 2 to 1 on, by Hiawatha ; Brindisi by Ipswich, and White Anarchist by Coady, each with 7 to 4 on. Other beaten favourites were Hackney Wick by Mirko, Minchmuir by Benedict, Racster by Glenbridge, Heel and Toe by Barlochan, Cockline by Howtown, Lady Adamant by Pioneer, and Keep Up by Age of Gold. The layers of odds were better on the mark in the second round, though they were much at fault when Newcastleton beat Ipswich, Coady beat Submarine, Hiawatha beat Glen Groudle, and Staff Surgeon, after his long course with Firth of Forth, was still

able to beat Glenalbane. The leading favourites for the event
were nearly all routed, Hoprend being the only one left in, and
he was deservedly made a warm favourite at night. The grand
character of the coursing, whilst all right from the spectators
point of view, had a somewhat searching effect upon our
present breed of greyhounds, and it cannot with truth be said
that many came through the test with credit. Hoprend, since
he was able to show superiority to both, was fortunate enough
to have smart bitches like Formula and Neolithic in opposition :
each of them floored the hare in reasonable time. Waterloo
winners have often owed their successes to early opponents
being handy with their teeth. I well remember how Mr. J.
Bell-Irving's smart bitch Corsica in 1914 cut Dilwyn's first
course short, whilst her more fancied kennel companion
Distingué got a stiff dose that told its tale when they met in
the semi-finals.

There was a well-filled room on Wednesday night when
Colonel M'Calmont called the card. 500 to 200 was taken
about Hoprend, other inside prices being 6 to 1 Mandini,
9 to 1 each Dividend Deferred and Pioneer, and 1,000 to 80
Parson Parkes.

Mist was again in strong evidence on Thursday morning,
when Lydiate was reached, and it was nearly midday before
friendly old Sol succeeded in dispersing the vapoury veil.
The trials hardly partook of all the earlier grandeur, but it
was nevertheless a magnificent day's sport, and not a few of
the courses were very well run.

Hoprend showed to advantage in each effort. He rattled
up to his hare a long way ahead of the handicapped Handsome
Cup, and commanding his game with splendid force as puss
tried a break to the left at once shot out for a fine kill. He
was then in luck's way, the south-country-bitch Mirko, whose
form on the opening day was exceedingly smart, being so
severely run against Newcastleton, that she was not sent to
slips again. Hoprend ran his bye with the smart runner
Shake a Fut, and the style in which he shot away from a fresh
greyhound and held possession for several points, was very
meritorious, the little fawn then rendering good service by
quickly killing.

At night slight odds were laid on Hoprend, Benedict being

second favourite at 85 to 20, Mandini 100 to 15, and Dividend Deferred 100 to 14.

On Friday there was no " misty morn " to worry us ; the weather from beginning to end being as though made to order, whilst running was simply superb, at stout running hares over a perfect surface. The opening spin in the Plate between Neolithic and Cost Price was perfectly run by both, and the succeeding ones between Rhythmical Footsteps and Glenbridge, Howtown and Peerless De Wet, Age of Gold and Glenalbane, and Formula and Hackney Wick were all such as to satisfy the most hypercritical enthusiast. Then followed a still more prettily and desperately-contested course between Birkdault (a Barbican Cup winner) and Holland Countess, whilst the succeeding one between Game 'Un and Lady Adamant was a perfect display on the part of both. And so it went on, both in the minor events and the Cup, the wind-up being one of the grandest ever witnessed.

In the semi-finals Hoprend and Dividend Deferred proved too good for Benedict and Mandini, though both courses were stoutly contested and well run.

Deciding Course.

Hoprend beat Dividend Deferred. Betting, 75 to 20 on Hoprend. From a smooth delivery Hoprend soon began to draw in advance, and was over two lengths in front when the white and black changed sides as puss bore to the left and considerably reduced the gap. Hoprend came round in strong command of his hare for a stylish start, and though Dividend Deferred imparted excitement with two game challenges, Hoprend always held the trump card, and when he wound up a grand trial with a smart kill he was an undisputed winner.

Waterloo Cup: Mr. H. Hardy's f d Hoprend, by Forgotten Fashion out of Heirloom, beat Mr. S. S. Death's w bk d Dividend Deferred, by Grampus out of Black Dame.

Waterloo Purse: Mr. R. J. Hannam ns Mr. A. Forster's f b Formula, by Pateley Bridge out of Forest Fairy, and Mr. W. Ward ns Mr. T. Graham's bd b p Game 'Un, by Tara out of Glenvera, divided.

Waterloo Plate: Mr. H. Birkbeck's bd b Neolithic, by

Father Flint out of Fillagree, and Mr. Whitworth ns Mr. H. Hardy's bd d p Howtown, by Father Flint out of Heirloom, divided.

The issues of this Waterloo Cup, both in the semi-finals and in the decider were brimful of excitement, and the trials were as perfect and satisfactory as in the minor events—a splendid contrast, indeed, to the conditions which obtained the previous year. Hoprend's defeat of Benedict, whilst perhaps never seriously in doubt, was not destitute of exciting phases, and the same remark applies to the trial between Mandini and Dividend Deferred. The last-named won his course meritoriously under great difficulties, for Mandini obtained a winning position from the turn, and was a second time splendidly placed. As illustrating how easy it is to obtain a deceptive view of the minutiæ of a course, it may be mentioned that from the members' side of the Withins it appeared as though Dividend Deferred finished the course with the kill. As a matter of fact, Mandini legged the hare, though puss was still swinging when the white and black grabbed her.

The final embodied at least two exciting touches. For a moment Hoprend, after leading, looked like winning in a canter, but Dividend Deferred, as soon as he got an opening, made a desperate challenge, and even a second time it seemed as though he might still turn the tables. Hoprend, however, never for a moment flinched, his last points and a good kill making his victory clear and decisive.

In this connection I may mention that Forgotten Fashion, the sire of the winner, was himself a wonderfully stout greyhound as well as splendidly bred and a grandson of Miss Glendyne. He was for a considerable period regarded as the hack of the great Saughall group, and had accordingly to do extra duty simply from the fact that there were a few leading swells amongst his kennel companions at the time.

As enhancing the merit of Hoprend's victory, it may be pointed out that his first two vanquished opponents—Formula and Neolithic—were respectively successful in the Purse and Plate. Mr. Hardy's Wild Night won the Cup in 1898, so that he can boast of two Waterloo triumphs in nine years; Hoprend's success, too, was supplemented by Howtown dividing the Plate.

CHAPTER XXXIV.

Waterloo, 1907—Long Span's Splendid Triumph.

A FEATURE of this anniversary was the fact that the last four in the previous year's Cup—Hoprend, Dividend Deferred, Benedict and Mandini—were again entering the fray, as well as the dividers of the Purse—Formula and Game 'Un. Others that at the same time had shown good Waterloo class were again included, in Flag of the Free, Glenbridge, Stalwart, Dashing Hero, Handsome Cup, Cost Price, Newcastleton, Parson Parkes and Hackney Wick, the youngsters therefore having a rather redoubtable opposition to contend with. As it turned out, however, a first-season greyhound not only won the Cup, but showed himself clearly to be the best of the 64, and just as " coming events cast their shadows before," three puppies oddly enough, started as the three best favourites. The pride of place fell to San Franciso, at 100 to 15, in the Countess of Sefton's nomination. She had recently shown smart form at the Altcar Club January meeting in carrying off the Members' Plate (for all ages), beating the Netherby Cup winner (Laureate), Firth of Forth, Horrid Weather, and Mandini. Long Span had a strong following, especially from the north, at 100 to 14, though his sparkling display at the commencement of his course with Flag of the Free, at the Altcar Club November meeting had been his only appearance in public. The third puppy favourite was Bachelor's Acre, whose good form in dividing the Home-produce Stake at the Altcar Club January meeting had not passed unnoticed : he was backed freely at 100 to 9. Amongst the senior brigade the previous year's winner, Hoprend, led the way at 100 to 8.

Before Mr. Mugliston had got quite through the list, great commotion was caused by Mr. Tom Graham being attacked with a sudden seizure, and though medical aid was immediately at hand, death ensued very quickly. Of course the sad event naturally at once cast a gloom upon the room, and the proceedings immediately closed.

Wednesday was one of the worst days (perhaps the very worst) ever experienced at a Waterloo meeting.   After a terribly stormy night matters were still bad enough when Hill House was reached, but after an hour's wait matters mended a little, and a move was made down to the Rye Heys where 24 courses were run off.   After the crowd again got into position on the Withins bank, however, the storm burst with renewed violence, and the thousands present rapidly melted into hundreds.   The leading features were the fine form of Long Span in his second course, and the good impressions made by his younger kennel companion, Benedict, and the previous year's winner, Hoprend.

On Wednesday evening Sir R. W. Buchanan Jardine was in the chair, and opened the proceedings with a sympathetic and feeling allusion to the tragic event of the previous night, paying a graceful tribute to Mr. Graham's qualities as a courser and his knowledge and judgment of the sport to which we were all so much attached.

With San Franciso and Bachelor's Acre on the retired list, Long Span now advanced to the position of pronounced favourite at 7 to 2, and his kennel companion, Benedict, was " next best " at 100 to 14.

A transformation scene made matters meteorologically pleasant at the second stage, and an interesting day's sport at Lydiate was greatly enjoyed.   Results were strikingly in accordance with the judgment of " the talent "—at any rate, so far as the Cup was concerned—scarcely a favourite being beaten in either the third or fourth round.

Of the previous year's final quartette Mandini had already gone out, and now Hoprend, Dividend Deferred and Benedict followed suit, the four left in to contend for final honours being the three puppies—Long Span, Platonic and Such a Mark—and the previous year's runner, Glenbridge, all the four having attained their forward positions by meritorious running. Long Span was out and out the star performer, for though he had not much in hand of Little Mercury, the course was well run by both, whilst against the previous year's winner, Hoprend, the Scottish puppy gave a sparkling and polished display.

Long Span's form having been quite convincing, he was a strong favourite at 11 to 10 on Thursday night, Glenbridge being second best at 7 to 2, with 5 to 1 against Platonic, and 100 to 14 Such a Mark.

Everything was favourable at the final stage : pleasant weather, good hares, and a splendid wind-up.

Semi-Finals.

Long Span beat Platonic. Betting, 2 to 1 on Long Span. After a perfect delivery Platonic fully held the favourite for a hundred yards—in fact, it looked as if he was going to lead. Long Span then put on high pressure and drew out very nearly two lengths at the finish. He moved at his hare with splendid life, and after a strong wrench made a smart attempt to kill. He recovered quickly, but as puss broke round Platonic got a good opening, which he instantly took, and, commanding his hare in fine style, looked like turning the tables until he made a fatal trip. Long Span thereupon dashed to the front as the hare bore his way, and instantly brought his teeth into play.

Glenbridge beat Such a Mark. Betting, 7 to 4 on Glenbridge. After another splendid slip it was a grand race for some distance, but in crossing the filled-in drain the last-named faltered, whereupon Glenbridge quickly dashed out for a two-length lead. Sweeping with his hare in grand style as she came round, he held close possession for a second, and went on in splendid command for a sequence of a dozen points. Such a Mark at last succeeded in displacing him, and made a gallant show, but the issue was now beyond doubt, Glenbridge still sticking well to his work, a rare hare at last making the sough.

Deciding Course.

Long Span beat Glenbridge. Betting, 3 to 1 on Long Span. Coming from slips this time with a rare rattle, Long Span quickly shot clear, and, widening the gap rapidly, reached his hare four lengths in front. He then swept brilliantly on the scut as puss broke to the right, and added a couple of strong wrenches before winding up a splendid victory with a smart kill.

Waterloo Cup : Sir R. W. Buchanan Jardine's f d p Long Span, by Pateley Bridge out of Forest Fairy, beat Mr. A. D. Gaussen's bd d Glenbridge, by Spytfontein out of Get Along.

Waterloo Purse : Earl of Sefton's r b Shake a Fut, by Father Flint out of Quadrille, and Colonel J. M'Calmont ns

Duke of Leeds's r d Lottery, by Fiery Furnace out of Luck's Reward, divided.

Waterloo Plate : Hon. C. B. Hanbury ns Mr. S. Hill-Wood's bk d Mandini, by Gallant out of Kaffir Queen, and Mr. F. Alexander ns Mr. Birkbeck's f d p Bachelor's Acre, by Farndon Ferry out of Fillagree, divided.

Coincidence strongly marked the year of Long Span's famous victory. It was the Waterloo Cup's Jubilee since it became a 64-dog stake, and as in the opening year (1857) when King Lear won, another Scottish greyhound was now fittingly triumphant. King Lear, in his final, beat a good English dog in Sunbeam, the property of the always smartly-dressed Capt. Spencer (it used to be said that he had a suit of clothes for every day in the year) ; but Long Span's last vanquished opponent was an Irish greyhound. This at once recalled the fact that the two countries had before been in Waterloo final opposition, and Scotland had then to strike her proud flag when Bab at the Bowster attempted to lower the colours of Master M'Grath. It was now an easy reversal of the earlier result, for Long Span, as on each of the previous days, running his second course better than his first, ran the final like a really great greyhound. The fact is he came to Waterloo only half-trained. The Castlemilk district had been so locked up in a wintry embrace that he could neither be walked nor galloped, and as a desperate resort he was slipped at two or three hares when the snow was soft : this being the chief extent of his training so far as exercise was concerned.

Long Span's victory was immensely popular, Sir Robert and Lady Jardine, and Long Span and his trainer all being cheered again and again. Perhaps the fact that there had not been a Scottish victory since Lord Haddington's with Honey-wood in 1880 helped the enthusiasm ; but Sir Robert's personal popularity, and the fact that he evidently possessed a splendid puppy of brilliant promise, were the prime factors. How Long Span came so unluckily to grief the following year will be told in connection with the success of his sister, Hallow Eve.

The excellence of the season's puppies was made abundantly clear, for, in addition to the striking successes and form of Long Span, Platonic and Such a Mark in the Cup, Bachelor's Acre " stood out " clearly in the Plate.

E. Hulton & Co., Ltd.
THE DUKE OF LEEDS.

E. Hulton & Co., Ltd.
SIR EDWARD HULTON, Bart.,
Owner of Hallow Eve and Harmonicon.

Jas. Bacon & Sons.
Captain The Hon. W. C. ELLIS,
To whom we owe the present reliable pedigrees
of the Greyhound race.

Elliott & Fry, Ltd.
SIR R. W. BUCHANAN JARDINE,
Owner of Long Span and Jabberwock.

CHAPTER XXXV.

Waterloo, 1908—Hallow Eve's Year.

THIS was an eventful year from first to last. At the outset we were deprived of the always-welcome presence of the Earl of Sefton, his Lordship, together with Lady Sefton and a distinguished party being out in Abyssinia, enjoying the more exciting sport of big-game hunting ; and there was also an unfortunate drawback in the fact that several Waterloo kennels had suffered from the dire scourge of distemper. This was partly reflected in the less than usual number of puppies included in the entry, only twenty-three being considered good enough. The Duke of Leeds occupied the chair on Tuesday evening, supported right and left by Earl Enniskillen, Sir R. W. Buchanan Jardine, Mr. H. Brocklebank, Lord Kenyon, Colonel J. M'Calmont, Mr. D. J. Jardine, Mr. J. Bell-Irving, Mr. J. Mugliston, Mr. Hartley Bibby, Mr. G. F. Fawcett, Mr. O. H. Jones, Mr. W. Paterson, Major Hugh Peel, etc. The amenities of the chair having been gracefully discharged, the " calling over " was, as usual, capably carried out by Mr. J. Mugliston. Long Span became a hot favourite, 700 to 200 being at last taken. Friendly Foe was also heavily supported at 6 to 1, Bachelor's Acre at 100 to 9, and Dendraspis at 100 to 7.

Favourable weather and good coursing were pleasant characteristics of the opening day, and backers of the favourite were on good terms with themselves for nothing went like him. " The talent," however, got several " sets back," and made an ominous start by laying 7 to 2 on Horrid Weather, only to see him cleverly beaten by Spearmint. Other prominent reverses were those of Bradmoor by Sheelah (3 to 1), Parson Parkes by Glen Ferry (9 to 4), Hortensius by Dooley (2 to 1), Flag of the Free by Royal Crest (9 to 4), and Punchestown by Kilby (100 to 30).

It was in the second round, however, where disaster was most conspicuous, High Almoner flooring the odds of 5 to 1 laid on Friendly Foe, and even leading him to the hare. One bold speculator laid the odds in hundreds, thus going down for £500 on one course.

On Wednesday night 9 to 4 was the best odds offer against Long Span, and Bachelor's Acre was well befriended at 9 to 2.

It cannot be said that the meteorological accompaniments were pleasant at the middle stage, but they were not seriously bad, and the stirring character of the sport made amends. An exceptionally level draw had imparted little enlivening colour at the outset, but there was plenty of excitement as the Waterloo Cup of 1908 progressed. The defeat of Friendly Foe, combined with other startling results, gave a memorable character to the opening stage, and there was quite a sensational scene on Thursday afternoon, although the denouement was not, after all, so tragic as it threatened to be. The favourite, in his course against Royal Crest, was slipped to a demon of a hare, and got such a gruelling that his chance of winning the Cup seemed hopelessly gone. In many quarters it was assumed that he would be drawn rather than be exposed to the imminent danger of defeat, but when the time came Long Span again appeared upon the scene, and not only started favourite for the course, but won it without allowing his opponent to score a point. Nor must it be said that he was beating nothing. Dooley, in fact, had run his three previous courses extremely well, and in his bye, obtained through Handsome Cup's withdrawal, showed himself a faster, as well as a better, dog than Boulter's Lock. Long Span covered himself with glory in coming again so brilliantly, and the way he and his trainer were cheered as the crack was led back after the course showed that this feeling had already penetrated the hearts of those who admire gallant deeds. Another leading feature was the great form shown by Bachelor's Acre in both spins, and the chief topic of conversation at night was, what a battle royal the final will be between the two!

At night the betting was 11 to 10 against Long Span, 11 to 8 Bachelor's Acre, 8 to 1 Silhouette, and 100 to 3 Hallow Eve, her gruelling in the fourth round seeming to have extinguished her chance.

Fine Weather and good trials marked the wind-up, and Hallow Eve's Waterloo will linger long in the memories of all who witnessed it, for the finish was of a sensational, I might almost say tragic, character. The two courses in the semi-finals were regarded as foregone conclusions, in favour of Long Span and Bachelor's Acre, yet both were signally defeated.

Bachelor's Acre, with 3 to 1 on him, led several lengths, and moving with fine force at his hare, shot out to kill, coming an awful cropper in the attempt. Silhouette at once took a fine position, and though the fawn rejoined, the bitch out-worked him, being an easy winner when she killed.

Odds of 11 to 2 were laid on Long Span, and, after leading quite as far, his attempt at the death brought him similarly to grief. Hallow Eve then quickly ran up a smart sequence, and still being the cleverer after the crack rejoined was a decisive winner when she killed.

Deciding Course.

Betting, 11 to 4 on Silhouette. From a pretty slip the favourite gradually forged to the front, having an advantage of two lengths as she reached her hare, and went wide at the turn. Hallow Eve, coming cleverly round, was well in front for the second turn, and easily held her place for the third. Silhouette then dashed up, but again went wide as puss broke round, whilst the red, as before, swept cleverly on the scut. The black again shot up for a point, but now running loosely, never scored twice in succession, and Hallow Eve all the while running truthfully and cleverly was a clear winner when she effected the death.

Waterloo Cup : Mr. E. (now Sir Edward) Hulton's r b Hallow Eve, by Pateley Bridge out of Forest Fairy, beat the Countess of Sefton's ns Earl of Sefton's bk b p Silhouette, by Strange Mystery out of Slish.

Waterloo Purse : Mr. Whitworth ns Mr. H. Hardy's bk d p Hydrus, by Wartnaby out of Nid Nodding, and Mr. R. Hyslop's bk b Skiddaw, by Farndon Ferry out of The Nigger, divided.

Waterloo Plate : Mr. D. Graham ns Mr. W. Graham's bd d Glacier, by Wartnaby out of Gravity, beat Mr. E. Dobson ns Mr. A. Brown's bd d p Royal Flint, by Father Flint out of Royal Gem.

Recognising the fact that Long Span and Bachelor's Acre were indisputably the best two greyhounds in this year's Cup, it is impossible to enthuse over the winner and runner-up ; yet Hallow Eve, who was a good-class bitch when Mr. Hulton bought her as Forest Kitten, deserved more commendation than she received at the time. It was a great tribute to her sterling character to come out as she did on Friday morning, after being " run to death " in the fourth round, causing the previously unheard-of odds of 100 to 3 to be laid against her in the last four. It was also a fine feat of young Reynolds (Alf. Reynolds's son) to bestow the necessary nursing and attention that the bitch must have required. In this connection, too, Long Span must have been in sore straits, for his case was almost equally bad, as after his heart-breaking course in the third round with Royal Crest, he had to be " bucked up " the same afternoon to vanquish his fourth opponent. Experience tells, that it is not the severe course that is such a deadly settler as the exhausting process of having to " come again " without a night's rest.

For Bachelor's Acre there was less excuse, on the face of it, than for Long Span ; but in his case there had been illness in his kennel, and the taint perhaps began to show itself in a third successive day's effort. Silhouette's performance was the redeeming feature of the poor general show made by the puppies, but she cut up very indifferently at last, after leading well to the hare. Hallow Eve's success was wonderfully well received after the downfall of two such popular favourites, quite a levee being held at Mr. Hulton's 'bus until long after the subsequent final of the Plate had been decided.

It ought to be recorded that Hallow Eve was not originally intended to represent her owner. Platonic was at first Mr. Hulton's Waterloo hope, and afterwards Fancy Lass found most favour, but both had suffered from the ailment that had affected the kennel, whilst Hallow Eve escaped, so that she was really only third choice. The Waterloo of 1908 was thus something of a romance all through. Hallow Eve and Silhouette each started at 1,000 to 15.

CHAPTER XXXVI.

Waterloo, 1909—Messrs. Dennis's First Success.

JUST as Hoprend gave the tip direct in 1906, so did
Dendraspis, this year truthfully foreshadow his great
Altcar triumph. He made an early mark at the Ridgway
Club meeting, run at Aintree, by dividing the Clifton Cup
in the first week of October, but it was his grand performance
in running clean through the Border Union Netherby Cup, at
the end of the month, that stamped him as the probable
Waterloo winner, even in the face of two cracks like Long Span
and Bachelor's Acre. Of this redoubtable pair, the latter had
suffered some injury and was relegated to other duties ; but
Long Span again entered the fray, and was made a hot favourite.
100 to 30 was taken freely, the closing odds being 3 to 1. There
was close rivalry between Dendraspis and Face the Foe for
the position of second favourite. 400 to 50 was taken several
times about the first-named, but 8 to 1 was still on offer.
About Face the Foe the first offers of 1,000 to 80 were readily
taken, then 1,000 to 90, and ten fifties, the closing price being
100 to 12.

The opening day was marked by much upsetting of previous
form, and this was not at all attributable to the character of
the running, the trials being even exceptionally genuine. This
remark applies especially to the trials on Rye Heys, where,
by the bye, the feat of going once through the Cup in 1906
(Hoprend's year) was now repeated. This particular portion
of the Altcar ground was never conspicuous for giving good
tests of speed to the hare, but this year the hares nearly all
went forward in a straight line, and the way Wilkinson got
dead behind and delivered his charges smoothly together was
a treat to witness.

It was here where so many hot favourites were bowled
over, Long Span amongst the number. The crack, with the
big odds of 13 to 2 on him, had not disposed of Recitress
without giving chances, and there were plenty takers of the
odds when 3 to 1 was laid on him against his old opponent

L

Royal Crest. Long Span, as in his previous course, went up well in front, but he failed to hold possession as puss broke sharply to the left and Royal Crest quickly rattled in a smart sequence. The favourite shot to the front immediately he got an opening, but was not very tight on his hare, and Royal Crest, again getting merrily to work, had a good balance in hand when Long Span at last wrenched and killed. Other big upsets in the round were the defeats of Glacier by Silver Charm, with 5 to 2 on, Perranwell by Writ (3 to 1 on), Conover by Star of Doon (2 to 1 on), Face the Foe by Heavy Weapon (15 to 8 on), and Hidden Depth by Happy Kate (15 to 8 on).

With Long Span and Face the Foe knocked out, undisputed favouritism fell upon Dendraspis at night, 7 to 2 being the closing price. Second Barrel was a good second favourite at 11 to 5, all the sixes being snapped up. Friendly Foe's price was 9 to 1, and Platonic's 10 to 1, Royal Crest having backers at 100 to 8.

A most excellent day's sport was thoroughly enjoyed at Lydiate on the Thursday, 'midst pleasant surroundings, and everything worked quite smoothly. Sir Robert Jardine pursued a sportsmanlike and popular policy in pulling out his dethroned idol for the Plate, and from the improved form Long Span now displayed it looked as though he might have been short of hare practice.

In the Cup the sensational features at the opening were not repeated, though after Broad Arrow's smart defeat of the faster Star of Doon, his overthrow by Writ came as something of a surprise. Dendraspis and Such a Sell were clearly the best performers of the four eventually left in. Second Barrel gave a polished display against Gilderoy, but only an extra-stout hare enabled her to turn the tables upon Heavy Weapon, and the severity of the course extinguished her chance of winning the Cup. Such a Sell was the only puppy left in at the end of the third round.

A bigger last day's crowd than usual mustered at Hill House on Friday morning, Three better or more satisfactory trials have rarely if ever marked the final stage of a Waterloo Cup. The lesser events, too, were full of interest, especially the Plate, in which Long Span re-invested himself with some of his lost glory.

In the semi-finals big odds were laid, both on Such a Sell beating Writ, and Dendraspis beating Second Barrel, and each course was decisively won and well run.

Deciding Course.

Betting, 5 to 4 on Dendraspis. The favourite, as usual, quick on his legs, was soon slightly in front, and although the hare bent a little from him to the left in the first eighty yards, he had by that time drawn clear. Such a Sell then began to gradually catch him, and as they neared the hare had drawn level. At this crucial point, however, puss went more strongly to the right, enabling Dendraspis to clearly take the turn, and he held smart possession for the next two points. The red collar then began to take a good share of the course, and after exchanges put together a sequence which momentarily raised the hopes of his backers. He never, however, held a winning balance, and when Dendraspis finished so strongly and floored his hare his victory was quite clear.

Waterloo Cup : Messrs. S. M. and J. E. Dennis's r d Dendraspis, by Wartnaby out of Gleneva, beat Mr. G. Mayall ns Mr. E. H. Sikes's f d p Such a Sell, by Father Flint out of Fan o' the Forest.

Waterloo Purse : Duke of Leeds's bd b Liquid Fire, by Fighting Fire out of Lemon Squash, and Mr. R. F. Gladstone's f d Garpool, by Father Flint out of Glen Garpool, divided.

Waterloo Plate : Sir R. W. Buchanan Jardine's f d Long Span, by Pateley Bridge out of Forest Fairy, and Mr. G. F. Fawcett's bd d Face the Foe, by Father Flint out of Forest Fury, divided.

It will be noticed that all the six which figure in this year's Waterloo record are pretty much of a colour, four being red or fawn, and the other two brindled ; such a similarity had never previously occurred in my long experience. Dendraspis is not entitled to rank amongst the *great* Waterloo winners of his own sex like Master M'Grath, Fullerton, Herschel, Honeywood, Fabulous Fortune, Farndon Ferry and Long Span, but he gained his honours in quite great style, and proved himself a worthy champion of his day.

CHAPTER XXXVII.

Waterloo 1910.
Heavy Weapon wins without a Final Victory.

HEAVY WEAPON'S year was signalised in quite an exceptional way. The divisions between Miss Glendyne and Bit of Fashion in 1885, and between Herschel and Greater Scot in 1887, robbed those occasions of the always interesting and exciting phase of a final tussle, and now we had undue tameness imparted to the finish through one of the finalists being unable to come to slips. Full Steam was not absolutely *hors de combat*, but he was so very severely run in his course with Calabash that it would have been as cruel as it would have been unwise to ask him for another effort.

One of the most interesting features this year was the appearance, for the fourth time, of Long Span. Upon this occasion he was not elected first favourite, the honour falling upon the previous year's runner-up, Such a Sell (at 6 to 1), Long Span being second favourite at two points longer odds. Lanthorn, who had won the Altcar Members' Plate the previous month, and Heavy Weapon were each backed at 1,000 to 100. Calabash was backed at 1,000 to 1 several times, and he ran into the last four.

At night Long Span once again figured as Waterloo Cup favourite, 85 to 20 being taken. 600 to 100 was accepted about both Postage Paid and Stepdance, and 100 to 15 about Carnforth. 7 to 1 was the best offer against Conover, and Heavy Weapon was well supported at 9 to 1.

On Thursday Rye Heys was the scene of operations, the ground having dried considerably, and comprehensive drives being taken the whole of the 44 courses on the card were run off without a move. The 1,000 to 1 chance Calabash was quite the surprise packet of the day, beating both Agile and Stepdance decisively.

The exciting course of the day was between Heavy Weapon and Long Span. It was a great race between the pair, and it

E. WILKINSON, Slipper.

was only through being quicker on his toes that Heavy Weapon proved the faster, for he got nearly the whole of his length's lead in the first fifty yards. It was also thought that Long Span would beat him for style, but instead of overshooting his game, as on the previous day, Heavy Weapon went round with no little smartness as puss broke sharply to the left. Mickey the Mill effected yet one more surprise in his somewhat fluky defeat of Steam Whistle, but against Heavy Weapon he was too far behind for one of his dangerous spurts at last to be successful, though even as it was he rendered good service to the now favourite for the Cup by shortening puss's career. Carnforth again showed to great advantage in both spins.

In the evening the card was called over by Mr. W. Paterson, Heavy Weapon being pronounced favourite at evens. 3 to 1 was the best offer against Carnforth, whilst 500 to 100 was taken about Calabash, and 750 to 100 about Full Steam.

Thanks to the blow, and the absence of further rain, the surface of the Withins was all right by Friday morning, that well-known arena being the scene of the wind-up. The running was eminently satisfactory, the only drawbacks being that at least two of the hares proved too good, destroying Full Steam's chance in the Cup, and Strange Idea's in the Plate, and that there was no final in any of the three events. In the fourth round of the Purse Solway Ferry beat Lanthorn, the Duke of Leeds's good bitch thus going down a second time before a Croxteth representative, but I may mention that she was fearfully hard run in a trial on the Saturday before the meeting. Strange Idea had to be drawn in the third round of the Plate through the distressing length of his course with the game puppy Enniskillen.

Semi-Finals.

Full Steam beat Calabash. Betting, 6 to 4 on Calabash. In a tremendous race Calabash had drawn his neck in front as they neared the hare, but, puss at last bearing to the right, Full Steam, under the white flag, just gained the initial point. Coming round beautifully as puss broke to his side, he held close possession for a strong start, and always had the course won, a demon hare running both to a standstill.

Heavy Weapon beat Carnforth. Betting, 11 to 8 on Heavy Weapon. There was another splendid race between this pair,

Heavy Weapon being only just clear as he scored the turn. Puss breaking sharply to the left gave Carnforth a fine opening, and she showed splendid smartness by at once shooting on to the scut. Being so well placed, her admirers thought her success was now certain, but Heavy Weapon was splendidly on his mettle, and the bitch had only scored twice before the brindled, with a magnificent dash, shot clean past for a fine kill.

Decider.

Heavy Weapon declared the winner, Full Steam being drawn through distress.

Waterloo Purse : Earl of Sefton's bk d b Solway Ferry, by Prince Charming out of First Ferry, and Colonel Chichester ns Mr. R. N. Stollery's bd d Sincere, by Wartnaby out of Gravity, divided.

Waterloo Plate : Mr. H. Hardy's bd d p Hostage, by Pioneer out of Heirloom, and Mr. E. Smith ns Mr. H. Birkbeck's bd w d Back to the Land, by Farndon Ferry out of Fillagree, divided.

If robbed of the eclat of a final victory, Heavy Weapon's performance was nevertheless a fine one on the whole, and his course with Carnforth alone entitles him to unstinted praise. The bitch was placed in a winning position from the turn, and it was quite an electric stroke with which the brindled saved the situation, and, as it turned out, won the Cup. His owner, Mr. S. Hill-Wood, having been unwell, was not present on the first two days, but as illustrating how the mind can conquer the body, Thursday evening's wire that Heavy Weapon was standing, effected a sudden cure, and he put in an appearance on Friday, and had the pleasure of seeing the son of Wartnaby and Garbitas give his best performance of the week. At the same time, his displays at the middle stage against Long Span and Micky the Mill cannot be disparaged ; indeed, they both earned high commendation. His disposal of the Irish dog was really a smart performance, and against Long Span he could claim the honour of having fairly beaten the Scottish flyer in point of speed. It is not a little remarkable that Heavy Weapon and the previous year's winner, Dendraspis, are full brothers in blood. They are both by Wartnaby, and their respective dams, Gleneva and Garbitas are sisters, by Gallant out of Gladiole, though, of course, Gleneva is from an earlier litter.

CHAPTER XXXVIII.

Waterloo, 1911.
Jabberwock's Success: A Puppies' Year.

IT was not a little singular that after the 1907 winner, Long Span, had figured as the Castle Milk champion upon four consecutive occasions, the kennel should send forth another winner in the very next year. Jabberwock's name did not remain famous for long, but it can fairly be said that he was a good greyhound the week in which he gained his Blue Riband honours. It was not a year in which enthusiasm ran high at the outset, though the short prices at which Hillcourt and Sylph were supported quite suggested great greyhound excellence. 5 to 1 was Hillcourt's starting price, 1,000 to 200 being accepted, and 700 to 100 was taken about Sylph.

A bright balmy atmosphere enhanced the enjoyment of a clipping good day's sport at the opening stage, but calculations were often upset, especially in the second round. Nor was this conduced to by the character of the running, hares going straight, and the trials being legitimate tests of greyhound merit. Sylph, however, may be classed amongst the few unfortunates. With 3 to 1 on her she went up well in front, but puss nicking short back enabled Horseman's Green to gain possession, and he just did sufficient before killing to floor the odds without Sylph getting a second chance.

Conspicuous amongst the upsets in the second round were the defeats of High Le Brian by Highacre (9 to 2), Horseman's Green by Modus (9 to 4), Postage Paid by Jabberwock (2 to 1), Hobos by the hard-run Beaded Brow (4 to 1), and White Orris by Silk and Scarlet (15 to 8). In the latter case the odds were hardly justifiable, as Silk and Scarlet had already shown fine speed in the previous round. The best performers were clearly Hillcourt and Lanthorn, though several of the puppies had acquitted themselves well, notable Mandate, Jet and Jabberwock. No fewer than ten youngsters were included in the sixteen now left in.

Thursday's running at Lydiate was again of a worthy Waterloo type, though the earlier features of bright sunshine, and the graceful manœuvring of a flying machine overhead were missing. The day was disastrous to the favourites for the Cup, and in the four courses in the fourth round the odds were three times floored. Hillcourt and Lanthorn were both beaten a bit unluckily. The first-named was fairly led to the hare, but he shot up well ahead for the second point, and was in fine command of his hare when Silk and Scarlet nicked in from the side for a lucky kill. Lanthorn, on the contrary, had fairly the foot of her opponent, and had drawn well clear when the rain storm, blowing across the ground, caused the hare to bear away to the right, and Jabberwock, under considerable favour, gained the turn. The course was afterwards well contested and almost hung in the balance until Jabberwock's finishing stroke.

Of the other three that reached the semi-finals, best words can be written of Mandate, whose defeats of Jet and Mickey the Mill were marked by considerable fire. Silk and Scarlet was served by his fine speed, and Raby Bachelor was distinctly good all round.

In the semi-finals Mandate, with 6 to 4 on him, was outpaced for the early points by Silk and Scarlet, and when he looked like winning, killed too soon.

Jabberwock outfooted Raby Bachelor, and was up first on an outside, but puss curving still more strongly to the left, the non-favourite shot to the front. Jabberwock, however, instantly returned the spurt, dashed past, and flecked strongly, Raby at once giving the finishing touch.

In the decider it was guineas to pounds on Jabberwock, and in a worthy Waterloo final he asserted clear superiority, though Silk and Scarlet led nearly three lengths and scored a second time before swinging out as puss broke clean round.

Waterloo Cup : Sir R. W. Buchanan Jardine's r d p Jabberwock, by Bachelor's Acre out of Forrester's Favour, beat Mr. A. J. Humphrey ns Mr. P. Storey's f d p Silk and Scarlet, by Earl's Court out of Gay Feather.

Waterloo Purse : Mr. J. W. Fullerton's r d Full Steam, by Prince Plausible out of Grammarian, and Mr. R. N. Stollery's bk b p Sylph, by Such a Mark out of Game 'Un, divided.

Waterloo Plate : Mr. H. Birkbeck's bd d p Boanerges, by Bachelor's Acre out of Bustard, and Mr. R. Hyslop's bk d Strange Idea, by Glenfield out of Daily Sport, divided.

Jabberwock's final success over Silk and Scarlet, enabling Scotland to inflict defeat upon England, was a counterpart of earlier years—1880, when Honeywood defeated Plunger ; 1873, when the Castle Milk bitch, Muriel, defeated Peasant Boy ; 1861, when Canaradzo defeated Sea Rock ; and 1857, when King Lear defeated Sunbeam.

It must be regarded as a striking piece of good fortune on the part of the popular Scottish baronet to so quickly supplement Long Span's Waterloo victory with another, and it would seem that the fates were propitious in preventing the smart puppy, Jibstay, from taking the place that Jabberwock filled. Oddly enough, Jabberwock is closely related to the great Castle Milk crack. Forrester's Favour (dam of Jabberwock), and Forest Fairy (dam of the two Waterloo winners, Long Span and Hallow Eve), being sisters, by Under the Globe out of Fantine. It has been a great winning family, and it is wonderful what can be achieved when you once get a dam that begins to throw good ones.

Both Long Span and Jabberwock strained to Herschel on the sire's side. Pateley Bridge, sire of Long Span, was out of Thoughtless Beauty by Mr. Hornby's great dog, and Bachelor's Acre, sire of Jabberwock, was by Farndon Ferry, son of Herschel's daughter, Fair Florence.

In running second Silk and Scarlet achieved a most wonderful performance, for, after the first day's running, he developed such a terrible thirst that a large quantity of water, left in his kennel at night, had all disappeared on Thursday morning ; and the same treatment was a dire necessity again the next night ! In more experienced hands, Silk and Scarlet must have done still better. He ought not to have been fed, either night, until the thirst was allayed. A few laps at a time, of three-parts water and one-part milk, as warm as he would take it, would have given relief, if persevered with ; if not, the yolk of a raw egg ought to have been his supper, and he would have been ready for six o'clock breakfast of boiled bread and milk.

CHAPTER XXXIX.

Waterloo, 1912—Tide Time's Success.

LIKE the previous anniversary, this was a puppies' year, the winner and runner-up (Adversary) both being first-season greyhounds. Favouritism fell upon Mr. R. N. Stollery's smart, but unfortunate, dog, Saracen, 900 to 100, then 800 to 100, being readily taken. Beaded Brow was nominally second favourite at 1,000 to 80 (o.), but Jibstay and Hillcourt were each strongly supported at 1,000 to 70.

For once in a way hares ran badly, and the poorest day's sport seen at Waterloo since Misterton's year (1879) had a depressing influence. It was an unfortunate fiasco, but was nobody's fault, and arose from the stickiness of the fallows that the hares had to cross in the drives, the hares' rough, hairy feet getting clogged before they had to run for their lives. These conditions improved somewhat later in the day, and the blemish did not in any way attach to the later stages.

Saracen having failed to survive the second round (it was the winner, Tide Time, that led and just beat him), Beaded Brow was promoted to the position of first favourite at night, 5 to 1 being taken. Hillcourt, Stepdance and Tide Time were each supported at 100 to 15.

There being no greasy plough to first cross at Lydiate, the hares at the second stage showed their usual stamina, and a fine day's sport resulted. Unluckily the weather broke down badly, and all the favourites were bowled over, though those who backed Tide Time overnight were now on good terms.

On Thursday night Tide Time was a slightly better favourite than Adversary, though the latter was backed at 225 to 100. Hidden Smoke was well backed at 9 to 2, Hyson's price being 11 to 2. On the night of the draw Tide Time and Adversary each stood at 40 to 1.

At the concluding stage the trials were even better than on the previous day, and in delightful weather, a great final gave a splendid finishing touch.

Semi-Finals.

Tide Time beat Hyson. Betting, 7 to 4 on Tide Time. From a pretty slip the favourite gradually drew ahead and reached his hare a length and a half in front. Steadying himself beautifully, he went on in strong possession for half-a-dozen points before giving an opening. Hyson then immediately shot to the front, but his couple of wrenches and good kill still left him in a minority.

Adversary beat Hidden Smoke. Betting, 7 to 4 on Adversary. In another fine stretch Adversary gradually forged to the front, being a length and a half ahead for the turn, at which he lost his place. Hidden Smoke scored the next two, and then exchanges followed, the black, with a sequence of three, for a moment looking dangerous. Adversary, however, never flinched, and made a fine finish, his victory being quite clear when he killed.

Deciding Course.

Tide Time beat Adversary. Betting, 5 to 4 on Adversary. This was one of the grandest finals ever seen in connection with the Waterloo Cup. They came away beautifully together, but Tide Time soon began to go a little the faster, and had drawn clear at one point. The hare then began curving slightly to the right, and Adversary, on the inside, squeezed up for the first point, and came well round with his hare for the second. The black shot to the front as the hare again shifted, and held possession for a smart innings, but Adversary soon challenged, and the course was desperately contested, each having the better of it in turns. Tide Time was a little the steadier, but the brindled kept on with rare determination, and the issue of the splendid fight fairly hung in the balance until the black took the last few points, and finished a great and gallant display with a good kill.

Waterloo Cup: Mr. J. W. Fullerton ns Mr. E. L. Townshend's bk d p Tide Time, by Friendly Foe out of Fast Waves, beat Mr. F. Alexander's bd d p Adversary, by Glenfield out of Alternative.

Waterloo Purse: Mr. G. F. Fawcett's r d Fly to the Front, by Force the Fight out of Fleet Footed, and Mr. E. V. Rayner's bd d Rostrum, by Prince Plausible out of Glen Huntly, divided.

Waterloo Plate : Mr. R. N. Stollery's w bd d Saracen, by Such a Mark out of Game 'Un, and Sir T. V. S. Gooch's w f d p Grey Muzzle, by Such a Mark out of Wilgate Daisy, divided.

The early blemish that attached to Tide Time's year was effectually blotted out. Thursday's improved trials were supplemented with a glorious finish, the three Cup courses in particular being as perfect tests of merit as could be desired, and a more strenuously contested final was perhaps never witnessed. In the Purse and Plate, too, the trials were superb, and the weather was as grand as the sport was good. It must have been a proud satisfaction to Mr. Mulgiston, in his opening year as Waterloo Secretary, to see such a culminating success after such dark promise on the opening day. His predecessors, Mr. Hartley Bibby and Mr. Harold Brocklebank, had each, I well remember, some anxious years with long postponements and fresh draws. Mr. T. D. Hornby, after a long tenure of office, retired in the season 1882-83, so that Mr. Brocklebank and Mr. Bibby discharged the honorary and arduous duties, between them, for twenty-nine years. Other changes marked Tide Time's year. Mr. Brice, after a triumphant run of fourteen years, did not seek re-election, and the choice of the nominators, as was fully expected, fell upon Mr. Joseph Walker, who had already shown his capability and given full satisfaction at Altcar Club meetings. A change, too, was made in the then important office of Flag Steward. Mr. Horace Ledger had officiated with great efficiency through some very difficult days for some years, but Mr. Mugliston, with characteristic kindness of heart, thought that as Jack Bootiman did so well at the Altcar Club meetings, he deserved the larger emolument that attached to the duties at Waterloo. The slipper, of course, remained the same : there was only one Edward Wilkinson.

Some credit for the victory of Tide Time is due to young Harold Wright, for he had the dog splendidly fit, or he would not have won the final course. The name of Wright " looms large " in Waterloo records. Harold's father, Joe Wright, trained the 1888 and 1895 winners—Burnaby and Thoughtless Beauty, and his uncle, Tom Wright, trained Fabulous Fortune, Fearless Footsteps (double winner), Farndon Ferry, and Father Flint.

A TRINITY OF JUDGES.

E. Hulton & Co., Ltd.

Mr. JOSEPH WALKER.

Mr. JAMES HEDLEY.

Mr. R. A. BRICE.

CHAPTER XL.

Waterloo, 1913—Hung Well's Year.

WHETHER the glamour that often attaches to the previous year's winner had a moving influence or not, there was an extra big demand for dinner tickets this year, many applicants being disappointed, and the fact that Tide Time was made favourite showed that he was, at any rate, much in men's minds. The Earl of Sefton presided, and we had the unique incident of three Waterloo secretaries on his immediate left, Mr. Harold Brocklebank, Mr. Hartley Bibby and Mr. John Mugliston side by side. On the noble chairman's immediate right sat the Duke of Leeds, and he was further closely supported by Earl Enniskillen, Mr. J. Bell-Irving, Mr. J. J. Bell-Irving, Major Hugh Peel, and the late Mr. Oliver Jones. The betting took a wider range than usual, though there were two good favourites in Tide Time (at 900 to 100) and Broadmoor (at 1,000 to 100). Hirundo and Hung Well were each well backed at 1,000 to 80, and so was Nimble Ninepence, at 1,000 to 70.

Frost delayed the start until midday on Wednesday, and it was decided to miss the Rye Heys flat in favour of the better going on the Withins. It was not one of the really fine day's coursing generally seen there, many of the hares running indifferently, and an occasional stout one only made matters worse in spoiling uniformity. Home in the Twilight and Hirundo were two special victims, having to be withdrawn after winning their first courses. Apart from these incidents the day was not specially marked by features, though there were fully the usual number of Waterloo surprises.

Tide Time acquitted himself well, and maintained his position of favourite at night at 4 to 1. Hung Well, who had also pleased, supplanted Broadmoor as second favourite, 5 to 1 being taken. Broadmoor stood at 100 to 14, Saracen at 8 to 1, and Distingue at 100 to 9.

Thursday's running at Lydiate was a vast improvement upon that of the earlier stage, for not only did the hares run exceptionally well—too well in many instances—the majority of the courses were also well run, on the good going, several of them being such inspiriting displays as to suggest high-class greyhounds. This was strongly marked when Hung Well and Tide Time tried conclusions, the exchanges being quite brilliant in their quickness, and the issue hanging in the balance until Hung Well killed.

Mr. George Mayall presided on Thursday night, and before calling the card announced that in consequence of Fellow from Wales being so hard run he might be drawn. This necessarily damped speculation, and as Dancing Dervish was in little better plight, they both stood at extreme odds. 2 to 1 on Hung Well was freely laid, the odds against Huldee being 11 to 4.

Mixed memories attached to this Waterloo Cup, and rarely has the great coursing event of the year been so strongly marked with fateful incident. Fellow from Wales (who ran so gallantly) and the sturdy Dancing Dervish were victimised like Home in the Twilight and Hirundo, whilst Saracen, who looked not unlike atoning at last for all his previous ill-luck, was equally a victim of misfortune in another direction. He was very nearly incapacitated at the outset by the viciousness of his brother, Sultan, who seized Saracen's upper jaw and dislodged a tooth. This did not prevent his surviving the opening day, but in the third round he dislocated a toe and limped off the ground a poor cripple.

Disasters of lesser account also spoiled some of the interest in the minor events, but these were trifling compared with the tameness that was so unfortunately imparted to the final tussles of the Cup. On Thursday night there was no attempt to speculate on the issues between the two pairs in the semi-finals ; and after Hung Well had disposed of Dancing Dervish, and Huldee had beaten his helpmate in his bye, misadventure again came in the way. Before Huldee could be picked up a fresh hare came along, and he was run to a complete stand-still.

Deciding Course.

Hung Well beat Huldee. Betting, 5 to 2 on Hung Well. Unable to jump off, Huldee was quickly left in the rear, and for some distance it looked as though Hung Well would draw clear away. Huldee, however, then began to feel his feet, Hung Well being a little less than three lengths in advance as he reached his game.   Huldee made a fine spurt at the turn, but the red collar retained possession for the next two points before Huldee, as the hare came his way, shot fairly to the front.   He was, however, unable to come round with sufficient closeness to show a really dangerous resistance, and though he continued to contest the course gallantly was always in a minority, Hung Well (who never flinched) being a clear winner when Huldee gamely killed.

Waterloo Cup : Mr. S. Hill-Wood's bd d Hung Well, by Mandini out of Pocahontes, beat Mr. E. Hulton's bd d p Huldee, by Little Mercury out of Full Way.

Waterloo Purse : Sir R. W. Buchanan Jardine's bd d p Jonc, by Mandini out of Jenny Howlett, beat Mr. A. F. Pope ns Messrs. Dennis's r d p Dinuba, by Bachelor's Acre out of Denwa, ran-up.

Waterloo Plate : Mr. G. W. White's r d p White Optic, by White Rubicon out of White Ouida, and Colonel Chichester ns Mr. J. Baily's f d Ballyrameen, by Glenfield out of Borrowed Beauty, divided.

It was not an inspiriting final for the Cup, neither greyhound being in a condition to give his best.   Hung Well's course with Dancing Dervish was a punishing one, whilst Huldee's go at the fresh hare was " a settler."

Hung Well is a well-shaped greyhound, of powerful build, and, scaling as he does, nearly 68lb., he combines remarkable cleverness with first-class pace.   On the second day he was seen to the greatest advantage, and his magnificently-run course with Tide Time will long be remembered.   I have little hesitation in saying that it has only been eclipsed twice in my time at Waterloo, and it is not greatly overshadowed by the recollection of those never-to-be-forgotten electric flashes between Master M'Grath and Bab at the Bowster, and little Penelope and Miss Glendyne.   Mention of Penelope reminds me that Hung Well is descended from Mr. Leonard Pilkington's blood, his dam (Pocahontas) being by Strange Mystery from Pensive Beauty, one of the celebrated Mellor Moor and Thoughtless Beauty family.   Hung Well is thus inbred to Under the Globe, his sire, Mandini, being out of Kaffir Queen (daughter of Under the Globe), whilst Strange Mystery is a son of the same celebrity.

CHAPTER XLI.

Waterloo, 1914—Dilwyn follows Dendraspis.

A SORROWFUL note was struck on the eve of this Waterloo Cup, the news reaching the Exchange Station Hotel, on Tuesday afternoon, that Mr. William Paterson, owner of Winning Number, had passed away suddenly at Bournemouth, as he was preparing to start for Liverpool. Mr. Paterson was amongst the most highly-esteemed coursers of the kingdom, his purity of character and charming manners making him a general favourite. The Duke of Leeds, who occupied the chair through the Earl of Sefton's indisposition, alluded to the unhappy event in graceful terms, and paid a high tribute to the deceased's qualities both as a courser and as a gentleman. It was a peculiarly tragic ending to Mr. Paterson's career, for he had endured many blighted Waterloo hopes, and now when he had a greyhound that promised to atone for previous disappointments—Winning Number having shown exceptionally great form by the style in which he ran through the Corrie Cup in December—he was called away. I may at once mention that Winning Number won the Cup for Sir Thomas (now Lord) Dewar the following year.

The withdrawal of Winning Number's name (Mr. Paterson's nomination being also transferred) had no doubt considerable influence on the wagering, for he would have had a host of north-country followers, the 1912 winner, Tide Time, now being made favourite at 100 to 14. Distingué was second favourite at 800 to 100, and Husky Whisper also followed closely at 900 to 100.

A series of grand trials marked the opening stage both on the Rye Heys and the Withins, and with a considerable proportion being brilliantly run, the day's sport was most inspiriting.

The most sparkling performance of the day was Dilwyn's defeat of Jaunt. The Scottish bitch had run a beautiful course against Bradawl, the style in which Dilwyn polished her off being thus extra meritorious.

Mr. Martin Alexander presided on Wednesday night, and the " calling over " led to some lively speculation. For the event Tide Time was still favourite at 100 to 30, 425 to 100 Distingué, 600 to 100 Dilwyn, and 100 to 11 Token.

Another magnificent day's sport was witnessed at the middle stage, over the Lydiate ground, and it is not often that a series of better displays in the Cup have been witnessed. The trials, too, were all genuine tests of merit, and the only favourite beaten in the twelve Cup courses was when the faster Gay Swell was outworked and outstayed by Competition.

On Thursday night there was almost disputed favouritism for the Cup, the prices being 7 to 4 against Distingué (taken and wanted), 7 to 4 Tide Time (taken and offered), 6 to 1 Dilwyn, and 7 to 1 Leucoryx.

The wind-up on Friday was in happy accord with the earlier stages, the sport being of superb character, with the accompaniment of perfect weather.

Semi-Finals.

Dilwyn beat Distingué. Betting, 9 to 4 on Distingué. From a pretty delivery Dilwyn was not long in showing in front, and, gradually forging ahead, was well clear when she scored the turn. The hare now broke to her side, and, sweeping on the scut in beautiful possession, she held command for what was clearly a winning sequence. Distingué at last got to the front, and made a game effort, but he was still far in arrears when Dilwyn displaced him, and finished a brilliant victory with three strong wrenches and a smart kill.

Leucoryx beat Tide Time. Betting, 5 to 2 on Tide Time. It was a grand race for some distance, Leucoryx going just a shade the faster. Towards the finish of the run-up, however, the hare bent to the left, and Tide Time, under the red flag, shot out well clear for the first point. Puss breaking clear round at the turn, the white collar came back more smartly than his opponent, being well ahead for the second point. At once setting grandly to work, Leucoryx then ran up a telling sequence, and though Tide Time made a few faint challenges the issue was never again in doubt, the white collar driving his hare over the Withins bank and killing her.

M

Deciding Course.

Dilwyn beat Leucoryx. Betting, 2 to 1 on Dilwyn. Feeling her feet more smartly than her lame opponent, Dilwyn very quickly showed in advance, and was two lengths and a half ahead for the turn, at which she came round with a rattle for the second. Leucoryx then made an attempt to challenge, but stumbled in the effort, the fawn going on in command for several other points. Persevering gamely, the black tried again for possession, but faltered as before, and Dilwyn, maintaining splendid fire, was the easiest of winners.

Waterloo Cup: Mr. A. F. Pope ns Messrs. Dennis's r b Dilwyn, by Bachelor's Acre out of Denwa, beat Major (now Colonel) R. M'Calmont ns Duke of Leeds's bk d p Leucoryx, by Lottery out of Gaysfield.

Waterloo Purse: Mr. H. Brocklebank's f d Brummagem, by Such a Sell out of Bibelot, and Duke of Leeds's f d p Legal Letter, by Postage Paid out of Love's Reward, divided.

Waterloo Plate: Mr. Brann ns Mr. Oscar Asche's f b Once Australia, by Yankee Doodle out of Ena, beat Mr. W. Cockerill's bk d Fast Sam, by Friendly Foe out of Fast Waves.

Huge attendances marked this year's Waterloo Cup, and there was probably a record crowd for a last day, the fact of the two favourites, Distingué and Tide Time, being left in being, perhaps, the special attraction. Both, as matters turned out, were destined to defeat, and it was something of a coincidence that the pair to finally contend for premier honours should each figure as the second string. Messrs. Dennis, knowing Distingué to have the superior speed, preferred him to Dilwyn, leaving the latter to fill Mr. Pope's nomination, whilst the Duke of Leeds similarly elected Legal Letter to run in his own name in preference to Leucoryx, Major M'Calmont being thus the fortunate nominator of the latter. Whilst still denying her favours to the Yorkshire nobleman, the fickle goddess was extra kind to Messrs. Dennis, as five years previously they achieved an equally brilliant Waterloo triumph with Dendraspis. Dilwyn's final victory was rendered comparatively easy, the lameness from which Leucoryx suffered, quite disabling him at last.

E. Hulton & Co., Ltd.

TIDE TIME, Winner of Waterloo Cup, 1912.

E. Hulton & Co., Ltd.

HARMONICON, Winner of Waterloo Cup, 1916.

CHAPTER XLII.

Waterloo, 1915—Winning Number's Year.

THIS Waterloo Cup was marked by the quite exceptional success of a third-season greyhound, that events had prevented from running the year before, when at the top of his form. The well-named son of Lottery was then the property of the late Mr. W. Paterson, and Sir Thomas (now Lord) Dewar buying him for 280gs., won the Waterloo Cup in his first year of holding a nomination.

Memories of his great Corrie form, in the December of the previous season, having partly died out, and having done nothing very striking in public since, Winning Number was not amongst the leading favourites. These were Hopsack (at 1,000 to 100), Jawleyford, Harmonicon and Bugleman (each at 1,000 to 80).

A notable feature of the dinner this year was the presence of three distinguished Indian officers—keen sportsmen—who had obtained special leave to see the English great coursing event. The whole of the first day's 48 courses were this year run on the Withins, and hares running well, the trials were of distinctly high class. There were, as often happens at Waterloo, many surprises ; and a good many extreme outsiders figured in the sixteen survivors of the day.

The favourite, Hopsack, was beaten very unluckily in the first round by Nip Near (who was the lucky dog of this year's Waterloo Cup, and ran into the last four), and Harmonicon and Bugleman both went down in the second round. Amongst the surprises Mr. H. Brocklebank's pair, Brummagem and Balderdash, figured conspicuously, and Dionysius (at 1,000 to 10 overnight) raised two flags in most commendable style.

Songstress, who unluckily fell against her kennel companion (Earlston) in the draw, ran two good courses. She was led by Babylon, but gave him a rare licking afterwards. Winning Number's first success was gained under difficulties by a sparkling display as puss circled away from him, and he commenced his second course in equally brilliant style, though Phidias finished it.

Leucoryx gave, perhaps, the most brilliant display of the first round in his one-sided victory over Real British, and might not improbably have gone to slips with his half-brother for the final but for his unfortunate accident. He struck his hare in flying the drain at the top left-hand corner of the Withins, and landing on some broken ground injured himself so severely that he had to be drawn—another stroke of cruel luck for the Duke of Leeds.

Jawleyford's running was quite impressive. He was "flying" to the hare against Once Australia, whom Mr. Oscar Asche brought back with him from the colony; he also took a strong lead from Dubiety, and ran both courses with considerable cleverness and determination. It came as a great shock next day to see him " hang fire " and " look on " when being tackled by Balderdash.

His own fine form, together with the other three leading favourites knocked out, led to Jawleyford being a strong favourite at night, 700 to 200 being taken ; 600 to 100 was accepted about Winning Number, and Dionysius was supported at 100 to 14.

The intermediate day's running at Lydiate did not, during the third round of the Cup, reach the high level of its predecessor, though hares ran better when the beat was changed from the Carr side to the other end, on the left of the crowd ; and, speaking comprehensively, it was a very fine day's sport. Every one of the early hares proved much too good for her pursuers.

Junco, in easily defeating Hopeful Still, got such a gruelling that she was drawn in the next round, giving Nip Near another bye. There was also " a victim " in the fourth round, Happy Challenge's course with Balderdash (whose damaged toe gave way) being of distressing length. This was bad luck for Mr. M. G. Hale, one of the very few of the old guard now left, as his dog in the previous round had outfooted and given short shrift to the Scottish bitch Songstress, who had shown smart form in her previous courses.

Winning Number quite sustained his previous day's great

form, both in his defeat of the hard-run Hedda, and the way in which he polished off Brummagem. Hadfield, too, ran both his courses extremely well, though each of his opponents—School and Dionysius—infused some excitement.

At the calling over on Thursday night Winning Number was a strong favourite, opening at 5 to 4 and closing at 11 to 10. Hadfield was at 3 to 1, Nip Near 4 to 1, whilst 1,000 to 55 was offered against the hard-run Happy Challenge.

Showery weather accompanied the wind-up on the Withins, but the coursing was again good, though neither the semi-finals of the Cup, nor the short final developed the usual excitement, whilst both the Purse and Plate were divided.

In the semi-finals Happy Challenge, with odds against him, outpaced Nip Near, and made short work of his hare, and Winning Number outfooted and polished off Hadfield in great style.

Deciding Course.

Winning Number beat Happy Challenge. Betting, 4 to 1 on Winning Number. Like the two spins in the semi-finals, this was also, oddly enough, quite short. Wilkinson effected another perfect delivery, but Winning Number soon began to go the faster, and was fully two lengths ahead as he scored the turn. Sweeping on the scut in perfect style as puss shifted to the right, he held close possession, and again wrenched strongly before the brindled with a fine spurt shot up inside and destroyed whatever chance he might have had with a smart kill.

Waterloo Cup : Sir T. Dewar's f d Winning Number, by Lottery out of Shady, beat Mr. M. G. Hale's bd d Happy Challenge, by Heavy Weapon out of Ferryman's Guide.

Waterloo Purse : Mr. O. H. Jones's r d p Jules Mumm, by Beaded Brow out of Tipula, and Mr. G. Mayall's bd d p Martini, by Heavy Weapon out of Mark Up, divided.

Waterloo Plate : Mr. G. F. Fawcett's f d p False Forecast, by Friendly Foe out of Pensa, and Mr. E. Hulton's bd d p Harmonicon, by Heavy Weapon out of Camorra, divided.

Winning Number's triumph naturally carried the memory back to his former owner, and breeder, Mr. William Paterson (so well liked by everybody), who was, unhappily, not spared to see a Waterloo Cup won by the best greyhound he ever possessed. It was a proud achievement of Sir Thomas (now Lord) Dewar to win a Waterloo Cup at his first attempt— an honour that many old coursers have striven for in vain ; but it was deservedly and meritoriously gained, and that always adds to the pleasure and prestige of victory.

Smartly as he won his first course, under difficulties, and well as he ran his next three, it was on the last day that he showed to the greatest advantage. But even then those who only know Winning Number, the Waterloo winner in his third season, have but a faint knowledge of Winning Number at his best.

In the Corrie Cup of December, 1913, he made an impression on my mind that will never be effaced as long as memory lasts.

It is worthy of mention that Winning Number would not have been the chief hope of Denny Smith's Waterloo team had all gone well with Husky Whisper. They were tried at Mr. Horace Ledger's Witham enclosure (a favourite venue for Waterloo trials at this period), and Husky led a couple of lengths and well won the course.

This was quite in accordance with expectation on the part of both owner and trainer, but, most unfortunately, " Husky " injured a toe so badly that there was no prospect of getting him to Waterloo. Oddly enough, when hopes again ran high the following year, he broke, or severely injured, a hock in a trial at Wappenbury, and this finished Husky's unlucky career —two cruel blows at the time for his popular owner, Mr. C. A. Mills.

That Husky Whisper must have been a really good greyhound there can be little doubt, and though his field activities were so spoiled, his splendid success at the stud could hardly have been greater even with the prestige of a Waterloo Cup victory.

CHAPTER XLIII.

Waterloo, 1916—Harmonicon's Year.

NEVER was a better Waterloo tip given than when Harmonicon, just as Hoprend did in 1906, carried off the Members' Plate at the Altcar Club meeting the previous month. He gave conclusive proof of his great speed by the way he stretched ahead of Babylon (who had shown all his fine pace in his previous spins), and although a big dog (71 lbs.) his recovery from a sharp angle, in his course with Princely and his brilliant shoot up for the next point, which it seemed impossible for him to take, was most striking.

Then, in addition to having shown great fleetness, extra cleverness, and the nimbleness of a smart bitch, he gave evidence of being able to use his head. In the final he looked like losing the run-up, and probably the early points, as puss was circling in Simla's favour, but Harmonicon at last made a sharp cut across behind, and eventually was first up.

Mr. Harold Brocklebank occupied the chair at dinner, and received an ovation upon rising to give the loyal toasts. Cheers were also given when he proposed the health of Commander the Duke of Leeds and Colonel the Earl of Sefton, absent respectively on naval and military duties. I may perhaps appropriately mention here other coursers who were absent engaged fighting their country's battle.

Prominent names like Colonel Lord Tweedmouth, Colonel R. M'Calmont, Colonel R. S. Chichester, Captain Cuthbert Blundell, Major Sir George Noble, Major Sir Wyndham Hanmer, Colonel H. C. Legh, Captain D. P. Wormald, and the Hon. Piers St. Awbyn are easily re-called, the last-named being, unhappily, amongst those who fell. The Duke of Leeds, like some of the others mentioned, had a lucky escape.

At first he was engaged on scouting duty in the North Sea on H.M.S. *Aires* (formerly his own yacht, lent to the Government), and shortly after his Grace had been transferred to a battleship the *Aires* struck a mine and went down, seventeen of the Duke's old crew being amongst those who perished.

The betting this year truthfully foreshadowed the final result, Harmonicon and Hopsack clearly heading the quotations, with the first-named slightly the better favourite. Harmonicon closed at 100 to 14, and Hopsack at 8 to 1.

A strong blow, interspersed with frequent bursts of hail, rendered the opening day the reverse of pleasant, and also now and then interfered with progress; but the quality of the sport suffered surprisingly little except just at one point when the hares had to cross a piece of sticky plough as they came forward.

It was quite a favourites' day, Hopsack, Harmonicon and High Legh Teaser being out and out the best performers, though the recent Irish Cup winner, Lord Protector, ran fast and with plenty of fire. The Castle Milk puppy, Jessop, whose debut was accompanied by a loud flourish of trumpets, ran his courses in workmanlike style, but was obviously not as fast as the gossip-mongers represented. High Legh Foam and Songstress each survived the day in most commendable style, but False Forecast figured as a disgraced favourite, the slower Minstrel Coon giving him a severe licking in a good trial.

At night speculation took a lively turn both on individual courses and for the event. Harmonicon and Hopsack maintained their leading positions, but in reversed order, Hopsack closing the better favourite at 7 to 2, whilst 4 to 1 was offered against Harmonicon. High Legh Teaser was third favourite at 7 to 1.

Better weather favoured the second day, though a cold wind was still in evidence. The sport was of excellent class, and all the 44 courses were run from one position, the hares being driven from the Carr end on to the big Lydiate flat. The two cracks again acquitted themselves in first-class style, especially Hopsack, who made a splendid recovery after being thrown out by the hare's sharp break to the right, and beat Tattenhall pointless. Harmonicon began his course against Gryphon in great style, and, with the worst of the handicap, went up in front of High Legh Foam, then going at his hare with fine fire quickly floored her.

Songstress was beaten very unluckily, but Minstrel Coon was too clever and resolute for both his faster opponents, Flying Man and Lord Protector, upsetting big odds in each instance. A cablegram reached his owner in France, " 'Coon ' in the last four," and caused joyous excitement on the real field of battle.

Rataine again won both her courses easily, and ran them both with considerable fire. Amongst those fairly beaten Jessop and Princely earned commendation, each having once won his course respectively against Lord Protector and Hopsack, if he could have killed.

On Thursday night Hopsack took a decided lead in the betting, being backed at evens until bookmakers at last asked for 11 to 10. It was 9 to 4 against Harmonicon, 9 to 2 Rataine, and 25 to 1 Minstrel Coon.

At the outset the weather threatened to spoil the wind-up, a drizzle and a misty atmosphere interfering, but a smart shower cleared the air and brightness followed. The semi-finals were somewhat discounted through Minstrel Coon having damaged some of his toes in his long course with Lord Protector, and being unable to go to slips with Hopsack, whilst, as expected, the trial between Harmonicon and Rataine was not invested with great excitement. The Purse and the Plate, in addition, were cut disappointingly short ; but the grandeur of the final for the Cup atoned for all.

Final Course.

Harmonicon beat Hopsack. Betting, 2 to 1 on Hopsack. After a beautiful delivery it was a fine tussle for some distance, but Harmonicon then began to go the faster and was once nearly two lengths in front. The hare then bearing a little to the left, Hopsack, under the red flag, drew closer, and Harmonicon had to put in all he could to score the turn on the outside. Puss shifting further to the left, Hopsack secured the third point, and the hare still favouring him he stuck to the scut like glue. Harmonicon, displaying fine resolution, forged up time after time, but just as he got his head in front the hare continually bore from him, until the fawn had stylishly scored what looked a certain winning sequence.

Puss, however, instead of going on for the refuge in the bank, was so hard pressed that she at last broke back. Upon this Harmonicon instantly shot up for possession, and he in turn held command for several brilliant points. Hopsack was not long in joining issue, several exchanges being desperately contested before the fawn again obtained clear possession.

He then a second time looked uncommonly like winning, but Harmonicon, persevering with splendid determination, made a grand point by displacing his opponent under difficulties, and having all the best of what followed before a game hare escaped at the corner of the Withins on the members' side, a closely-balanced issue ended in his favour, the result being hailed with loud cheering from the big crowd, from whose point of view it was a clear win.

Waterloo Cup: Mr. E. Hulton's bd d Harmonicon, by Heavy Weapon out of Camorra, beat Mr. H. Hardy's f d Hopsack, by Hoprend out of Heart of Freedom.

Waterloo Purse: Fourth round, Simla beat White Fleet; Bryn Peril and Staff Officer did not go to slips. Stakes divided between Mr. J. Mugliston ns Lord Sefton's bd d Simla, by Friendly Foe out of Glen Yuba, Major H. Peel's bk d Bryn Peril, by Duplicate Deed out of Pen-y-Bryn, and Earl of Sefton's f d p Staff Officer, by Friendly Foe out of Higher Walton.

Waterloo Plate: Captain D. P. Wormald ns Mr. H. Birkbeck's f d p Bisley (late Horstead Claymore), by Heavy Weapon out of Sweet Sauce, and Mr. Cockerill ns Mr. R. Dunn's r d Enoch, by Earl's Court out of Forest Lassie, divided.

This was probably the finest contested Waterloo final, having regard to its length, that was ever witnessed, and it was certainly a case of "honours easy" between victor and vanquished. It was, moreover, in my opinion, a case of the best two greyhounds in the Waterloo Cup fighting it out—a pleasing feature that does not often conspicuously and clearly mark the final struggle, though there could be no two opinions on the point when such a pair as Master M'Grath and Bab at the Bowster opposed each other. Fullerton never disposed of a final opponent quite worthy of his steel.

It was a fine achievement of Mr. E. (now Sir Edward) Hulton to win a second Waterloo Cup in eight years, to say nothing of having also, in the meantime, run second, and if his earlier honours were gained by a bitch hardly up to the standard of Waterloo winners, the remark does not in the least apply in the present case. Harmonicon proved himself distinctly a greyhound of superior class.

He gave great promise at the outset of his career, but a dog of over 70lbs. weight was not likely to be sufficiently matured to win a Waterloo Cup as a puppy. His fine powers, however, in his second season were beyond dispute, and his excellent and well-respected trainer, Harry Hoad, had him in splendid bloom in Waterloo week. It was a lucky stroke for Irish coursers, as well as for himself, when Mr. Gorey bought him for 600 guineas at the sale of Mr. Hulton's greyhounds.

Of Hopsack, the runner-up, only good words can also be written. Like his sire, Hoprend, and the Waterloo winner, Dendraspis, Hopsack "trained on," and was a better dog in his third season than at any earlier period of his life — a characteristic that does not generally apply. This is a subject that might receive more attention : I feel sure that many greyhounds would develop much greater powers if they were more tenderly treated in their puppyhood—and also last longer.

On account of the war, there was no Waterloo Cup in the years 1917-18-19, but in the latter year, though there was not sufficient time to make the necessary preparations for a Waterloo, after the Armistice Lord Sefton gave permission for a substitute meeting to be held on February 5th, 6th and 7th. It was a joyous gathering, nearly all the leading lights of the coursing world being present, and the meeting was rendered memorable by two owners each gaining a double success. Sir R. W. Buchanan Jardine's pair, Jakin and Jock's Lodge, shared the honours of the Victory Cup; and Mr. H. Sawtell's two puppies, Melksham Nellie and Melksham Mollie, similarly distinguished themselves in the Peace Cup.

CHAPTER XLIV.

Waterloo, 1920—Fighting Force's Victory.

AFTER three blank years, owing to the war, the recommencement of Waterloo Cup history was signalised in both a romantic and tragic manner. Leaving out his suggestive name, the winner was bought from Miss Ruth Fawcett only a few days before the meeting by the young courser, Mr. S. W. Beer, who was thus enabled, like Mr. Rogers in 1899 and Lord Dewar in 1915, to gain Waterloo Cup renown at the first attempt.

Good luck, combined with exceeding cleverness and striking resolution, carried him into the final, but all his gallantry would at last have been in vain but for a tragic ending. Mr. M. L. Hearn's Honeyman had him well beaten when they reached the fatal spot from whence Honeyman had bolted at the end of his previous course with Staff Job, through being scared by the rush of some too eager, would-be, pickers up.

They were then again close to the crowd, and the roar from a thousand throats so frightened the Irish dog that he deliberately left his hare and galloped away for safety, leaving Fighting Force to go on and win. No doubt many an owner will have thought that he had the Cup, so to speak, " dashed from his lips," but this was a clear case of the Waterloo Cup having been virtually won, and yet lost !

The interval of four years led to many changes in the personal of this year's Waterloo, only 46 of the nominators in Harmonicon's year now figuring in the 64. The ruthless scythe bearer was responsible to a great extent, Mr. G. F. Fawcett, Mr. A. J. Humphery (father of the present Sir John), Mr. O. H. Jones, Mr. R. N. Stollery, Mr. W. Wing, Captain D. P. Wormald, Mr. W. M. Haywood and Mr. W. H. Smith being familiar figures whom we shall, unhappily, see no more.

An influential and enthusiastic company marked the reunion at dinner, with the Earl of Sefton in the chair. A pleasant and much-applauded feature of the evening was embodied in

Lord Sefton's acknowledgment of the toast " the Lord of the Manor," proposed in such choice terms by the Duke of Leeds. His Lordship expressed his regret that it had latterly become the fashion to divide the Purse and the Plate, and to encourage these being run out, like the Cup, he had decided to present a £50 Cup to the winner of each.

The betting took lively shape, favourites for the event being Staff Job and Derringer at 1,000 to 90 each. Jemadar was third favourite at 1,000 to 80, and Jack in Office fourth at 1,000 to 70.

It was a novelty for old Waterlooers to go to Lydiate for the opening day, but the Withins being—or having been—in plough, through war regulations, there was no other place where the huge crowd could be sufficiently well placed.

Fighting Force was the first to show marked cleverness and resolution, but he was led too far by Jamie to make many friends. H.S. One and Barr-na-Maidne each made short work of his game in rather smart style ; but Wingle, in giving Corby Hero a terrible licking, was unlucky enough to get a hare that was too good for him.

Jack Spraggon and Hidden Harp were also severely gruelled, which was very bad luck for " Jack," as he began his course brilliantly. Mornington made a capital impression in perhaps the best display of the round, and Honeyman was also brilliant with his hare. Guards' Brigade and Staff Job each rattled up several lengths ahead and, also showing plenty of fire in short spins, won in decisive fashion.

The second round at the outset introduced four short spins, in the second and fourth of which Fighting Force and Boy Ben showed to advantage. Wingle also ran well, especially bearing in mind his morning's dose, but he unluckily got another grueller. Mornington, who won all hearts in the morning, stretched out several lengths from Halston, but slipped up badly at the turn, and was well beaten in a long course.

His defeat was, of course, exceedingly unlucky, but he ought, perhaps, to have " come again " better than he did. Yet he did no worse than Long Span and Bachelor's Acre after their memorable successive mishaps in Hallow Eve's year.

Betting on the event was now 4 to 1 against Staff Job, 9 to 2 Honeyman, 6 to 1 A, 10 to 1 each against Great Form and Party Truce. Terrible weather attended the middle stage, and even the continuous rain was not the worst, a misty veil soon shutting many of the courses out of view. The wet, slippery ground was much against the dogs, and not a few of the trials were of distressing length.

At the outset Great Form won well, but in a course of terrific length, Fighting Force outstayed him. This, combined with his deficiency of speed, seemed to settle all chance of Fighting Force winning the Cup, and, on the spur of the moment, a leading bookmaker offered 1,000 to 5 against him, the tempting odds being taken four or five times.

H.S. One was beaten in an unlucky and unsatisfactory course, and his victor, Boy Ben, was the victim of equally bad luck in the next round. Wingle, like Fighting Force, displayed wonderful recovery after his earlier gruelling, but another " long one " gave the finishing touch, and he was drawn.

This gave A a bye, which he ran fast and well, as he did his previous course against Halston. Without fully sustaining his first day's brilliance, Honeyman again acquitted himself like a good greyhound, though he was stoutly challenged by Another Attempt in the middle of the course. Staff Job, too, was in danger of defeat by Hailfellow—in fact, the latter, after being led and beaten for the early points, had fairly turned the tables, before Staff Job's last few points and the kill.

At night Staff Job and A were equal favourites at 6 to 4, 7 to 2 being laid against Honeyman, and 25 to 1 against Fighting Force. It was a tragic finish, bringing vividly to mind Hallow Eve's year (1908).

The two overthrows in the semi-finals were not, as upon that occasion, the result of accident, A and Staff Job being both beaten on their merits by the extra cleverness and determination of slower opponents ; but the flooring of the odds again in the final, with the success of a greyhound whose price in the last four was 25 to 1, together with the tragic manner in which it was brought about, as previously explained, constitutes an equally romantic phase in Waterloo Cup history.

CHAPTER XLV.

Waterloo, 1921—Shortcoming's Splendid Success

AFTER a good many disappointing years, the Earl of Sefton at last tasted the sweets of a Waterloo triumph, and that the victory of the Lord of the Manor strongly appealed to the vast crowd was clearly demonstrated by the cheers—again and again renewed—which greeted the Earl and Countess of Sefton as they walked back again— Lord Sefton leading Shortcoming—from where they had advanced to bestow their adorations upon the winner.

It was a dramatic last day in another respect. The judge's horse—one of Mr. J. J. Bell-Irving's clever hunters—during one of the Plate courses, came an awful cropper, through breaking the crust of a grown-over rabbit burrow, and before Mr. Mulcaster could get clear the horse rolled over him. It was at first feared that he was seriously injured, and much concern, if not excitement, was at once manifested.

Two doctors were quickly on the scene, and with their help the unfortunate judge was, in a short time, enabled to walk to Lord Sefton's luncheon hut, 'midst the warm sympathy of everyone. The doctors' diagnosis was, happily, that there seemed to be no very serious injury, though bad enough, in the shape of a broken collar-bone. The services of the two stewards present—Mr. J. Bell-Irving and Col. R. M'Calmont— were now called into requisition, but there was no difficulty as Mr. Hector Clark was present with a retaining fee, as second judge, and he filled the unfortunate and much regretted void, with entire satisfaction.

In order to make a faithful recital of events it ought to be explained that Mr. Walker had still fully retained the confidence of the nominators, but fearful of getting an imperfect view, declined to take the risk of judging from a ladder, and Mr. Mulcaster, having the second largest number of votes, become the elected judge.

The Earl of Sefton, as usual (except when unavoidably absent), occupied the chair at the banquet, and, as in the previous year, had a pleasing announcement to make. His Lordship said that the well-deserved testimonial, in recognition of Mr. Mugliston's lifelong and untiring efforts in the interests of the sport, had been entirely successful, and he had great pleasure in handing him a cheque for £1,000. Mr. Mugliston's acknowledgment was brief, but charmingly appropriate, and uttered with much feeling.

In connection with the little friction there had been regarding ladder versus horse, Lord Sefton explained that though there was ample scope and the necessary hares on other portions of the ground, it was only on the Withins and at Lydiate that the huge first day's crowd were enabled to get a fair view of the running. Lydiate could only yield sport for two days, so that it was in the best possible interests of the spectators to run on the Withins where the biggest crowd would obtain the best view ; and as it had been ploughed during the war, it was not yet sufficiently covered with herbage to safely carry a horse.

A longer price than usual was offered on the field this year, Guards' Brigade heading the quotations at 1,000 to 70. Closely on his heels came Skeets, Jassiona and Sir Berkeley each at 1,000 to 60, and a quartette were all on the same lower mark of 1,000 to 50, viz., Shortcoming, Mornington, and the Irish pair, Three Speed and Irish Steeple.

The opening spin was between the favourite (Guards' Brigade) and Staff Job—two old opponents. It was a tight race until nearing the hare, when Guards' Brigade, under a little favour, got his head in front, but puss, from bearing to the right, at last curved to the left, whereupon Staff Job shot forward, wrenched and killed—a mere apology for a trial, and a lucky win. A second short spin followed, but here Barnacle showed very decided superiority.

The prettiest course in the round was run by Jassiona, the smart bitch, Littleton Mars, only getting in at the finish to quickly wrench and kill. Irish Steeple had far too much speed for Jevenesse, and January, after outfooting Merry Cutthroat, gave him no chance. Wingle and Bryn Fancy were well matched, but Mornington and Magog were both much too good for their opponents.

As in the previous round there was no striking feature until Jassiona came upon the scene. She was perhaps hardly as brilliant as in her previous effort, but she even beat the speedy Diapason in pace to the hare. Shortcoming, I think ran even better than before, and after leading three lengths never relinquished possession this time until she killed.

On Wednesday night Shortcoming advanced to the position of first favourite at 900 to 200, Hailfellow following closely at 500 to 100, Irish Steeple, Jassiona and Thalia being next best.

Staff Job, as previously, was one of the first brace, and, though he well led Matrimony to the hare, he made an indifferent exhibition, and was severely beaten. Hailfellow ran a beautiful course in his easy defeat of Dry Goods, and performed equally well against Matrimony until a demon hare took it all out of them both.

Thalia's efforts against Mutter and Mornington were both unimpeachable ; but the star performers were clearly Jassiona and Shortcoming. The Scottish bitch showed nearly as good pace as the speedy Denny, and gave a spectacular display that is nowadays not often seen on the coursing field. Her effort against Nebulous Nike was equally, if not more, brilliant, this clever bitch never getting a look in. Shortcoming was hardly so splendidly tight on her hare as on the previous day in her course with Woodcut, though no exception could be taken.

Irish Steeple fairly had the foot of Lord Sefton's bitch, being two lengths in front until nearing the hare, when the fawn closed up a little as the Irish dog dwelled slightly upon seeing the hare's movement to break round. Shortcoming was very nippy as puss broke short back, and, shooting up well in front, wrenched twice, killed, and gained the fiat.

Lydiate was the closing scene of operations, and it was a great wind-up—one of the greatest except in the Master M'Grath and Fullerton days, and perhaps when Miss Glendyne and Penelope ran off. Jassiona and Shortcoming each sustained their previous brilliant form in the semi-finals, and the decider was looked upon as a battle royal.

Jassiona had at first slightly the call, 1,100 to 1,000 being laid ; but when it became known that she had damaged a

N

toe in her course with Hailfellow, which she had run so
splendidly, the betting veered round to 5 to 4 on Shortcoming,
and the injury no doubt affected the result. Shortcoming
would, I think, have shown slightly the better speed to the
hare in any case, but when she fell in the middle of the course
she would hardly have got another chance had Jassiona
possessed four sound feet.

It was certainly a stroke of very bad luck for Sir Robert
Jardine, but, like the good sportsman that he is, he took it in
the right spirit, bearing in mind that he had already won two
Waterloo Cups, whilst this was the Earl of Sefton's first taste
of the sweets of victory.

The Countess of Sefton must also be associated, for Shortcoming ran in her ladyship's nomination. She was bred by
the late Mr. Oliver Jones, and gave great promise as a puppy
when she divided the Whinfell Stakes at the Border Union
(Lowther) meeting, but was amiss at Waterloo time, and did
not run.

In connection with the Purse, it can be said that Guards'
Brigade showed such marked superiority over all his five
opponents that it was seemingly very unlucky for Colonel
Lord Tweedmouth that he was snuffed out of the Cup in such
a miserable course by Staff Job. The way in which Diapason
disposed of his Plate opponents also enhanced the merit of
Jassiona's form in the Cup.

So ended my fifty-sixth Waterloo, and of the fifty-one I
reported from Brigadier to Harmonicon, I can add—I hope
not boastfully—that I never missed a Cup course.

Previous Runner-up never won a Waterloo Cup.

A feature in connection with the great event is the fact
that a previous runner-up has never won it, though both
Rebe and Peasant Boy went very near : each ran-up twice
in successive years. It is also a little singular that of the
24 successful bitches since its becoming a 64-dog stake in 1857
(against 33 of the stronger type) not one has bred a winner
of her own sex. Bit of Fashion, of course, scored heavily
through Fullerton, and Thoughtless Beauty produced two
runners-up in Paracelsus and Prince Plausible.

CHAPTER XLVI.

Remarkable Successes.

MR. PILKINGTON's first success was dividing the Ridgway Club Clifton Cup, in December, 1873, with Protector, and between then and his retirement in 1909 he won or divided 339 stakes! The wins included two Waterloo Cups, with Burnaby and Thoughtless Beauty ; nine Altcar Members' Cups, with Palmer, Penelope II, Petrutha, Prism and Pennegant (first and second), Pateley Bridge, Pensive Beauty (twice in 1901 and 1902), and Paracelsus ; and five Altcar Club Cups, with Prince Rupert, Penelope II, Peregrine Pickle, Pensive Beauty, and Pentonville.

Mr. Pilkington " farmed " the Corrie Cup for four successive years with Pensive Beauty, Pretty Lassie, Priestlaw and Paracelsus, and four years later won Sir Robert Jardine's always handsome trophy again with Punchestown. Another fine achievement was dividing six Netherby Cups with Pins and Needles, Pennegant, Pelerine, Pursebearer, Paracelsus and Prince Plausible.

Lytham was the most frequent scene of Mr. Pilkington's and Joe Wright's successes : they included wins in eight Clifton Cups and nine Lytham Cups ; also ten divisions of the latter. The kennel was equally triumphant in the junior events, four divisions in the North Lancashire, eight in the South, and five in the United North and South being recorded.

Notable successes were also scored far and wide. Phœbus won a Kempton £1,000, Paracelsus won a Barbican Cup, Pontypool won a Newmarket Champion, and Burnaby divided one of the big Gosforth Park stakes. Three of Colonel North's Yorkshire Club Cups were captured and a like number of Scottish National Cups ; and Carmichael, Ashdown, Beckhampton, Plumpton, Haydock Park, Bangor, Purdysburn, Heatley, Brigg, Eccleston, were all scenes of success.

The Great Saughall Kennel.

Messrs. Fawcett's coursing triumphs did not come as quickly as Mr. Pilkington's, but they were equally pronounced at one period, and, of course, more splendidly conspicuous through their great Waterloo victories with Fabulous Fortune, Fearless Footsteps (twice), Farndon Ferry and Father Flint. Both at the Altcar Club meetings and at Corrie their successes were almost phenomenal, and at the Border Union meeting, when the programme was a 64 Netherby Cup and a 64 puppy, they one year won the Netherby Cup with Fitzfulke, and were first and second in the junior event with Famous Forrester and another puppy whose name I forget.

They were also hugely successful with their Waterloo victors as sires. Farndon Ferry and Fabulous Fortune were perfect gold mines, and Father Flint was also largely patronised. Fiery Furnace, Fecht Fair, Father o' Fire, Faber Fortunæ, Fortuna Favente, Fighting Fire, and others, all brought "grist to the mill."

The Fame of Short Flatt.

No man won greater celebrity in the coursing world than Mr. Edward Dent, Master of Short Flatt. His first good ones that I remember clearly were Miss Glendyne, Bit of Fashion, London, Lights o' London and Jester, and the speedy Huic Holloa. He sold Miss Glendyne, however, before her first Waterloo Cup to Mr. C. Hibbert, after she had made a successful debut at Gosforth Park, though she remained at Short Flatt to be trained. Bit of Fashion won 21 courses as a puppy, and two as a sapling, before going to Waterloo and dividing with her kennel companion ; and London, Jester and Lights o' London all made their marks. The last-named won 67 courses in public, and Jester was successful four times at Gosforth. Huic Holloa won £1,900, including the Kempton Park £1,000.

A Great Sale.

Mr. Dent chose an opportune period to break up his kennel, or rather to sell off, and a remarkable sale it was, yielding towards £3,000. Fullerton had shown such great form at Haydock that Colonel North had to bid up to 850gs.

Miss Glendyne, sold at the same time, was the next highest-priced lot, Colonel North again being the buyer at 510gs.

Five brothers and sisters to Fullerton sold well, Mr. O. H. Jones giving 200gs. for Yooi Over (afterwards Jupon Vert), and Miss Kitten (by Jester out of Tender and True) brought 160gs. Colonel North gave 200gs. for Bit of Fashion, and four of her saplings (by Jester) fetched nearly £300. Col. North bought two of these, and also Miss Kitten, and Fullerton's sister, Kate Cuthbert.

The Short Flatt kennel was not broken up, for Col. North's numerous purchases remained there to be trained, and it was now that Mr. Dent won the great fame to which I have previously referred, adding Fullerton's four Waterloo Cups to the two already won—firstly by Miss Glendyne and Bit of Fashion jointly, and then by Miss Glendyne outright.

These three kennels each owed the chief of its splendid successes mostly to Bab at the Bowster's blood and the co-mingling of " Bab's " and Bed of Stone's. Messrs. Fawcett's towering strength was with the Herschel—Fair Future first litter. Herschel was a direct descendant of Bab's son Contango, and Fair Future's dam (Reformation) was a grand-daughter of Bed of Stone's son, Bedfellow. The same admixture was afterwards renewed more closely with Herschel's sons or grandsons and the daughters or grand-daughters of Greentick and *vice versa*.

Mr. Pilkington's sweeping successes came mostly through Thoughtless Beauty and her sons and splendid daughters, and she was by Herschel out of Thetis, daughter of Greentick. There was also a valuable outcross here. Thetis's dam, Tonic (a very smart bitch), was by N. Dunn's Herrera, by the good Border dog Fugitive.

Mr. Dent and Short Flatt, I need hardly say, acquired their chief fame through Greentick's champion son Fullerton, and it is almost superfluous to add that Greentick combined both "Bab's" and Bed of Stone's blood. But Mr. Dent made a big mark in his earlier days mainly through the Ptarmigan—Gallant Foe family, though he always maintained that Pretty Nell, dam of Bit of Fashion, was the foundation of his success.

CHAPTER XLVII.

Training Methods.

IN offering a short chapter on this subject, I may at once premise that I regard book learning, in connection with training greyhounds, as of comparatively little worth ; hence I must not stultify myself by attempting to teach, and to take rank amongst other book exponents of the art, at any rate, except in a perfunctory sort of way.

To my mind, the application of intelligent common sense is the golden method. The trainer must be in entire sympathy with his charges : he must be ever watchful, so that he always knows exactly the state of his dogs' health ; he must, in fact, love his greyhounds, and not regard anything as a trouble that will in any way conduce to their comfort or well being.

Above all things they ought to be well housed, and have sufficient air space, so that a pure atmosphere can always easily be maintained, without risk of draughts or occasional rushes of cold air. Drains inside the kennel, or indeed contiguous, ought to be quite taboo ; and the kennel floor, and at least a foot upwards of the walls should be quite non-absorbent. In connection with warming the kennel, stoves are a great danger if not well attended to and of proper construction. An overheated stove exhausts the oxygen out of the atmosphere, not only rendering it unhealthy, but even poisonous. Hot-water pipes are safer. But in a well-constructed kennel, with a snug arrangement of the benches and proper attention with regard to clothing, even these are hardly necessary where a reasonably equitable temperature can be maintained.

Food in these days of such excellent dog biscuits as a basis, is a simple matter. Sheep head broth, with a good beef bone occasionally added, is recognised as the staple food, and as extra to a liberal admixture of good-class vegetables, such as celery and leeks, or onions, the addition of a little rice, barley and linseed (not linseed meal), also a breakfast cupful of oatmeal, are desirable. The latter ought never to be used new. Porridge made of oatmeal less than six months old possesses heating properties which are hurtful. Care ought also to be taken in the use of salt. It is not necessary to use it at all ; dogs relish their food just as well without it, and it will soon destroy the bloom of the coat if used to excess. I have known greyhounds come to Waterloo with bare hips, purely through its too liberal use. In speaking of the broth, I ought to have mentioned that cabbage ought to be used sparingly, when added : it is the better plan to boil it separately, and not use the water.

What I have written so far is, of course, quite elementary, more for the novice than the experienced trainer. With regard to the amount of exercise necessary, it is impossible to lay down any standard rule for general practice. The old book-teaching of inordinately long walking exercise could never have been sound ; with our present breed of greyhounds it is ridiculous, and spells ruination to speed and fire. More than once I have seen good greyhounds come to Waterloo utterly unable to show their real form through being over-walked. Compare the speed of a tailor, who sits on his sewing bench most of the day, with that of the man who follows the plough. ·

The great desideratum is to have a dog clean in his wind. The tongue must be red (and not white), with the watery saliva dropping clean off the tongue after his smart gallops. Reasonable exercise will soon produce this effect, when dogs are in a clean, healthy condition, and neither over-fed not under-fed. If not, they must have a proper " opening out " with a course of good length. This, indeed, is nearly at all times a preliminary necessity with second, third and fourth-season greyhounds ; indeed, I could cite instances where good greyhounds have never been able to show the best that was in them until after having had an extra severe course. This applies particularly to savage dogs that resolutely refuse physic ; but even they can, of course, be circumvented.

Upon the point of whether walking exercise is best done on the road, or in fields, different views are held. Mr. Dent, in all his great successes, very rarely resorted to the road. He varied his walks as much as possible in fields, and took directions where they were likely to see game of any sort, with the object of keeping his dogs always on the look out, and never took them home too tired.

In training for a special occasion—say, the Waterloo Cup— a dog that has been kept in special reserve, either through choice or force of circumstances, might first have a dose of medicine to touch the liver. He ought then to have a couple of fair courses to clean him well out in December. A short easy time would then follow, before he was gradually trained up to the desired perfection, with, say, half-a-dozen courses, care being taken that not one of them was long. So long as he kept killing his hares without any distress, there need hardly be a limit to the number of spins. The dog would then come to slips with his heart fully in his work, under the happy conviction that he was sure to kill. The last week should be an easy one in the matter of work, but should include a dose of oil and an emetic. And, after medicine, the breakfast should consist of boiled bread and milk—stale bread and new milk. This, by the way, is also the desirable breakfast, in running, after a hard course : it is more soothing than soup, or broth, or strong jelly : these latter each have a tendency to develop a thirst. The evening feed, during a meeting, ought never to be given after a long course until any thirst that had been developed was entirely allayed by a weak mixture of milk and water as warm as the dog would take it.

In the last two weeks of training legs of mutton are preferable to beef, and they ought to be a fortnight old.

Milk is a valuable adjunct — both new milk and buttermilk—either during special training or in a general way. An occasional feed of boiled bread and milk—always stale bread, and when not old enough carefully toasted—will be greatly relished as a change, and the occasional addition of a little buttermilk to either the breakfast or evening meal is a great help in ensuring the stools to be of the desired consistency. If the main bowel become loaded, the dog will be unable to give his best, and too drastic treatment near the end of training is undesirable.

JUDGES OF THE WATERLOO CUP SINCE IT BECAME A 64-DOG STAKE.

1857—Mr. NIGHTINGALE.

1858—Mr. McGEORGE.

1859 and 1860—Mr. A. DALZELL.

1861 to 1873—Mr. G. WARWICK, 13 years.

1874 to 1897—Mr. J. HEDLEY, 24 years.

1898 to 1910—Mr. R. A. BRICE, 13 years.

*1911 to 1920—Mr. J. WALKER, 7 years.

1921—Mr. GEO. MULCASTER. (Mr. Walker was elected, but declined to judge from a ladder.)

Mr. Mulcaster had an accident on the last day, through his horse falling, and Mr. HECTOR CLARKE judged the last ten courses.

* *There was no Waterloo Cup in* 1917–18–19.

THE BEST TEN GREYHOUNDS "VINDEX" HAS SEEN.

MASTER M'GRATH, the best Altcar greyhound.

BAB AT THE BOWSTER, the best over all countries.

FULLERTON and MISS GLENDYNE, next best.

HERSCHEL, clearly fifth best.

COOMASSIE and BED OF STONE, equally good.

FARNDON FERRY, next best.

HONEYWOOD, perhaps equally good

LONG SPAN, very little behind them.

THE NEXT BEST SEVEN BITCHES.

LOBELIA, CHAMELEON, HONEYMOON, REBE, THOUGHTLESS BEAUTY, FEARLESS FOOTSTEPS, LAVISHLY CLOTHED.

INDEX.